WAR
IN THE
HOLY
LAND

FROM MEGGIDO
TO THE WEST BANK

ANDREW DUNCAN
AND MICHEL OPATOWSKI

FOREWORD BY
PROFESSOR ROBERT O'NEILL

SUTTON PUBLISHING

First published in 1998 by
Sutton Publishing Limited · Phoenix Mill
Thrupp · Stroud · Gloucestershire · GL5 2BU

British Library Cataloguing in Publication Data
A catalogue record for this book is available from the British Library.

ISBN 0-7509-1500-5

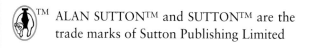

Typeset in 10/13pt Sabon.
Typesetting and origination by
Sutton Publishing Limited.
Printed in Hong Kong by
Midas Printing Limited.

CONTENTS

LIST OF MAPS

KEY TO MAPS

I T A L Y	country		cavalry		✕	battle site
Rome	town		infantry			fortified position
Cassino	village		armour			minefield
Beitar	locality/settlement		mechanised infantry		xxxx	army
Mt. Maiola	geographical feature		paratroops		xxx	corps
Station	military feature		chariots (ancient)		xx	division
——·——	armistice/ceasefire line		artillery		x	brigade
——·——	international border		aircraft		ⅲ	regiment
▬▬▬	railway		helicopters		ⅱ	battalion
▬▬▬	highway		ships (ancient)		ⅰ	company
———	road		naval ship		•••	platoon
- - - -	path		command post		•	section
·········	river		command post (ancient)			
·········	wadi					
•	location					
∴	ruins					
▲	hill					

The two sides on each encounter are displayed in red and blue.

Blue has been used for: the Israelites, the Crusaders, British in World War I and the Israelis.

FOREWORD

BY ROBERT O'NEILL

CHICHELE PROFESSOR OF THE HISTORY OF WAR

UNIVERSITY OF OXFORD

This book throws light on an extremely important and currently relevant topic. The Middle East has been the most contested region of the world. Any reader seriously interested in warfare or the peaceful management of international relations requires knowledge of the history of this area. It is all too easy to develop simplistic ideas on the basis of slight knowledge of the region's geography and the aims of its governments. One needs a deeper insight into what the strategic characteristics of the region are, what are the underlying enmities, what has been tried and failed, and the reason for those failures before anything useful can be said about ways of bringing peace to the peoples of the Middle East. The causes of their conflicts sometimes reach back over centuries of bitter rivalry which has undermined the basis for trust and given rise to profound senses of injustice and hostility which dominate public and communal thinking in the region today. This book not only grounds the reader thoroughly in the history of war in the Middle East but also includes a forward-looking analysis, 'Peace at Last?' In this the authors appraise the progress achieved over the past twenty years and the balance of risks and opportunities in the major proposals which continue to be the subjects of negotiations.

Andrew Duncan and Michel Opatowski have provided in this volume a comprehensive and succint examination of the past three millennia of conflict in the Middle East. The foundations of the book are Colonel Duncan's expertise in Middle Eastern affairs and Mr Opatowski's skill as a cartographer. Colonel Duncan served as British Defence Attaché at the Embassy in Israel from 1977 to 1980. He went on after retirement to head the analytical staff at the International Institute for Strategic Studies which prepares and publishes the well-known annual survey of the world's armed forces, *The Military Balance*. That volume offers the fullest publicly available data on the strength, composition and equipment of land, sea and air forces, and its reputation owes not a little to the rigour and extensiveness of Colonel Duncan's work. His experience and knowledge have equipped him well to prepare the text of this book, in which he has shown his capacity to combine breadth and accuracy within tight word limits. Michel Opatowski's work as a cartographer in Israel has given him the necessary command of techniques and context to complement Duncan's knowledge of military history. His maps are among the best I have seen in years of teaching the conflicts which are at the heart of this volume. And I also commend the text for its comprehensibility in describing battles and campaigns which were intricate in their development. The reader can then make his or her own tactical analysis on the basis of the sound information and historical context provided.

I have much pleasure in commending the work as a whole to students of warfare, the history of war, and Middle Eastern affairs.

INTRODUCTION

The Holy Land is the most fought-over region in the world. It is holy to the three great monotheistic religions – Judaism, Christianity and Islam; all have fought to control it. It has no recognized borders but is generally accepted as being the land lying between the Mediterranean and the Jordan River; its capital is Jerusalem, a city sacred to all three religions. The Holy Land is also the junction between the three continents of Europe, Asia and Africa, and connects to a fourth area, Arabia. Invaders have come from all four directions, often their aim not to take the Holy Land itself but to conquer the lands beyond; a number of wars have also been waged here on purely religious grounds. The Israelites conquered it as it had been promised to them by God; the Crusaders fought for it to regain Christian access to Jerusalem; the Mamelukes recovered it for Islam. The Jews fought to establish the state of Israel; they and their Muslim neighbours have fought virtually continuously ever since. Today peace is, slowly and painfully, being achieved with peace treaties signed by Israel with Egypt and Jordan; a start has been made on a solution for the descendants of the land's original inhabitants – the Palestinians.

This book covers the history of the Holy Land as represented by the battles fought for or through it. The story begins with the Battle of Megiddo in 1482 BC, the first battle in history about which there are detailed records, carved on the walls of the Temple at Thebes. It ends within weeks of the book's publication date. It is not possible in the space available to cover every battle nor any in any real detail (there are many volumes covering different periods in detail and a list of these is provided for those who wish to study some aspect in greater detail) but this is the first book to cover the whole story from the Israelite conquest to the possibility of peace at last. No attempt has been made to assess the tactics, leadership and fighting ability of the many nations and forces that have fought over the Holy Land.

Throughout the book, place-names of the period in question have been used and where possible today's name is also given. The correct spelling of names is a particular problem in a part of the world where certain letters, for instance Q and K, are interchangeable. The 1:250,000 maps contained in the *Israel Atlas* published by the Survey of Israel and the Elsevier Publishing Company have been used as the source for names in Israel and the territories it has occupied. Wherever possible historical place-names have been taken from the historical maps in the same Atlas, and where the Atlas does not cover the area the names used in the *Times Atlas of the Bible* have been used. Names elsewhere are taken from the *Times Atlas of*

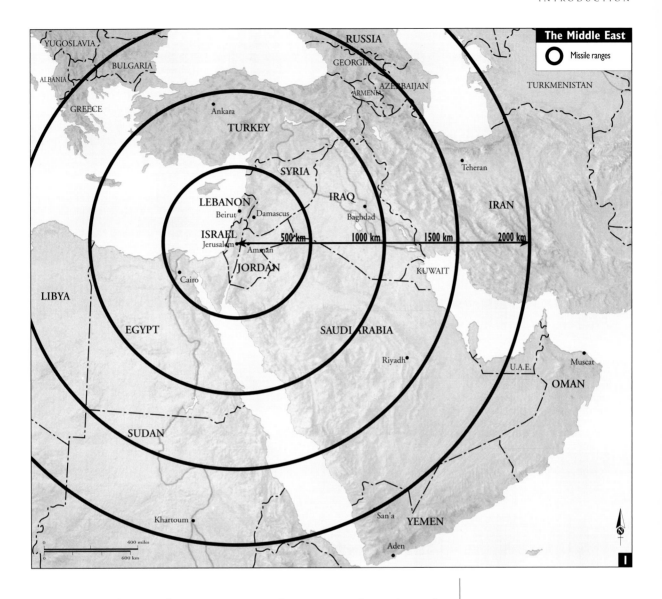

the World. Selecting the correct names for groups of people or for geographical regions which have changed over the years is difficult; for example, the Crusaders are often also called the Franks or the Latins. Where appropriate, the contemporary name has been used, otherwise today's name is used. The term Israelites is used in the years before the Romans, Jews between then and Israel's Independence, and Israelis after Independence. The term Palestine has only been used after the Romans named it.

A description of the terrain faced by invaders and defenders of the Holy Land and its neighbouring territory in this introduction will avoid having to repeat it in the descriptions of the many battles fought there. The coastline from Israel's northern border with Lebanon to Gaza is roughly 200 km long and from the tip of Israel at Metulla to Elat on the Gulf of Aqaba, following the line of the Jordan, Dead Sea and Arava, is 440 km, both as the crow flies. The distance from the Mediterranean to the Jordan/Arava is on average some 70 km. Throughout history the coastline from Gaza northwards has been the most developed and populated area

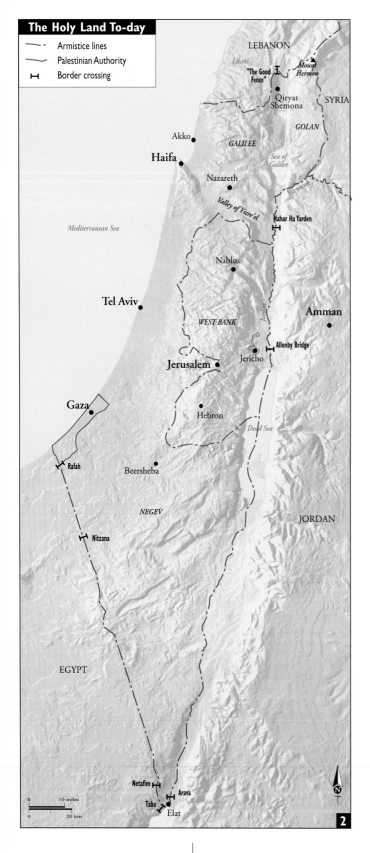

The Holy Land To-day

- — · — Armistice lines
- — Palestinian Authority
- ⊢—⊣ Border crossing

LEBANON

Litani

"The Good Fence"

Mount Hermon

Qiryat Shemona

SYRIA

Akko

GALILEE

GOLAN

Haifa

Sea of Galilee

Nazareth

Yarmuk

Valley of Yizre'el

Nahar Ha Yarden

Mediterranean Sea

Nablus

Jordan

Tel Aviv

Amman

WEST BANK

Allenby Bridge

Jerusalem

Jericho

Gaza

Hebron

Dead Sea

Rafah

Beersheba

NEGEV

JORDAN

Nitzana

EGYPT

N

Netafim

Arava

Taba

Elat

0 — 10 miles

0 — 20 km

2

with the cities of Gaza (Middle and Late Bronze Age, 2000–1200 BC), Ashkelon (Early Bronze Age, 3150–2200 BC), Ashdod and Jaffa (Middle and Late Bronze Age), and Acre (Akko) (Hellenistic Period, 332–30 BC) all having long histories. The coastal road, or 'way of the sea', was the main route for invading armies between Egypt and Syria (and on into Europe or Asia). The other main route, known as the King's Highway, lay to the east of the Arava and Jordan Rivers, passing Petra, Ader (Early Bronze Age), 5 km north-east of Karak, and Rabbat Ammon (Amman) (Middle and Late Bronze Age). A third route kept to the high ground between these two. From Beersheba (Iron Age, 1200–586 BC) it went through Hebron and Jerusalem (Early Bronze Age), Shekhem (Nablus) (Middle and Late Bronze Age) and then either to Megiddo (Early Bronze Age) or the Jordan Valley.

To the south of the Holy Land lies the Sinai Desert, stretching 195 km from the Suez Canal to the Israeli border and 270 km from the Mediterranean to Ras Muhammad on the Red Sea. Sinai links Africa to Asia and Europe but also forms a barrier, more difficult to cross before the days of motor transport but even now shortage of water can be a problem. Sinai is in the shape of an inverted triangle. Along the Mediterranean coastline the topography is mainly sand dunes and ridges, often making travelling difficult off the main El Qantara–El Arish–Gaza road. Further south the going is easier, being mainly gravel plain, but movement here is channelled by the Gebel el Maghara and Jebel Yiallao. There is a line of hills running north–south some 48 km east of the Suez Canal at its north end, down to 16 km at the southern end. The hills rise to between 600 and 800 metres and can be crossed only through three passes, the Gidi, Mitla, and Sudr. The southern part of the peninsula comprises steep mountain ranges divided by deep waterless wadis; going is virtually impossible except down the coast of the Gulf of Aqaba.

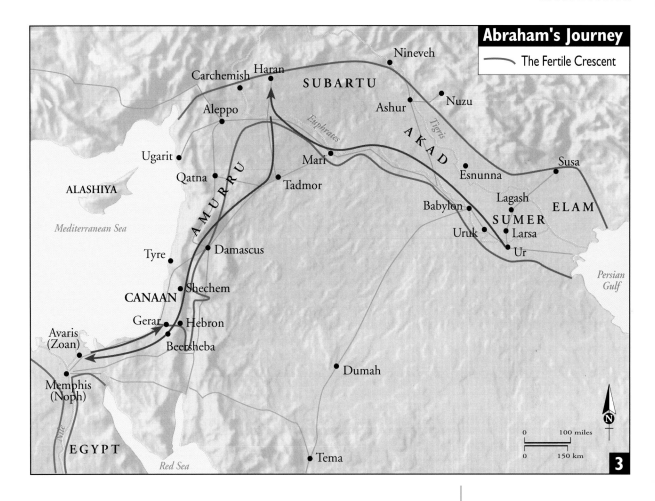

The desert continues northwards over the Israeli border and, apart from the coastal strip, stretches as far north as a line from Rafah to Beersheba and the southern end of the Dead Sea. A strip of desert continues northwards west of the Dead Sea and the Jordan River to about 16 km south of Bet Shean and westwards towards the ridge line, the only exceptions being the oases of Jericho and Jiflik.

From Beersheba to the Yizreel Valley the land between the Mediterranean and the Jordan/ Dead Sea is divided by the Judaean Hills which rise to a ridge varying between 800 and 1,000 metres above sea-level. To the west lies the coastal plain; at its widest it is no more than 32 km from the sea to Latrun, and it narrows to only 200 metres where Mount Carmel reaches the Mediterranean. North from Tel Aviv to Hadera the average distance from the sea to the 'Green' line (the 1949 cease-fire line) is only 16 km, a distance that can be crossed by a tank force in a matter of minutes, cutting Israel in two. There are few east–west routes from the Jordan to the coastal strip, the most important being those that pass through Jerusalem and Nablus; all are relatively easy to block. While the Jordan River provides little in the way of an obstacle, the Jordan Rift through which it flows is a major barrier, and tank egress on the western side is limited to a handful of places. The Yizreel Valley, whose width varies between 13 km between Nazareth and Jenin and narrows to a few hundred metres at Qiryat Tivon, runs north-west to south-east from Haifa on the Mediterranean to Bet Shean in the Jordan Valley; it passes north of Mount Carmel and Megiddo and south of Nazareth and Mount Tabor.

North of Yizreel is Galilee. Again there is a well-cultivated coastal strip, and between this and Lake Tiberias and the Upper Jordan the ground is rocky and extremely hilly, rising to over 1,000 metres at its highest point. The hills carry on northwards over the border into southern Lebanon. Before reaching the Upper Jordan the hills descend to the Hula Valley, an area of swamp and lake which was drained by Jewish settlers in the 1930s. Lake Tiberias (Sea of Galilee, Yam Kinneret) is over 200 metres below sea-level. To the east of the lake and the Upper Jordan the ground rises steeply, between 500 and 800 metres in less than 1.5 km, to the Golan Heights. The Golan is bounded by the Mount Hermon range in the north and, 70 km to the south, the Yarmouk River gorge. The plateau, which ascends gradually towards Damascus, is strewn with lava boulders and a number of volcanic hills (known as tels) dot the area, providing observation points and fields of fire. The map of the Middle East showing missile ranges is intended to show both the area which lies within range of Israeli missiles and equally the places from which missiles of various ranges could be fired at Israel.

The story of the Holy, or Promised, Land begins sometime between 1000 and 3000 BC with the migration from the region of Ur, a city on the Euphrates in southern Mesopotamia, of an Aramean clan led most probably by Abraham's father Terah. Why they left Ur is not known; one suggestion is that it became necessary after an Elamite invasion had replaced the Sumerian order in the region. The death of Terah is believed to have taken place at Harran (close to the Turkish–Syrian border), where he and his tribe had temporarily settled (*Genesis 11. 31–32*). The Lord then appeared to Abraham and said, 'Get thee out of thy country . . . unto a land that I will shew thee: And I will make of thee a great nation. . . .' (*Genesis 12. 1–2*). After Abraham had reached Canaan the Lord appeared to him again saying, 'Unto thy seed will I give this land.' (*Genesis 11. 7*). Further south Abraham found there was a famine and so journeyed on to Egypt. On leaving Egypt Abraham returned to Canaan, travelling as far north as Bethel, where on the journey south he had raised an altar. Here he split from Lot, his nephew, who crossed the Jordan to settle there. The Lord then appeared again to Abraham saying, 'Lift up now thine eyes . . . for all the land thou seest, to thee will I give it, and to thy seed for ever . . .' (*Genesis 13. 14–15*).

And when Abram was ninety years old and nine, the Lord appeared to Abram, and said unto him . . . and I will make thee exceeding fruitful, and I will make nations of thee, and kings shall come out of thee. . . . And I will give unto thee, and unto thy seed after thee, the land wherein thou art a stranger, all the land of Canaan, for an everlasting possession; and I will be their God.
Genesis 17. 1–9

THE FIRST BATTLE OF MEGIDDO

The Battle of Megiddo was not strictly a battle for holy land but it has been included as it is the first battle to have been recorded in any detail. The account, which includes the official log of the campaign, can be found carved on the walls of the Temple of Amun at Thebes. The date of the battle is not certain but all sources suggest it took place between 1468 and 1482 BC.

Some details about the Egyptian Army have been gained from the temple carvings. The army was organized in divisions of some 5,000 men, including both infantry and chariots, and normally named after Gods. The smallest unit was commanded by 'the greatest of the fifty', and four or five 'fifties' were commanded by a 'standard bearer'; the next highest rank was *ts pdt* (captain of a troop) and above that *hry pdt* (troop commander). For the first time the core of the army was made up of regular soldiers.

Egyptian (above) and Canaanite chariots.

At this time the Egyptians, who had recovered their land from the Hyksos invaders some eighty years earlier, were ruled by a woman, Hatshepsut, the aunt of her successor Tuthmosis III. Hatshepsut had been militarily inactive so that the rulers of Egypt's 'Asiatic' provinces had grown increasingly independent and they decided to combine in a move against Egypt. As a preliminary, they assembled an army, led by the Syrian King of Kadesh, on the plain of Esdraelon (Emeq Yizreel) close to the city of Megiddo. Tuthmosis reacted quickly and marched out with an army estimated to be between 10,000 and 20,000 strong; they reached Gaza in ten days, taking a further ten to reach Yaham (probably close to Baqa el-Gharbiya).

There were three roads by which Megiddo could be approached: the direct route followed Wadi Arah (Nahal Iron); to the south another route reached the plain at Taanach (Ta'nakh) about 6 km south-east of Megiddo; and to the north a road led to Jokneam (Yoqne'am), 13 km north of Megiddo. Overruling his generals' advice, Tuthmosis chose the Arah route, which was the narrowest; the generals had ruled it out on the grounds that the army would be widely spread out when it reached the plain at Megiddo. But it was also a choice the Canaanites had not expected – they had positioned forces at Taanach and north of Megiddo to block the other two routes. It is supposed that they were planning to retire, luring the Egyptians on to the plain where their infantry would be overrun by the Canaanite chariots which lay hidden just north of Megiddo.

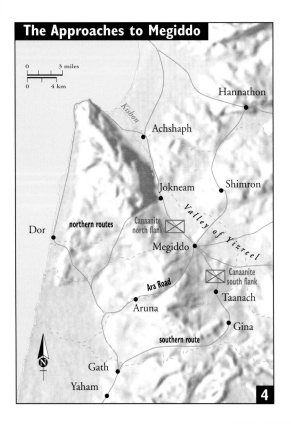

The Approaches to Megiddo

0 3 miles
0 4 km

Hannathon

Achshaph

Kishon

Jobneam

Shimron

Dor

northern routes

Canaanite
north flank

Megiddo

Valley of Yizreel

Canaanite
south flank

Ara Road

Aruna

Taanach

Gina

southern route

N

Gath

Yaham

4

The Egyptians advanced cautiously through the narrow pass, surprised to find no resistance, and they were able to fan out into battle formation as the northern end of the pass widened just west of the last hills before the valley. They camped on the southern side of the Qina (Nahal Ba'ena), as Tuthmosis had accepted his generals' advice not to deploy on to the plain immediately but to remain overnight in a strong position as the army closed up. The Egyptian army column took seven hours to pass a particular point, the rearguard leaving Aruna (Ara), where the army had spent the night, as the advance guard reached the northern end of the pass.

A detailed study of the Thebes texts, coupled with information derived from visits to the battlefield by an American scholar, suggests that the battle took the following course. The Canaanites would have formed up on the line of hills south of Megiddo but north of the Qina; the Egyptians sent part of their army, including their chariots, across the Qina and formed up to the north-west of Megiddo and to the west of the Canaanite centre; another part remained south of the

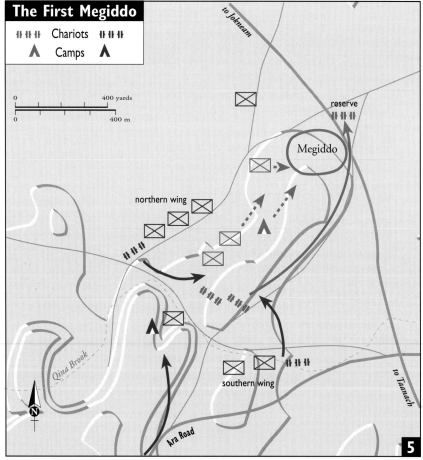

The First Megiddo

⫴ ⫴ ⫴ Chariots ⫴ ⫴ ⫴
Λ Camps Λ

to Jokneam

0 400 yards
0 400 m

reserve

Megiddo

northern wing

Qina Brook

N

southern wing

Ara Road

to Taanach

5

Tel Megiddo. (Photograph: Z. Radovan, Jerusalem)

wadi facing the Canaanite left. Little information is available on the actual fighting but it would appear that the Canaanites broke before the Egyptian attack and retreated into the fortifications of Megiddo, abandoning their horses and chariots. There were apparently few Canaanite casualties, possibly because the Egyptians were diverted by the search for booty in the Canaanite camp that they had to cross.

The Egyptians made no attempt to storm the city but set about a siege. Megiddo was not prepared for a siege and although there was no shortage of water it is unlikely that it held out for longer than a month. (The Thebes text records a period of six months between the start of the siege and Tuthmosis' return to Thebes, during which time the Egyptians had advanced into Lebanon, taken three other cities and returned to Egypt.) A good many of the Canaanites managed to escape from Megiddo, including their leaders who were not captured when the city fell. The Canaanites lost over 2,000 horses and nearly 900 chariots. The battle ended any chance of a successful revolt against the Egyptians.

THE ISRAELITE
CONQUEST

INTRODUCTION AND OVERVIEW

This section covers the 1,300 years between the Israelite crossing of the River Jordan into Canaan under the leadership of Joshua and the conquest of the Holy Land by the Assyrians. Four battles in this period are described in more detail: Joshua's capture of Jericho and Ai (Khirbet et Tell); the defeat of Sisera by Deborah; the Battle of Endor in the War of Gideon; and the campaigns of David. The Israelites were, like their modern Israeli counterparts, virtually continuously at war throughout their period of rule in the Holy Land, and this introduction can only give a broad outline of the period.

Following the defeat of the Canaanites at Ai, Joshua prepared to expand the territory occupied by the Israelite tribes but before he could do so he received a plea for help from the Gibeonites with whom he had made a pact after the capture of Jericho. Gibeon was about to be punished for having sided with the Israelites and an army had been gathered by the King of Jerusalem (though it must still have been named Jebus then) and four other Amorite kings (*Joshua 10.1–6*). Joshua reacted immediately and marching by night covered the 24 km from Gilgal (possibly Khirbet el Mefjer or Khirbet uin Ghafir) to Gibeon (Jib) undetected. His attack took the Amorites, who were then besieging Gibeon, by surprise and his army pursued them as they fled towards the Aijalon (Ayyalon) valley. The Israelites continued to harry them until they reached the fortress at Azekah (Tel Azeqa, about 13 km north of Bet Guvrin).

Joshua then extended his control throughout the mountains now known as the Judaean Hills as far as their western slopes. In the south, as *Joshua 10* relates, Joshua took and destroyed in turn the people of Makkedah, Libnah (Tel Burna), Lachish, Eglon (Tel Hasi), Hebron, Debir (Tel Bet Mirsham), Kadesh Barnea, and Gaza. He also conquered Galilee but to do so had to fight an alliance of northern Canaanites headed by the King of Hazor. The Canaanites were well equipped with chariots which the lightly armed Israelites would be unable to withstand if they encountered them on open ground. Joshua waited until the Canaanite army had camped in the gorge through which the Merom River flows (Nahal Meron); they were concentrating their forces in this central location in order to be able to deploy in any direction to meet the Israelites. After defeating the Canaanites in a surprise attack, Joshua

The Twelve Tribes of Israel

Asher
Benjamin
Dan
Ephraim
Gad
Issachar
Judah
Manasseh
Naphtali
Reuben
Simeon
Zebulun

turned back to the south and took the city of Hazor, destroying it and its population. However, he left the other Canaanite cities unharmed.

The tribes of Israel now settled the conquered territory. Gad, Reuben and half the tribe of Mannasseh had already settled on the eastern side of the Jordan. In the north, in Galilee and southern Lebanon, Asher, Issachar, Naphtali and Zebulun settled. To their south was the other part of Manasseh. Also in the central mountains were Ephraim, Benjamin and Dan but the Dan tribe was forced to migrate north by the Amorites on whose land they had attempted to settle. Judah took the southern mountains while the Negev was eventually settled by Simeon. However, the Israelites did not occupy nor control the whole country. The coastal plain was occupied as far north as the Yarqon by the Philistines, and further north from Tyre northwards by other 'sea-peoples' tribes. The Philistines, who had come from the Aegean, had first conquered Cyprus, then invaded Egypt where they had been defeated by Rameses III in 1188 BC. Shortly after this they established themselves on the coast of Canaan. They were a more advanced race than the Israelites, having learned how to process iron, a skill they attempted to withhold from the Israelites (*1 Samuel 13.19–20*). Inland there were still pockets of independent Canaanites: in the valley of Yizreel around Megiddo, Taanach (Tel Ta'nakh) and Bet Shean, and on the coast at Aphek (Afeq, north-east of Haifa), Acco and Akhziv. Further north they held Beth Shemesh and Beth Anath (Ainatha, Lebanon), and there was a strip of Canaanite-held land running from Gezer to Jebus (Jerusalem) which separated the northern Israelite tribes from those in the south.

The Judges followed Joshua's period of leadership; they were leaders who usually came into prominence at a time of crisis or danger, and who had authority over the whole or part of the country. During this time the Philistines made considerable inroads into Israelite territory. Also in this period a coalition of northern Canaanites was defeated by Deborah, and Midianite raiders were driven out by Gideon. The northern Israelite tribes formed a loose federation under the name of Israel. When the Israelites were attacked from the east by the Ammonites, who besieged Jabesh-Gilead (Tel el Maqlub, east of the Jordan in Wadi Yabis), Saul, the last of the succession of Judges, assembled an army at Bezek (north-east of Tubas) and totally defeated them. Samuel then led the Israelites to Gilgal where he anointed Saul as the first King (*1 Samuel 11*). Saul then set about creating a standing army some 3,000-strong and divided into two groups; the smaller group, of 1,000 men, was commanded by his son Jonathan and stationed at Gibeah (Tel el Ful) (*1 Samuel 13*). Jonathan's first operation was the capture of Geba (Jab'a) from the Philistines; as this success threatened Philistine control of central Judah they gathered a force at Michmash (Mukhmas). Saul attempted to concentrate his army at Geba but many of his soldiers had deserted and his force was very weak.

Discovering this, the Philistines sent out three separate raiding columns to ravage the countryside, leaving a blocking force south of Michmash at the saddle on the Geba road. Saul moved forward but his army was still not strong enough to risk an attack on the Philistines; meanwhile Jonathan, accompanied only by his shield-bearer, went into the deep gorge of Wadi Suweinit (Nahal Mickmas), climbing out behind the Philistine position.

> And when the Lord raised them up judges, then the Lord was with the judge, and delivered them out of the hand of their enemies all the days of the judge....And it came to pass, when the judge was dead, that they returned, and corrupted themselves more than their fathers.
>
> *Judges 2. 18–19*

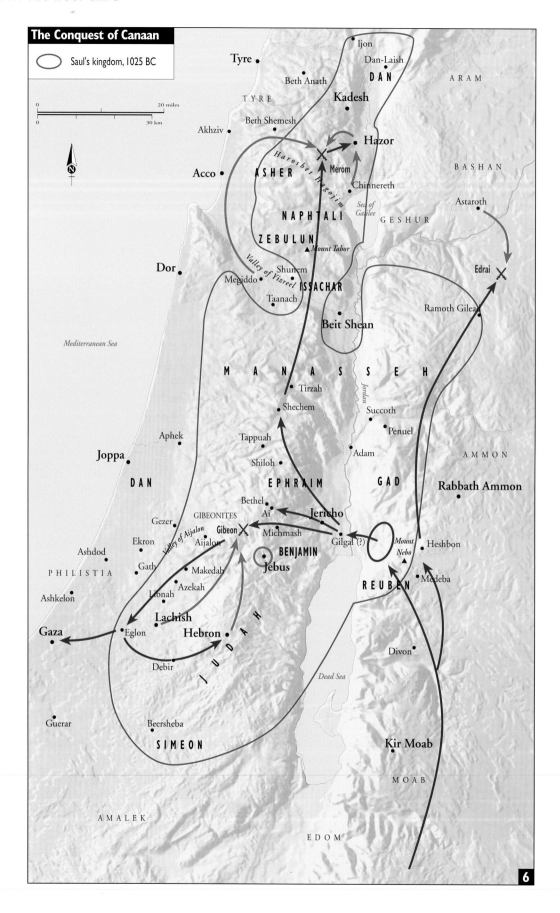

The Conquest of Canaan

Saul's kingdom, 1025 BC

0   20 miles
0   30 km

N

Tyre

TYRE

Ijon
Dan-Laish
DAN
Beth Anath
Kadesh
ARAM

Beth Shemesh
Akhziv
Harosheth-haggoiim
Hazor
Merom
Acco
ASHER
Chinnereth
BASHAN

NAPHTALI
Sea of Galilee
GESHUR
Astaroth

ZEBULUN
Mount Tabor

Dor
Valley of Yizreel
Shunem
Megiddo
ISSACHAR
Taanach
Edrai

Beit Shean
Ramoth Gilead

Mediterranean Sea

M A N A S S E H

Tirzah
Jordan
Shechem
Succoth
Penuel

Aphek
Tappuah
Adam
AMMON

Joppa
Shiloh

DAN
EPHRAIM
GAD
Rabbath Ammon

Bethel
Gezer
GIBEONITES
Ai
Jericho
Gilgal (?)
Mount Nebo
Heshbon
Ekron
Gibeon
Michmash
Valley of Aijalon
Aijalon
Ashdod
BENJAMIN
Medeba
Gath
Makedah
Jebus
PHILISTIA
Azekah
Libnah
Ashkelon

Lachish
Eglon
Hebron
JUDAH
Divon
Gaza
Debir

Dead Sea

Guerar
Beersheba

SIMEON

REUBEN

Kir Moab

AMALEK

MOAB

EDOM

6

They so surprised the Philistines that the pair were able to kill a number and force the others to retreat. In the confusion Saul attacked Michmash; the Philistines fled and were harassed throughout their flight by other Israelites who had earlier hidden from them in the hills. (*1 Samuel 14*).

In about 1006 BC the Philistines had regained their strength and set about attempting to divide the Israelite tribes in Galilee from those to the south. They first assembled their forces at Aphek (Tel Afeq, Antipatris) and then advanced up the coastal route to the Valley of Yizreel, camping at

The Ayyalon Valley, scene of several Israelite battles with the Philistines. (Photograph: Z. Radovan, Jerusalem)

Shunem (Solam). Saul and the Israelite army followed them northwards, using the central route and deploying on the western lower slopes of Mount Gilboa. David, who was a vassal to the Philistines at that time, brought his men to Aphek to support his liege but he was judged unreliable and was not allowed to join the operation. The terrain around Mount Gilboa allowed the Philistines to employ their chariots successfully and their chariot-mounted archers were able to continue the attack even after the Israelites withdrew higher up the slope. Saul, realizing that the battle was lost, committed suicide rather than be captured. The Philistines achieved their aim in that the Israelite nation then split into Judah, which was ruled by David, and Israel, ruled by Saul's son Eshbaal.

David's campaigns, which reunited the Israelites, defeated their enemies east of the Jordan, and expanded their territory, are described separately. David was succeeded by Solomon who built a network of fortresses throughout Israel and reorganized and modernized the army. He introduced the chariot and is said to have had 1,400 of these (*1 Kings 10.26*). While Solomon's achievements were of great importance they cost the people of Israel a great deal in both financial and labour terms. When Rehoboam, Solomon's son, asserted on his succession '. . . my

Mount Merom Gorge, scene of an Israelite battle with the Canaanites. (Photograph: Z. Radovan, Jerusalem)

father also chastised you with whips, but I will chastise you with scorpions' (*1 Kings 12.13–14*), the people rejected him, only Judah and Benjamin remaining loyal while the other tribes retained the name Israel under the rule of Jeroboam. Jerusalem remained the capital of Judah while Tirzah (Tel el-Farah) became that of Israel.

In 924 BC the Egyptian Pharaoh Shishak despatched two armies to ravage and weaken the Israelites, who, while strong and united, threatened Egypt's ability to expand its political influence and trading opportunities. One army was sent to destroy the infrastructure of the Negev and the port of Ezion-Geber (Elat/Aqaba), while the other advanced up the coastal route before turning inland to attack Judah. The Egyptians settled for a heavy tribute from Judah before attacking Israel, including a foray over the Jordan to Penuel (Jebel Osha); a fragment of a Shishak stele has been found at Megiddo. A list of the Israelite cities destroyed by the Egyptians is inscribed at Karnak.

Israel now faced three enemies: to the north were the Arameans, who had taken advantage of Shishak's invasion to capture a number of towns on the Golan; to the east the Ammonites and Moabites had regained their independence, and to the west the Philistines continued to be a threat. Israel failed in two attempts, in 906 and 882 BC, to recapture the Gibbethon area which controlled Philistine access to the Samarian Mountains from the coastal plain (*1 Kings 15.27* and *16.15*). Nor were Judah and Israel always at peace with each other; in about 911 BC Abijah, the King of Judah, made considerable inroads into southern Israel, capturing Bethel (Beitin), Jeshanah (Burj el-Isaneh) and Ephron (Ofra). This territory was recovered by Baasha who advanced a short way into Judah and began to construct a fortress at Ramah (E-Ram). But an attack by the Arameans distracted Baasha and Judah, now ruled by Asa, destroyed the work and used the materials there to develop its own forts at Mizpeh (Tel en Nasbeh) and Geba (*1 Kings 15.22*).

In about 882 BC Zimri, the army commander, led a revolt which killed Elah, who had succeeded his father Baasha, and all his descendants and supporters, and Zimri himself took the throne. Omri, the general who commanded that part of the army that watched Gibbethon, was supported by the people of Israel and in his turn attacked Zimri and was declared king (*1 Kings 16.8–23*). Omri greatly strengthened Israel's security and economy; an alliance was made with the Phoenicians, Moab was reconquered and a new capital was established at Samaria (Sabastiya). Omri's son Ahab fought three wars against the Arameans; in the first Samaria was besieged but the Israelites, employing a decoy force, broke out and drove the Arameans away with great loss (*1 Kings 20.19–22*). Ahab, to pre-empt another Aramean invasion, advanced on to the Golan south of the Sea of Galilee. He was blocked for eight days in a defile (possibly Wadi Mezar) but made two wide outflanking moves so that the Israelites could attack the Arameans from the rear; the Aramean army was broken completely (*1 Kings 20.26–30*). In the third encounter, at Ramoth-Gilead (Tel Ramith, Jordan) in 851 BC, Ahab was shot by an archer but continued fighting until he died later that evening, leaving the Arameans in control of the northern part of the country east of the Jordan (*2 Chronicles 18.28–34*).

Kings of Israel

1006 David
965 Solomon
928 Rehoboam

The Divided Kingdom

Israel	Judah
909 Baasha	911 Asa
886 Elah	870 Jehoshaphat
885 Zimri	848 Jehoram
885 Omri	841 Athallah
874 Ahab	835 Jehoash
853 Ahaziah	796 Amaziah
852 Joram	767 Uzziah
841 Jehu	740 Jotham
814 Jehoahaz	732 Ahaz
798 Joash	
782 Jeroboam II	
753 Zechariah	
752 Shallum	
752 Pekah	
732 Hoshea	

The next threat came from the Assyrians under Shalmaneser III who, in 853 BC, captured several cities in Hamath (northern Syria) including Qarqar on the Orontes. The Assyrians were faced by a 'league of twelve kings', including those of Hamath, Aram and Israel. A major battle was fought at Qarqar, and while Shalmaneser claimed a victory the Assyrians advanced no further. The Assyrians had, though, weakened the power of the Arameans and Judah took advantage of this to attack Edom and capture Salt (es Salt) and Sela (Petra). This success prompted Israel to attack Judah, defeat it and take the king, Amaziah, captive. Israel, under Joash and his son Jeroboam II, defeated the Arameans on three occasions as described in *2 Kings 13.25*, *Amos 6.13* and *2 Kings 13.17*. Jeroboam extended Israel's control beyond the Golan to the east and as far as Lebo-Hamath (Lebweh) north of Damascus.

In the mid-eighth century BC Judah, led by Uzziah, attacked the Philistines and gained control of the eastern part of their land but not the cities; Judah now held the coastline from Jabneh (Yavne) to the Yarqon. Uzziah also completed the conquest of Edom and the Negev, establishing a border from the Brook of Egypt (Wadi el-Arish) to the Red Sea south of Ezion Geber. Uzziah also headed another alliance to stem the Assyrian advance but after fighting in northern Syria the alliance collapsed and the Assyrians moved into Hamath and the Lebanese mountains. Ahaz, Uzziah's grandson, refused to join a further alliance against the Assyrians which caused both Israel, under Pekah, and the Arameans, under Rezin, to attack Judah. The Philistines also set about retaking their land, gaining as far east as Gimza (Gimzo), Aijalon (Ayyalon), Beth-Shemesh and Socoh (Khirbet Shuweikeh). In some desperation Ahaz appealed for Assyrian help even though he had been warned of the danger of this by Isaiah (*Isaiah 8.6–9*).

THE ISRAELITE ENTRY INTO CANAAN: THE BATTLES OF JERICHO AND AI

When Joshua looked at Canaan over the River Jordan from Mount Nebo he could see that the river crossing might not be easy and that his first task in establishing a bridgehead across the Jordan would be the capture of the walled city of Jericho which blocked the way into the hills lying between the Jordan and the sea. Joshua had also appreciated that the lightly armed Israelites would be no match for the more heavily armed and better organized Canaanites in the open plains, and that they must first establish themselves in the hills if they were not to be cut down by the Canaanite chariots. Joshua despatched a two-man reconnaissance party to check the crossing sites over the Jordan and the strength of Jericho's defences. Their exploits have been recorded in *Joshua 2*, and while in Jericho, where they were hidden by Rahab, the harlot, they learnt that morale was low as the news of the defeat of the Amorites had reached them.

The Israelites crossed the Jordan probably close to the site of the Damiya Bridge where there was a ford and where, on two more recent occasions, the steep banks of the river have collapsed and temporarily blocked the flow of water. This, rather than some miraculous event, may account for the report in *Joshua 3.14–17* that the Israelites 'passed over on dry ground'. Equally important was the fact that the Canaanites did not oppose the crossing. The Israelites were not equipped to lay siege to Jericho, which may explain the tactics adopted, but which Joshua claims he was instructed in by God (*Joshua 6.2–5*). Virtually no archaeological evidence of this period has been found in digs at Jericho so it cannot be proved that the walls collapsed at the Israelites' great shout. In any event the city must have fallen to a sudden attack after the garrison had been lulled by the Israelite routine into a sense of false security, and possibly a covert entry was made aided by Rahab. The assault is described in *Joshua 6*. After the capture of Jericho the Israelites established a camp at Gilgal (possibly Khirbet el-Mefjer or Khirbet um-Ghafir).

Joshua again sent out scouts to reconnoitre the routes to Ai (Khirbet et Tell) and Bethel (Beitin), the latter being some 25 km west of Jericho close to today's Ramallah and just below the ridge formed by the Judaean Hills, and to gauge the strength of their defences and garrisons. Joshua also made an alliance with the Gibeonites, a small group of tribes living in the hills just north-west of Jerusalem (then called Jebus) which would give him greater freedom of action. As a result of the scouts' reports Joshua decided not to attack Bethel as it was too heavily defended but to attack Ai some 4 or 5 km to the east and which dominated the approaches to the ridge. Unfortunately the scouts badly underestimated the Canaanite strength at Ai and recommended that only 2,000–3,000 men would be needed to take the town. The first attack on Ai was repulsed and the Israelites must have fled as only thirty-six casualties were reported (*Joshua 7.5*); Canaanite morale was restored.

Joshua decided to attack again straightaway and formulated a deceptive plan, taking advantage of the earlier setback, whose main aim was to draw the Canaanites away from their defensive positions at Ai and Bethel. Two detachments of Israelites were moved under cover of darkness to be in positions to take advantage of any Canaanite move on the Israelite main body out of their defended towns. The task of one detachment, lying up probably south-west of Ai, was to capture the town as soon as the garrison moved out, to set fire to it and then to fall on the rear of the Canaanites.

The second detachment, positioned to the north-west of Ai, was to outflank the Canaanite forces. The main Israelite force assembled, after an approach march, in Wadi Makkuk and advanced on Ai at dawn. Then, when the Canaanites came out to attack them as they had before, they began to withdraw; the deception worked and the Canaanites left both towns in pursuit. Once the two forces were a kilometre or two away from Ai, in the gorge of the Wadi, Joshua, who had climbed a nearby hill, signalled by flashing sunlight on the blade of his spear and the Israelite plan came into effect. Ai was

Joshua crosses the Jordan

0   3 miles
0   5 km

Bethel
Ai
Jericho
Gilgal (?)
Gibeon
Jordan
Jebus (Jerusalem)
Dead Sea

N

7

The view towards the hills west of Jericho.

taken and set alight, the main Israelite force turned about and attacked the Canaanites who were also attacked from the west by the captors of Ai and from the north, from high ground, by the outflanking group of 5,000 men. Ai was totally destroyed and all its inhabitants killed. The Israelites did not go on to take Bethel but returned to their base at Gilgal.

Joshua obviously appreciated the importance of intelligence and reconnaissance and his use of surprise, achieved by his deception plan, helped to ensure his victory at Ai.

DEFEAT OF SISERA BY DEBORAH: EARLY TWELFTH CENTURY BC

It is disputed whether the defeat of Sisera by Deborah in the Valley of Yizreel, the plain running from Mount Tabor west towards Acco, took place before or after the Battle of the Waters of Merom, following which the city of Hazor was destroyed. In the Bible it is described in the Book of Joshua, with the King of Hazor having the same name, Zabin, as that of the king at the time of Deborah. There is archaeological evidence that Hazor was burnt to the ground in the thirteenth century BC and Israelite pottery of the same period has been found there; Professor Yigal Yadin maintains that Hazor was destroyed in both the thirteenth and mid-twelfth centuries. However, the date has no implications for the conduct of Deborah's victory.

At this time, thought to be between the end of the thirteenth and middle of the

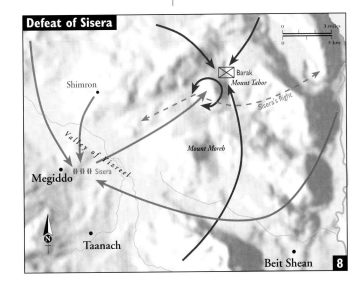

twelfth century BC, the Israelites had begun to make inroads into Galilee but after the death of Joshua no leader had emerged and the tribes were only a loose coalition. However, the Israelites did not drive the Canaanites out and they still occupied the main towns; the two races lived very much together with one or the other being dominant. (*Judges 1* describes the situation after the death of Joshua.) Nor were the Canaanites totally united either, though the tribes living in the lower Galilee had been brought together to oppose the Israelite intrusion by the unnamed 'King of the people in Galilee'. He was supported by the kings of the cities to the north and north-west of Yizreel of whom Jabin, King of Hazor, was the most important. After the death of Ehud, 'the children of Israel again did evil in the sight of the Lord' (*Judges 4.1*) and the Canaanites gained the ascendency and the Israelites were 'mightily oppressed for twenty years' (*Judges 4.3*) by Sisera, the Canaanite general whose army was positioned at Haroshet Hagojim (Ha Amaqim), blocking the pass between the Valley of Yizreel and the coastal plain.

The Hebrew prophetess, Deborah, who lived on Mount Ephraim (between Ramah (Ramallah) and Bethel (Beitin) *Judges 4.5*), rallied support from a number of the tribes and appointed Barak to lead their army. Her plan was to draw the Canaanites away from Haroshet Hagojim by positioning Barak, with 10,000 men from the tribes of Naphtali and Zebulun, on Mount Tabor where they would be safe from the Canaanite chariots which were said to number 900. They would also be deployed between Sisera and Hazor. Sisera would then be outflanked by Israelite forces, of the tribes of Benjamin, Ephraim, Issacher, and Manasseh, coming from the hills to the south.

Sisera, on learning from Heber the Kenite of the Israelite deployment on Mount Tabor, advanced towards it, as had been hoped, and the two armies faced each other for several days. The southern Israelite force advanced into the Valley of Yizreel where they encountered some opposition; Sisera turned to meet this threat to his rear. Barak then attacked. At this juncture, 'They fought from heaven; the stars in their courses fought against Sisera' (*Judges 5.20*) which has been interpreted to mean a fortuitous rainstorm which turned the valley into a quagmire in which the Canaanite chariots soon became bogged down. The rain also flooded the River Kishon where many fleeing Canaanites were drowned and their chariots swept away.

While the Canaanites mainly fled to the west, Sisera made his escape to the east where he met Jael, the wife of Heber, who led him into her tent and, having hidden him under a mantle, killed him by driving a tent peg into his forehead.

Many of the details of the battle come from the 'Song of Deborah' in *Judges 5*. The following chapter begins: 'And the children of Israel did evil in the sight of the Lord: and the Lord delivered them into the hand of Midian seven years'; so their victory did not last long.

THE BATTLE OF ENDOR

The lands in which the Israelite tribes settled were bordered to the east and south by deserts where nomadic tribes were entirely dependent on

---

Death of Sisera

And Jael went out to meet Sisera, and said unto him, 'Turn in, my Lord, turn in to me; fear not.' And when he had turned in unto her into the tent, she covered him with a mantle....

Then Jael Heber's wife took a nail of the tent, and took an hammer in her hand, and went softly unto him, and smote the nail into his temples, and fastened it into the ground: for he was fast asleep and weary. So he died.

Judges 4.18 and 21.

rain for survival. It was not surprising therefore that they should migrate into the Israelite lands in search of pasture for their flocks and from time to time carry out deeper marauding raids. These tribesmen were mounted on camels which enabled them to avoid having to fight a pitched battle, but at the same time they were strong enough to break through groups of lightly armed Israelites.

During the twelfth century BC there was no central control over the Israelite tribes, which made them more vulnerable to the depredations of the desert tribes. In the north Gideon, the leader of the Aviezer clan of Manasseh, decided to take action against the intruders and gained the support of Asher, Zebulun, and Naphtali, who provided him with fighting men. He had assembled a force of some 30,000 men to expel a large group of Midianites who were encamped at Endor on Mount Moreh (Givat Hamore) south of Mount Tabor (some 4 km south-west of today's Endor). Realizing that attempting a large-scale attack would only result in warning the Midianites who would immediately ride off, Gideon decided to attack at night with a small body of picked men and to hope to drive the intruders back to the Jordan and to harry them throughout their retreat with forces positioned in the hills on either side of the likely escape route.

Judges 7. 4–7 describes the way Gideon chose his selected assault party of 300 men, the final test involving the manner in which they drank at the Spring of Harod (En Harod, halfway between Afula and Bet Shean), which was dangerously near the Midian encampment. The choice was between those who knelt and brought the water to their mouths in their cupped hands and those who lay down and drank directly from the pool; different interpretations have been given to the choice. Mordechai Gichon suggests that those who lay down were chosen because they kept their weapons in their hands and so were always ready to react. Josephus saw it differently: God had instructed Gideon to choose those who hurriedly scooped up water in their hands because they were more frightened than those who drank calmly – a rather peculiar choice. *Judges 7. 4–7* does not really clarify matters: it states that they were divided between those who lapped with their tongues like dogs and those who knelt; then it muddles things by saying that 300 who lapped by putting their hands cupped to their mouth, unlike dogs, were chosen, the others having drunk from their knees.

Gideon then carried out a personal reconnaissance of the Midian camp. He equipped his assault party with earthenware jars, in which were hidden lighted torches, and trumpets; they approached the camp from three directions and at a signal sounded the trumpets and set fire to the camp with the torches, creating panic among the Midianites who fled towards the Jordan. They retreated through Beth Shittah (between Afula and Bet Shean) and on to Abel Mehola (15 km south of Bet Shean) and Tabbath (Pella), which Gichon suggests were forts that prevented them from crossing the Jordan there. At this late stage Gideon called on the tribe of Ephraim to hold the Jordan fords at Beth-barah (thought to be Adam/Damiya) which they did with some success, killing the Midianite chiefs Oreb and Zeeb. The tribe of Ephraim complained bitterly to Gideon for not having asked for their help earlier.

Gideon continued to pursue the Midianites across the Jordan but was refused supplies by the people of Succoth (Tel Deir 'alla) and Penuel

> So he brought down the people unto the water: and the Lord said unto Gideon, Every one that lappeth with his tongue as a dog lappeth, him shalt thou set by himself; likewise every one that boweth down upon his knees to drink. And the number of them that lapped putting their hand to their mouth were three hundred men.
>
> *Judges 7. 5–6*

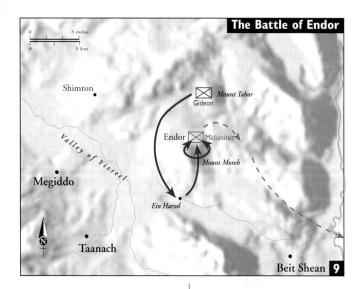

The Battle of Endor

Shimron

Mount Tabor
Gideon

Valley of Yizreel

Endor ✕ Midianites

Megiddo

Mount Moreh

Ein Harod

Taanach

Beit Shean **9**

(which lay in the Wadi Zarqa/Nahal Yaboq), of the tribe of Gilead (Gad). The Israelites took prisoner two Midianite kings, Zebah and Zalmunal, after a battle east of the Jordan. Gideon said to them, "'What manner of men were they whom ye slew at Tabor?" and they answered, "as thou art, so were they; each resembled the children of a king". And he said "they were my brethren"' *Judges 8. 18–19*. Gichon believes that this passage suggests that Gideon had despatched a force to Mount Tabor to block further Midianite movement to the north and to provide time for Gideon to concentrate his forces. He also suggests that the presence of this force kept the Midianites' attention and so allowed Gideon to approach Endor undetected.

Following the battle and defeat of the Midianites the Israelites called on Gideon to be their king, but he replied, 'I will not rule over you neither shall my son rule over you: the Lord shall rule over you.' *Judges 8. 22–23*. However, Gideon led the Israelites for another forty years of peace; but after his death they again turned away from God and turned to worship Baalberith.

THE CAMPAIGNS OF DAVID

While David may be best known for his killing of the Philistine champion, Goliath, as described in *1 Samuel 17*, he was the first Hebrew leader to unite the Jewish people of both Judah and Israel, and to conquer virtually the whole of the Holy Land and much of the surrounding territory.

Mount Gilboa and the Valley of Yizreel, scene of many Israelite battles. (Photograph: Z. Radovan, Jerusalem)

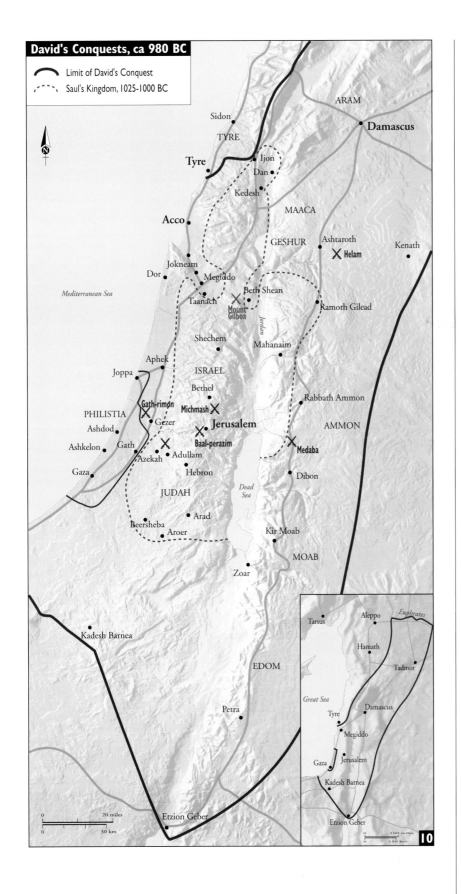

David's Conquests, ca 980 BC

- Limit of David's Conquest
- Saul's Kingdom, 1025-1000 BC

N

Main map labels:

ARAM

Sidon

Damascus

TYRE

Ijon

Tyre

Dan

Kedesh

MAACA

Acco

GESHUR

Ashtaroth

Kenath

✕ **Helam**

Jokneam

Dor

Megiddo

Beth Shean

Mediterranean Sea

Taanach

Mount Gilboa ✕

Ramoth Gilead

Jordan

Shechem

Mahanaim

Aphek

ISRAEL

Joppa

Bethel

Rabbath Ammon

Gath-rimon ✕

Michmash ✕

PHILISTIA

Gezer

✕ **Jerusalem**

AMMON

Ashdod

Baal-perazim ✕

Ashkelon

Gath ✕

Adullam

✕ **Medaba**

Azekah

Gaza

Hebron

Dibon

Dead Sea

JUDAH

Arad

Beersheba

Kir Moab

Aroer

MOAB

Zoar

Kadesh Barnea

EDOM

Petra

0   20 miles

0   30 km

Etzion Geber

Inset map labels:

Tarsus

Aleppo

Euphrates

Hamath

Tadmor

Great Sea

Damascus

Tyre

Megiddo

Jerusalem

Gaza

Kadesh Barnea

Etzion Geber

0   100 miles

0   150 km

10

Mount Tabor from the south.

And there went out a champion …
named Goliath, whose height was six
cubits and a span. … And he stood and
cried unto the armies of Israel …
choose you a man for you. … And all
the men of Israel … fled from him. …
And David put his hand in his bag, and
took thence a stone, and slang it, and
smote the Philistine in his forehead.

1 Samuel 17

After the battle with Goliath Saul's jealousy of David (*1 Samuel 18–19*) led the latter to adopt the life of an outlaw. Based at the cave of Adullam (Netiv ha-Lamed He) south-west of Bethlehem, he led a band of guerrillas who, for a price, protected the local people against the raids of the Philistines and the nomadic tribes. After the defeat of Saul and the tribes of Israel by the Philistines at the Battle of Gilboa (*1 Samuel 31*) where Jonathan was killed and Saul committed suicide, David was proclaimed King of Judah at Hebron and he set about gaining the confidence of all the Jewish tribes. It was seven years before he was accepted by all twelve tribes and proclaimed King of all Israel. His first act was to move the capital from Hebron to a neutral location; he chose Jerusalem, then known as Jebus, which lay between Judah and Israel and on the main east–west route from the Mediterranean to the Jordan. First, however, the Jebusite garrison had to be defeated. This was achieved by Joab in a surprise attack, possibly by climbing the water channel (now known as Warren's Shaft) which ran from the Gihon spring into the city. *2 Samuel 5.8* makes mention of a gutter. Joab was appointed commander-in-chief of the Israelite army as his reward.

The Philistines saw the risk from the newly united Israelites and decided to take action. Their first move was to send a force towards Michmash (Mukhmas) but David, who had moved his army to Adullam, shadowed the Philistines as they moved eastwards, before they reached Jerusalem. When the Philistines reached Baal-perazim (Manakhat) in the Valley of Rephaim (along which the railway to Jerusalem now runs), David attacked them from the rear and dispersed them. The Philistines advanced again up the Rephaim Valley. This time David, after abandoning his blocking position and so enticing the Philistines deeper into the valley, was able to mount a surprise attack from the cover of a wood of mulberry trees. The Israelites pursued the retreating Philistines, constantly attacking them until they reached Gazer (Tel Gezer). David finally defeated the Philistines at the Battle of Methegammah (on the coastal plain but otherwise unlocated) (*2 Samuel 8.1*); he then moved on to capture and occupy Gath (Tel Zayit) and a stretch of coastline from the Yarqon south to the Soreq. The port of Joppa (Jaffa) was allowed to remain independent.

David then moved north in order to consolidate Israel's control over the whole area and to eliminate the remaining Canaanite strongholds, including those in the Sharon and Yizreel Valleys. Next he crossed the Jordan to suppress first the Moabites, then the Edomites in a campaign which lasted six months, and finally the Ammonites. The Ammonites had had friendly relations with both Saul and David but after the death of their king his successor had insulted a mission sent bearing David's condolences: thinking that they were spies the Ammonites cut off the beards of the Israelite messengers. Realizing this had provoked David, the Ammonites sought help from their northern neighbours, the Arameans (Syrians), who despatched a large army. This meant that Joab and the Israelites found one army to their north and another, weaker, Ammonite army to the south.

The Israelites were besieging the fortress of Medeba (Madaba) when warning of the Aramean approach was given by the screen Joab had deployed to guard his rear. David's plan was to split his army, leaving the weaker part to face the Ammonites, while he with the stronger half attacked the Arameans. The results of these two battles were inconclusive but the Arameans resolved to restore their military credibility and summoned reinforcements. David moved to the Edrei gap, that part of the Yarmouk River which is neither in a deep gorge nor impassable because of the lava rocks. The battle took place north of the Yarmouk, at Helam (Aalma), and resulted in a total victory for the Israelites. David then returned to complete his defeat of the Ammonites. After this he controlled the land from the Mediterranean to the desert east of the Jordan and all three main routes from Egypt and Arabia in the south to Asia Minor and Mesopotamia in the north. However, he allowed both the Philistines and the Phoenicians a degree of independence in their cities along the coast, though this led to several minor wars with the Philistines.

And he said, If the Syrians be too strong for me, then thou shalt help me: but if the children of Ammon be too strong for thee, then I will come and help thee. . . . and Joab drew nigh . . . unto the battle with the Syrians: and they fled before him. . . . And when the children of Ammon saw that the Syrians were fled, then fled they also. . . . David, he gathered all Israel together. . . . And the Syrians set themselves in array against David, and fought with him . . . and David slew the men of seven hundred chariots and forty thousand horsemen.

2 Samuel 10.11–18

THE PRE-ROMAN
CONQUESTS

T his section covers the period from the Assyrian expansion, which began in the early ninth century BC, to the Seleucid conquest of Antiochus III and the Maccabean Revolt against his son, Antiochus IV, in 167. It describes also the conquests made by the Babylonians, the Persians and Alexander the Great.

THE ASSYRIAN CONQUEST

Assyria lay astride the River Tigris, centred on its capital Nineveh. In the ninth century BC Asshurnasirpal II began a campaign of expansion which took his armies through northern Beth-Eden (Syria) and into Phoenicia on the Mediterranean coast. Tribute was exacted from Arvad (Ruad), Byblos (Jubail), Sidon, and Tyre. Asshurnasirpal's son Shalmaneser III continued the campaign and by 859 BC he had reached the Amanus Mountains; in 853 he marched further south capturing Qarqar and other cities in Hamath (Syria). An alliance of the threatened kings assembled an army

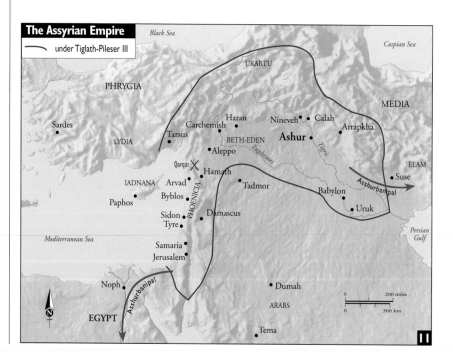

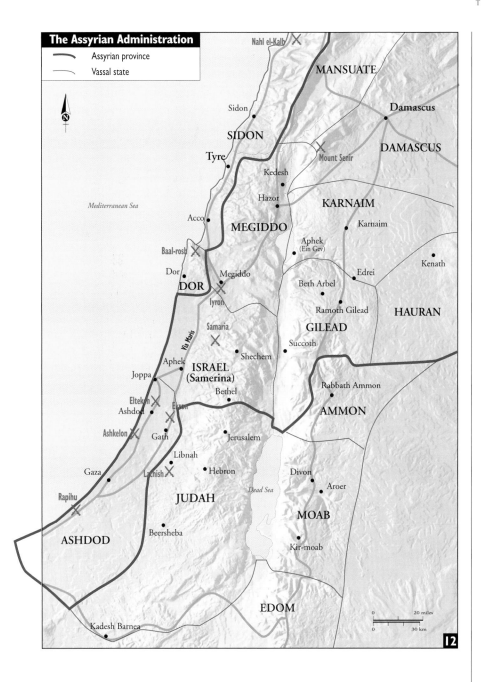

The Assyrian Administration

— Assyrian province

— Vassal state

Nahl el-Kalb ✕

MANSUATE

Sidon

SIDON

Damascus

DAMASCUS

Tyre

Kedesh

Mount Senir ✕

Hazor

KARNAIM

Mediterranean Sea

Acco

MEGIDDO

Karnaim

Baal-rosh ✕

Aphek (Ein Gev)

Dor

Megiddo

Kenath

DOR

Edrei

Iyron

Beth Arbel

Samaria

Ramoth Gilead

HAURAN

✕

GILEAD

Shechem

Succoth

Aphek

ISRAEL (Samerina)

Joppa

Bethel

Rabbath Ammon

Eltekon ✕

Ekron

AMMON

Ashdod

Jerusalem

Ashkelon ✕

Gath

Libnah

Gaza

Lachish ✕

Hebron

Divon

Dead Sea

Aroer

Rapihu ✕

JUDAH

MOAB

ASHDOD

Beersheba

Kir-moab

EDOM

0   20 miles

0   30 km

12

Via Maris

said to number some 4,000 chariots and 60,000 foot soldiers, with the main contingents coming from Damascus, Hamath, Israel and Phoenicia. A major battle was fought at Qarqar; although Shalmaneser claimed a victory for the Assyrians they were unable to renew their invasion attempt for four years. Campaigns were mounted in 849, 848 and 845 but none was successful owing to the opposition mounted by the alliance. However, after Hazael in Damascus and Jehu in Israel came into power, the alliance disintegrated. In 841 Shalmaneser was more successful, first defeating Hazael at Mount Senir (Mount Hermon) then mounting an unsuccessful siege of Damascus. Moving south he destroyed a number of cities in the Haurun mountains, then turning west destroyed Beth-arbel (Irbid) and, it is believed, Hazor (level VIII). He then crossed the Carmel mountains and marched north along the coast, setting up victory columns at Baal-rosh (Mount Carmel) and in the north at the mouth of the Nahr el-Kalb.

After this Assyria had to concentrate on problems in the north and east of their empire and this allowed Hazael in Damascus to mount a campaign to the south. In about 815 BC Hazael conquered all the land east of the Jordan as far south as Aroer (close to Wadi el-Mujib), while in Israel he is thought to have destroyed Hazor (level VII); he may well have also destroyed Aphek (Ein Gev), Shechem (Nablus) and Samaria. He reduced Israel's borders and imposed limits on its forces of 10 chariots and 10,000 soldiers (2 Kings 13.7). He reached Gath (Tel Zayit, near Qyriat Gat) where Jehoash, King of Judah, paid a ransom for Jerusalem to be spared.

Tiglath-Pileser III came to the throne of Assyria in 745 BC and spent his first years campaigning first to the south-east of Nineveh and then westwards into eastern Asia Minor where he exacted tribute from a number of cities. In 738 he fought a battle in northern Syria against an alliance led by Amaziah of Judah. Next he had to turn his attention back to Ullubu (the Dohuk-Zakho region of Iraq), Media (north-east Iran), and Urartu (around Lake Van). Tiglath-Pileser's conquest of Israel and Judah took place in 733–2, following his campaign down the Mediterranean coastline in 734, when he had conquered Philistia and reached as far south as the Brook of Egypt (Wadi el Arish). The Assyrians now incorporated their conquests into the empire as provinces rather than simply accepting tribute. Israel was divided into three provinces: Dor, Megiddo and, east of the Jordan, Gilead. What was left of Israel, an area around Samaria, became a vassal state. Judah had already accepted Assyrian suzerainty as Ahaz, who had not joined the alliance against the Assyrians, had appealed for Assyrian help when attacked by Aram and Israel from the north, and the Edomites from the east (2 Kings 16.6–7). The Assyrians then had to turn to quelling a revolt in Babylon.

The next king, Shalmaneser V, was occupied with troubles at home which allowed Israel to move its allegiance to Egypt. Shalmaneser sent an army to besiege Samaria but it only captured it after two years. Israel then became the Assyrian province of Samerina; part of the population was deported to Nineveh and Media, being replaced by Arabs from the south and captives from Babylon and Hamath (2 Kings 17.6, 24, 30–31). The next ten years witnessed a series of revolts encouraged by the Egyptians. After putting down the rebellions and defeating the Egyptians at Rapihu (Rafah) in 720 BC Sargon II extended Assyria's borders down to the Brook of Egypt and established a new province of Ashdod. After the death of Sargon in 705 a fresh revolt broke out in Judah and at Ashkelon and Ekron (Tel Miqne) in Ashdod/Philistia. Hezekiah, King of Judah, prepared for the inevitable Assyrian counter-strike. At Jerusalem he fortified the city walls and built a water tunnel from the Gihon spring, which lay outside the walls, to the reservoir at the Siloam pool so as to ensure the city's water supply in the event of a siege. Elsewhere he fortified the cities in the centre of Judah and captured a number of coastal cities like Gaza which had not joined in the revolt.

Sennacherib, Sargon's successor, began his reconquest of the Holy Land in 701 BC by advancing down the coastal route. Most cities submitted

Assyrian Kings

Sargon –705
Sennacherib 704–681
Esarhaddon 680–669
Ashurbanipal 668–627

without a fight, although Ekron and Ashkelon held out for a while but were forced to surrender. Turning inland Sennacherib besieged and destroyed Lachish. Earlier a detachment under Rabshakeh had been sent to Jerusalem, which it approached from the north, the route being described in *Isaiah 10.28–31*. Rabshakeh camped outside Jerusalem and negotiated the payment of a large ransom before moving on to Lachish as he did not have the necessary force to lay siege to Jerusalem. By this time Sennacherib was besieging Libnah (Tel Burna) and threatening Ekron, when an Egyptian army was reported marching up the coast. Sennacherib raised the siege and concentrated his army at Eltekeh (Tel Shalaf) where he totally defeated the Egyptians. He then laid waste to the country, recording the destruction of forty-six fortified cities; Jerusalem was not taken though, probably because a siege would have taken considerable time and effort. In any event Sennacherib had received news of another rebellion in Babylon and he hurried back to suppress this.

Judah and Assyria appear to have come to an understanding that if Judah did not oppose Assyrian movement along the Via Maris route to Egypt, Assyria would not invade Judah. The Assyrians mounted two campaigns against Egypt; the first, in 669, conquered Lower Egypt and the second, in 663, captured Upper Egypt as far south as the first Nile cataract. This was the peak of Assyrian power and it was to last for a further fifty years. In 609 Judah made the fatal error of attempting to block the movement of the Egyptian army which was en route to aid Assyria in its struggle with Babylon and Media. Josiah took up a position in the Yizreel Valley close to Megiddo, planning to attack the Egyptians as they came out of the Iyron Pass (Nahal Iron) when they would not be deployed for battle. The Egyptians concentrated their archers' fire on Josiah who was killed. The Judaean army was destroyed, and the Egyptian army marched on towards Assyria. In 605 the Egyptians met Nebuchadnezzer at Carchemish (Jarabulus) on the Euphrates where they and the remains of the Assyrian army were destroyed by the Babylonians.

The Bible describes things somewhat differently:
Then the angel of the Lord went forth, and smote in the camp of the Assyrians a hundred and fourscore and five thousand: and when they arose early in the morning, behold, they were all dead corpses. So Sennacherib king of Assyria departed.
Isaiah 37. 36–37

THE BABYLONIAN CONQUEST

Babylonia had first been subjected by Assyria in 1250 BC and had revolted against its rule on numerous occasions. These revolts were always subdued until a Chaldean chieftain, Nabopolassar, seized the throne of Babylon in 626 BC. After several years of fighting to keep control of Babylonia, Nabopolassar moved against Assyria in 616. Battles were fought at Gablini in August 616 and at Arrapkha (Kirkuk) and Takrit (Tikrit) in 615. The Medes, who came from east of the Zagros mountains, invaded and overran eastern Assyria in 615. They then joined the Babylonians in an alliance and together they overthrew the Assyrian Empire, capturing Ashur (Sharqat) in 614 after having failed to take Nineveh. The latter was captured in 612 after a siege lasting several months. The Assyrians managed to fight on from their new capital, Haran, but were forced to withdraw further west to Carchemish (Jarabulus) on the Euphrates. There they were joined by the Egyptian army which had defeated the Judaean army near Megiddo on their march north. The Medes had now returned

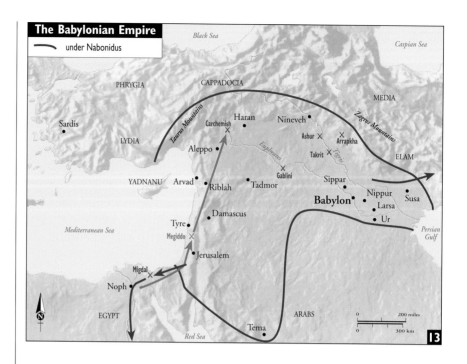

to their own country but the Babylonians, under Crown Prince Nebuchadnezzer, were strong enough to defeat the joint Assyrian/Egyptian army at Carchemish in 605.

After the defeat of Josiah by the Egyptians Judah became an Egyptian vassal. Internal divisions between Jehoiakim, who had come to the throne after the Egyptians had deposed Josiah's successor Jehoahaz, and the prophet Jeremiah led to the former relying on the Egyptians to maintain him in power. The Egyptian defeat at Carchemish led to Judah becoming Babylon's vassal.

Little is known of the Babylonian era as few records have been found other than those referring to the building of palaces and temples. Syria and Judah were incorporated into the Babylonian Empire but Babylon had to wage numerous campaigns to maintain its suzerainty. In 604 all the minor rulers, including Jehoiakim of Judah (*2 Kings 24.1*), assembled to pay their tribute. The ruler of Ashkelon did not submit and so was taken prisoner; at the same time Nebuchadnezzer reinforced his forces at Arad and other southern centres as a precaution against Egyptian attack. At the end of 601 a major battle was fought at Migdal (Romani) against the Egyptians in which both sides suffered considerable casualties, and it took the Babylonians a year to reform their army; shortly afterwards Judah re-aligned itself with Egypt. In 599/8 Moab and Ammon were encouraged by Nebuchadnezzer to attack Judah, and in 597 he besieged and captured Jerusalem. Nebuchadnezzer returned to Babylon with much treasure and many prisoners including Jehoiakim's son and successor, Jeoiachin, and 'his princes and officers' (*2 Kings 24.12*); he placed Zedekiah, another son of Josiah, on the throne of Judah.

In 593 BC Zedekiah, advised by Jeremiah, refused to join an alliance of Ammon, Edom, Moab, Sidon and Tyre in a revolt against Babylon (*Jeremiah 27.2–6, 12*). In 590 the Egyptian King Apries invaded and

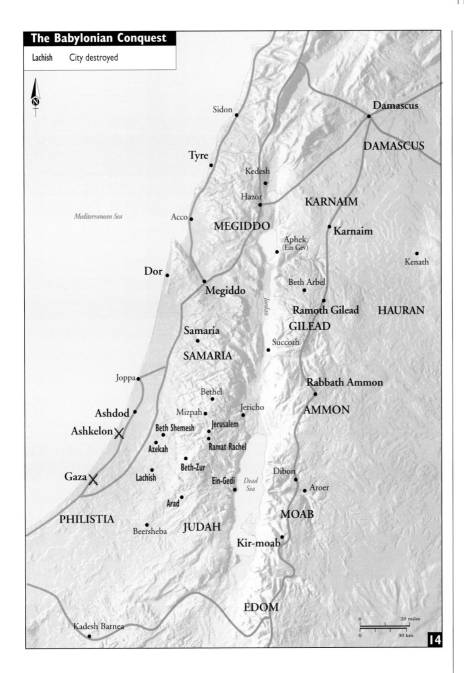

The Babylonian Conquest

Lachish   City destroyed

N

Sidon

Damascus

DAMASCUS

Tyre

Kedesh

Hazor

KARNAIM

Mediterranean Sea

Acco

MEGIDDO

Karnaim

Aphek
(Ein Gev)

Kenath

Dor

Megiddo

Beth Arbel

Ramoth Gilead

HAURAN

GILEAD

Samaria

Succoth

SAMARIA

Joppa

Rabbath Ammon

Bethel

AMMON

Ashdod

Mizpah

Jericho

Ashkelon

Beth Shemesh

Jerusalem

Azekah

Ramat Rachel

Beth-Zur

Gaza

Lachish

Ein-Gedi

Dibon

Dead
Sea

Aroer

Arad

MOAB

PHILISTIA

Beersheba

JUDAH

Kir-moab

Jordan

EDOM

Kadesh Barnea

0   20 miles

0   30 km

14

Zedekiah revolted against Babylon and joined the alliance. Nebuchadnezzer found this unacceptable and established himself at Riblah (on today's Syrian/Lebanese border) before laying siege to Jerusalem again. The Babylonians destroyed all the major cities of Judah including, as is known from archaeological evidence, Arad, Azekah (Kefar Zekharya), Beth-Zur (Khan et Tubeiqeh), Beth Shemesh, Ein Gedi, Lachish and Ramat Rahael. At one stage the Babylonians withdrew as an Egyptian army approached but the siege was continued once the Egyptians had departed two to three months later. In 586, after an eighteen-month siege, the walls of Jerusalem were breached and Zedekiah and the army fled the city which was captured. Zedekiah was soon taken prisoner, blinded and sent to Babylon along with a large number of other prisoners. The walls of

Jerusalem were broken down, the Temple and Royal Palace burnt, and Gedeliah, a trusted Jew, installed at Mizpah (Kafr Aqab south of Ramallah) as Governor.

After the fall of Jerusalem the Babylonians laid siege to Tyre which, as it could be supplied from the sea, held out until 573 BC. In 568 Nebuchadnezzer mounted another campaign against Egypt.

Nebuchadnezzer died in 562; within eight years there had been four kings and two revolutions in Babylon. The fourth king was Nabonidus who spent most of his reign campaigning, leaving his son, Belshazzar, in charge at home. Among his conquests were Edom and in north-west Arabia the huge oasis of Tema where he stayed for ten years. He returned to Babylon in 542.

THE PERSIAN EMPIRE

By 540 BC Babylon was coming under increasing pressure from the Persians in the south-east and the Medes, who had fallen to the Persians in 550, in the north-east. Extensive defensive preparations were made, which included building the 'Median Wall' at the narrowest point between the Tigris and the Euphrates. However, there the Babylonians were defeated by the Persians. Babylon was soon captured, and Nabonidus and Belshazzar were both killed. The entry of the Persian King Cyrus into Babylon on 30 October 539 marked the end of the Babylonian Empire. Earlier the Persians had concentrated their conquests in Asia Minor and in 546 had defeated Croesus, King of Lydia, and captured the capital, Sardis (in western Turkey close to Salihli).

Cyrus allowed the Jews of Babylon to return to Judah and authorized the rebuilding of the Temple in 538, though it was not completed for twenty years. Cambyses, Cyrus's son, invaded Egypt in 525 supported by the Phoenician fleet. He advanced through Syria and down the coastal route through Gaza. He defeated the Egyptians at Pelusium (in northern Sinai close to Romani), going on to take Memphis (Mit Rahina) after a siege. Penetrating further south, he established a garrison at Elephantine (north of Aswan). Cambyses then returned to Persia, where he failed to put down a revolt led by the Babylonian King Gaumata, and died. Gaumata in his turn was overthrown and killed by Darius, another of Cyrus's sons, in 521. Darius organized the Persian Empire into 'satrapy', each ruled by a Persian-appointed satrap, thus avoiding the risk of rebellion by vassal kings. The Vth Satrapy, Abar Nabara ('Beyond the River'), extended from the Euphrates in the north to a line from the Brook of Egypt to the Red Sea at Elath (Aqaba) in the south; Judah was a province of the Vth Satrapy.

The Persian Empire was constantly threatened by revolts. First Darius had to recover Babylon which had appointed another king after the death of Gaumata. In the west the Ionians' revolt, supported by the Greeks, led to the Persian invasion of Greece and Darius's defeat at the battle of Marathon in 490. The struggle with Greece continued throughout the era with Greece often supporting Persia's enemies while at the same time providing mercenary soldiers for the Persian army. Egypt revolted in 486

Persian Kings

Cyrus II 559–529
Cambyses II 529–522
Darius 521–486
Xerxes 486-465
Artaxerxes 465–425
Darius II 425–405
Artaxerxes II 405–359
Artaxerxes III 359–338
Arses 338–336
Darius III 336–331

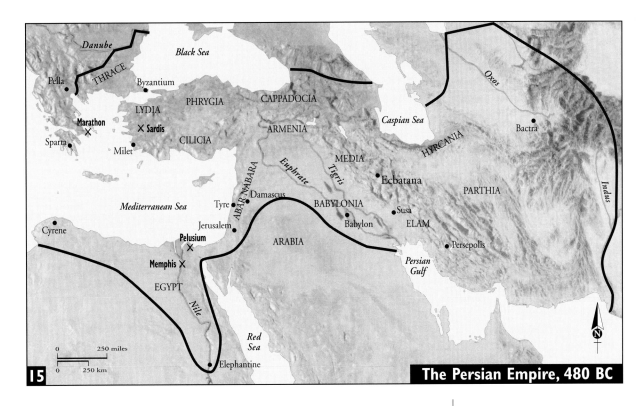

The Persian Empire, 480 BC

after the death of Darius but the rebellion was quickly put down by Xerxes. In 444, following a Samaritan attack on Judah, Nehemiah, who was a Jewish official in the court of Artaxerxes I, was authorized to rebuild the walls of Jerusalem. Other revolts followed until Egypt regained its independence. Campaigns by Artaxerxes II in 389–387 and 374 failed to subdue the revolt, and in 361 the Egyptians managed to invade the southern coast of Syria but were unable to hold it for long. Egypt was finally reconquered by Artaxerxes III in 343. Throughout the Persian era Syria and Judah were relatively peaceful, other than the revolt of the Syrian satrap, Megabyzos. Phoenicia, which was joined by the Jews, rebelled in 351 and, after Artaxerxes III's first failure to subdue Egypt, defeated a Persian army. The Phoenicians remained independent for three years until the rebellion was put down by an army led by Artaxerxes who afterwards destroyed Jericho and deported Jews to Babylon and Hyrcania (south-east Azerbaijan and the Iranian Caspian Sea coastal area).

The remaining years of the Persian Empire were marked by a series of court intrigues and the murders of two puppet kings followed by that of the murderer, leaving Darius III on the throne in 336, the same year that his eventual conqueror, Alexander, came to the throne of Macedonia.

ALEXANDER THE GREAT

Alexander was born in 356 BC and twenty years later succeeded his father, Philip, as King of Macedonia. After suppressing rebellions in Thrace, Illyria and Thebes, which he sacked, the rest of Greece accepted his leadership against the Persians.

Leaving a strong force to garrison Greece Alexander set out in 334 BC with an army of around 30,000 men including 5,000 cavalry. He fought battles at Granicus and Miletus (Milas) that year and at Halicarnassus (Bodrum) at the turn of the year. Alexander then marched across Asia Minor, establishing a base at Issus (Dörtyol) before pressing on to Myrandros. Here he learnt that the Persians under Darius had moved north to attack Issus, where they had massacred the sick. Alexander turned back to meet the Persians at the River Pinarus, the north bank of which Darius had fortified. Darius positioned a screen of 50,000 cavalry and light infantry across the river while the main army of some 90,000 men was forming up to its north.

Alexander began the battle by clearing aside the Persian screen with lightly armed troops and his cavalry and the Persians moved to the foothills of the Amanus mountains on his right flank. The main phalanx had difficulty in crossing the river and a gap opened in the Macedonian line which the Persians tried to exploit. But the phalanx stood firm and Alexander led his cavalry in a charge that forced the Persians to retreat. The Persian cavalry had crossed the river to attack the Macedonian left wing but when they saw the defeat of the Persian centre they too broke and fled, closely followed by Macedonian cavalry.

Alexander now approached the Holy Land where he first laid siege to Tyre. This was an important seaport for the Persians and he intended to leave no bases behind him as his advance continued. At the time the two harbours of Tyre were part of an island lying almost a kilometre from the mainland, and the city had a strong fleet and could be supplied by sea indefinitely.

Alexander had only a few transports so a seaborne assault was impossible. He therefore decided to build a mole to bridge the gap

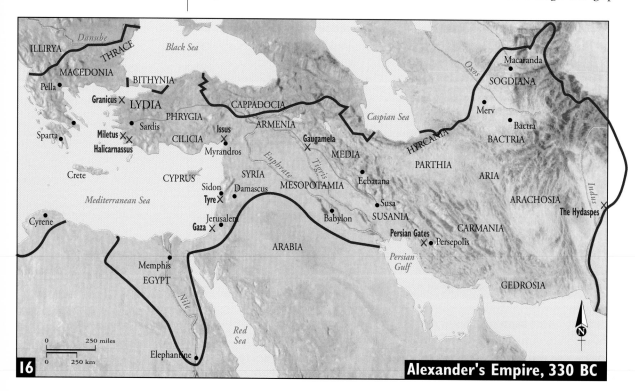

Alexander's Empire, 330 BC

16

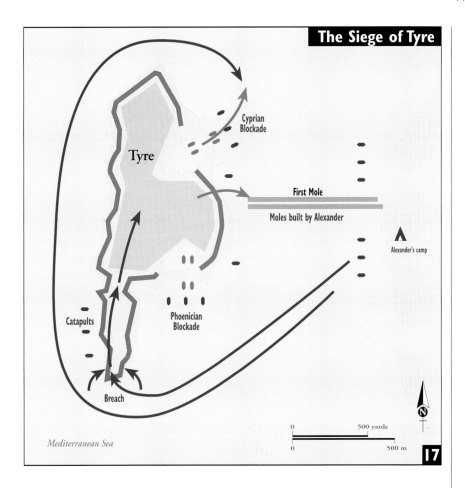

The Siege of Tyre

Tyre

Cyprian Blockade

First Mole

Moles built by Alexander

Alexander's camp

Catapults

Phoenician Blockade

Breach

Mediterranean Sea

0   500 yards

0   500 m

17

between the mainland and the island, but as it approached the island the Greek workers on the mole were bombarded both from the city and from ships. To protect the work two towers, armed with catapults, were constructed on the end of the mole. The defenders realized that the towers must be destroyed and a fire ship was prepared. The attack was a success: the towers were burnt down and raids were made along the length of the mole destroying its defences and other catapults.

Alexander ordered the mole to be rebuilt and to be widened so that there could be many more towers and catapults to defend it. At the same time he realized that he needed a naval force and so he set off to Sidon where his own few ships had been left. The Phoenicians, whose ships had served the Persians, had abandoned them after the battle of Issus and soon Alexander had gathered some 80 ships into his navy. The kings of Cyprus, wishing to be on the winning side, sent a further 120 ships to join Alexander.

Alexander hoped that the Tyrians would engage in a sea battle but when they saw the size of his fleet they wisely remained in harbour, the entrances to which were strongly defended. The Phoenician fleet was ordered to blockade the southern part of the island and the Cyprian fleet the northern part. A battle of wits ensued with the Tyrians harassing the blockading forces, and Alexander instituting counter-measures which in their turn were countered. Eventually Alexander managed to clear the approaches to the city wall on the landward side by towing away the rocks which had been thrown there to prevent an attack, and he positioned ships close to the wall.

The Tyrians now made a surprise attack out of the northern harbour and managed to sink a number of Cyprian ships, driving others on to the shore. Ensuring the southern harbour was properly blockaded to prevent another attack, Alexander sailed around the island and surprised the Tyrians who were concentrating on destroying the grounded boats. Few of the Tyrian ships escaped back into harbour: two were captured and the remainder disabled.

The assault on the city now began. Catapults mounted on ships were used to try to breach the walls; at first only a small breach, at the southern end of the island, was made and the assaulting troops were easily repulsed. Three days later a wider breach was achieved at the same spot and, while diversionary attacks were made all round the island and the two harbours were attacked by the navy, Alexander's troops broke into the city. After a bitter fight the city fell, leaving some 8,000 Tyrians dead; 30,000 prisoners were taken and sold into slavery. Only 400 of Alexander's men are reported to have been killed. The siege had lasted seven months.

Alexander now set out for Egypt and found no opposition to his progress except at Gaza which had been prepared to withstand a siege. The main problem in breaking into the defences was the height of the mound of debris of previous cities on which it was built. Alexander therefore had a bank of sand built around the city on which his siege catapults could be mounted; they were concentrated on the southern side which appeared to be the weakest. When the bombardment started the defenders made a strong sally in an attempt to burn the siege engines but they were repulsed by a counter-attack in which Alexander himself was wounded. The building work continued while heavier catapults were sent for from Tyre. Once these had arrived the bombardment was intensified and concentrated on the sections of walls which had already been damaged by the collapse of tunnels driven under them. The Macedonians breached the walls and captured the gates, and, with the aid of reinforcements, took the city, killing the men because the city had refused to surrender. The siege ended in November 332, having lasted only two months.

Alexander went on conquer Egypt, then turned back to the north, crossed the Euphrates and occupied Mesopotamia and Babylon. In 330 he marched south through Persia as far as Persepolis (Marv Dasht) where he fought two battles before turning north to the Caspian Sea. His campaigns, initially in pursuit of the Persian Emperor Darius, took him as far north as Samarkand and then across the Indus; he defeated an Indian army at Bucephela on the River Hydaspes, before reaching the Arabian Sea and returning to Babylon where he died in June 323.

THE PTOLEMIES AND THE SELEUCIDS

After the death of Alexander the Great his empire was split between his leading generals after a power struggle between those men, such as the

An Alexandrian ship.

regent Perdiccas, who wished to keep the empire intact, and the provincial governors who wanted to take power to themselves. A Macedonian, Ptolemy I, was Governor of Egypt and took control of that country. He was opposed by Antigonus who had gained control of the region from the Mediterranean into Central Asia. Ptolemy's first act was to invade Judah, Phoenicia, and Syria; he sailed up the coast while the army marched up the coastal route. The years 315–305 witnessed a succession of campaigns waged between Damascus and the borders of Egypt as Ptolemy and Antigonus fought to control the area. First Antigonus turned on Seleucus, the Governor of Babylon, who fled to join Ptolemy in Egypt. Next he advanced against Ptolemy himself, who withdrew to Egypt without offering any resistance. Ptolemy and Seleucus returned to Damascus in 312 after defeating the army of Demetrius, Antigonus's son, at Gaza. Again Ptolemy withdrew before the superior forces of Antigonus, and Seleucus returned to Babylon. In 311 Demetrius made two attempts to capture the Nabataean stronghold of Petra and gain control of the Red Sea trade routes, but failed on both occasions. In 306 Antigonus attempted to invade Egypt by land and sea; his land advance was halted at Pelusium (near Romani) and the naval attack was beaten off at Damietta.

Antigonus was defeated in 301 by the combined armies of Ptolemy, Seleucus, who had acquired a force of Indian elephants, and a third general, Lysimachus, who had earlier taken Thrace. The final battle took place at Ipsus, in western Asia Minor; the forces were roughly balanced in strength except that the Seleucids had over four times as many elephants as Antigonus. Ptolemy and his army did not take part. Antigonus was killed in the battle and his portion of the Alexandrian Empire was broken up. Demetrius was allowed to retain the Phoenician coast. Ptolemy was to have been given Syria but as he had not joined the battle at Ipsus it was awarded instead to Seleucus, who found Ptolemy already in possession of the southern part of the country. Syria was therefore split three ways – a situation that would inevitably lead to further fighting. Ptolemy quietly took Phoenicia while Demetrius was coping with problems in his other province in Macedonia.

Coin showing Seleucid elephant

The next hundred years saw a succession of wars between the Ptolemies and the Seleucids over control of Syria and the Holy Land. The first was between 274 and 271 when both sides claimed that they had won. The next lasted from 260 to 253 when Antiochus II captured Ionia, Lycia and Pamphylia on the Mediterranean coast of Asia Minor. From 246 to 241 Ptolemy III attempted to win the Seleucid throne for the son of Berenice; he failed but recovered the territory that had been lost in Asia Minor and captured Seleucia (Samandag). Between 219 and 217 Antiochus III recovered Seleucia, captured Tyre, Ptolemais (Acre) and Gaza but was then decisively beaten in battle at Rafah. Antiochus III launched another attack in 200 and met the Ptolemaic army under General Scopas at Panion (Banias). The Seleucids remained on the high ground in the foothills of Mount Hermon with cavalry positioned on either flank and with the elephants, which were larger and heavier than Ptolemy's African ones, in the centre. The right wing of the Seleucid cavalry charged and put the Ptolemaic cavalry to flight, then swung southwards so that the Ptolemaic centre was caught between them and the elephants, and it quickly

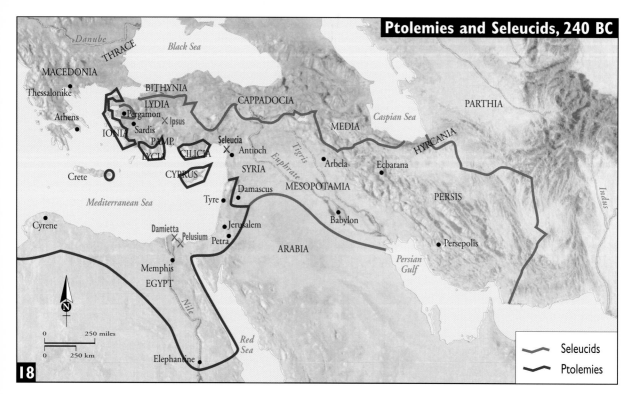

Ptolemies and Seleucids, 240 BC

Danube
THRACE
Black Sea
MACEDONIA
Thessalonike
BITHYNIA
LYDIA
CAPPADOCIA
PARTHIA
Athens
Pergamon
×Ipsus
Caspian Sea
IONIA
Sardis
MEDIA
HYRCANIA
PAMP.
Seleucia
LYCIA
CILICIA
× Antioch
Arbela
Ecbatana
Crete
CYPRUS
SYRIA
Euphrate
Mediterranean Sea
Tyre
Damascus
MESOPOTAMIA
PERSIS
Cyrene
Jerusalem
Babylon
Damietta
×Pelusium
Petra
ARABIA
Persepolis
Memphis
EGYPT
Persian Gulf
Nile
Indus
N
0   250 miles
0   250 km
Red Sea
Elephantine

18

— Seleucids
— Ptolemies

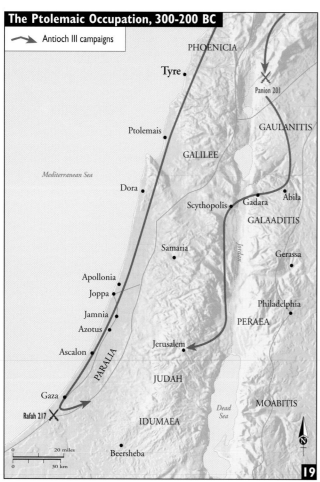

The Ptolemaic Occupation, 300–200 BC

→ Antioch III campaigns

PHOENICIA
Tyre
Panion 201 ×
GAULANITIS
Ptolemais
GALILEE
Mediterranean Sea
Dora
Gadara   Abila
Scythopolis
GALAADITIS
Samaria
Jordan
Gerassa
Apollonia
Joppa
Philadelphia
Jamnia
PERAEA
Azotus
Jerusalem
Ascalon
PARALIA
JUDAH
Gaza
Dead Sea
MOABITIS
Rafah 217 ×
IDUMAEA
N
0   20 miles
0   30 km
Beersheba

19

The Battle of Panion

N
Tel Hamra
phalanx
phalanx
Antiochus
Scopas   elephants
elephants
phalanx
Wadi Sr'ar
Banias
0   1 mile
0   1 km
Tel Azaziat
Tel Fakhr

20

disintegrated. The Ptolemaic right wing fared better but could not break through the elephants and so withdrew to Sidon where they were besieged and later surrendered. The Seleucids took control of the Holy Land and held it for a further forty years.

THE MACCABEAN REVOLT AND THE HASMONEAN ERA

The Maccabean revolt against Seleucid rule began as a quarrel between two groups of Jews: those who stuck to the traditional law of orthodox Judaism and those who wished to Hellenize the Jewish state. Antiochus IV appointed Jason as High Priest in Jerusalem in return for a large bribe; three years later, after a larger bribe had been paid, he appointed Menelaus as High Priest. Jason managed, while Antiochus was engaged in a war with Egypt, to oust Menelaus. Neither Jason nor Menelaus was supported by the orthodox Jews as both had been appointed by Antiochus. Menelaus was soon reinstated by Antiochus who regarded Jason's action as a rebellion and the Temple was therefore robbed of its wealth. Menelaus was even less acceptable to the Jews as High Priest and

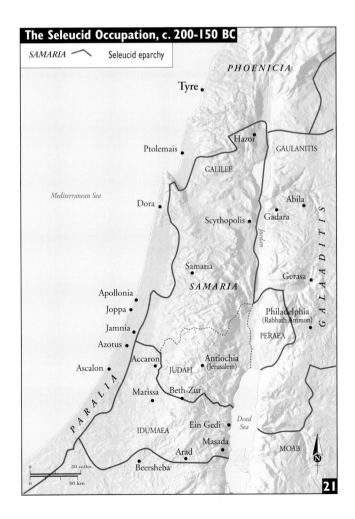

The Seleucid Occupation, c. 200–150 BC

SAMARIA — Seleucid eparchy

PHOENICIA

Tyre

Hazor

GAULANITIS

Ptolemais

GALILEE

Mediterranean Sea

Dora

Abila

Scythopolis • Gadara

Samaria

SAMARIA

Gerasa

Apollonia

Joppa

Philadelphia
(Rabbath Ammon)

Jamnia

PERAEA

Azotus

Accaron

Antiochia
(Jerusalem)

Ascalon

JUDAH

Marissa Beth-Zur

IDUMAEA Ein Gedi

Dead
Sea

Masada

Arad

MOAB

Beersheba

0   20 miles

0   30 km

N

21

their opposition resulted in Antiochus sending an official to impose his will on them; he punished the Jews severely. The Hellenistic Jews took advantage of the situation and began imposing their views on the traditionalists, often using force. Antiochus then gave his support to the Hellenistic movement and began eradicating the customs of the Jewish faith.

The spark which ignited the revolt, in 167 BC, was struck at the village of Modiin (Mevo Modi'im), near Lod, when Seleucid officials ordered a heathen altar to be set up and a sacrifice made. The local priest, Mattathias, refused and killed both the Jew who was about to make the sacrifice and the Seleucid leader. Mattathias and his sons then fled into the hills and one son, Judas Maccabeus, was appointed the revolt's military leader. The first battle between the Maccabean Jews and the Seleucids took place in the hills north-west of Jerusalem; the Governor of Samaria was killed and a rather larger Seleucid force, sent to suppress the rebellion, was ambushed as they climbed the pass of Beth-Horon (Beit Ur el-Foqa). In 165 the Maccabeans defeated a much larger army at the battle of Emmaus (Imwas). The Seleucids were camped at Emmaus where they received reinforcements. A strong detachment under Gorgias left under cover of darkness to be guided to the Maccabean camp at Mizpah; Maccabeus, hearing of the Seleucid plan, left Mizpah to attack the weakened force at Emmaus. When Gorgias returned to Emmaus he found his camp in flames and retreated to the coast. The Maccabeans then rededicated the Temple and fortified the Temple Mount against the Seleucid garrison which overlooked it from the fortress of Acra. They also fortified Beth-Zur (Khirbet et Tubeiqeh). In 163 the Maccabeans demonstrated and recruited in Idumea, Philistia, Galilee and across the Jordan, rescuing many Jews. After the Jews besieged the garrison of Jerusalem the Seleucids sent a large army under Lysias which approached down the coastal plain before swinging eastwards to Jerusalem. Lysias besieged Beth-Zur and then advanced, with his elephants and infantry in the valley and his cavalry on the slopes on either side, on the Maccabean army. They awaited him at the head of the valley near Beth Zachariah and here they were defeated. Advancing on Jerusalem Lysias besieged the Jews in the Temple but a threatened revolt in Syria caused him to break off the siege. Before leaving, Lysias dismantled the defences and a Seleucid garrison was left in control of Jerusalem.

Demetrius succeeded Seleucus in 161 and, following the appeals of Alcimus, the leader of the Hellenistic faction whom he had made High Priest, sent an army under Bacchides to support him. This force was unable to defeat the Maccabeans and a larger army under Nicanor was despatched; in the fighting which followed at Adasa (north of Jerusalem), Nicanor was killed and his army fled, pursued by the Maccabeans. Bacchides returned with a much larger army which met the Maccabeans at Elasa (just north of Adasa) in 160. Judas's army is reported to have suffered from large-scale desertion, but nevertheless he managed to push the Seleucid right wing back, only to be attacked from behind by their left wing. Judas was killed and the survivors fled. Bacchides ruled Judah, supported by the Hellenistic faction, but resistance continued under the leadership of Jonathan. Alcimus died and Bacchides returned to Antioch believing his work done. Jonathan spent the next two years building up the strength of his movement until the Hellenistic faction sent for Bacchides again; this time he found the guerrilla movement too strong for him to subdue and so negotiated a deal with Jonathan which in effect allowed the latter to take control of Judah.

Jonathan negotiated with both Demetrius and the rival claimant to the Seleucid throne, Alexander Balas, and gained concessions from both. Balas appointed Jonathan High Priest. When Demetrius was killed in battle in 150, Balas became king and Jonathan ruled Judah in peace for three years. In 147 Demetrius's son, also named Demetrius, sought to regain the throne and, as Judah supported Balas, he mounted a campaign against Jonathan which culminated in a battle at Azotus (Ashdod). The Maccabeans defeated the forces of Demetrius and were rewarded by being given the territory of Accaron (Eqron). Balas was killed after a battle with Ptolemy VI close to Antioch in 145 and Jonathan immediately switched his allegiance to Demetrius and was confirmed as High Priest and rewarded with three districts of Samaria (Lydda, Arimathaea, and Aphairema).

A new Seleucid civil war broke out when Tryphon claimed the throne for Balas's infant son, Antiochus VI, and occupied Antioch; initially Jonathan supported Demetrius by providing troops but changed sides when the promised Seleucid withdrawal from Jerusalem did not take place. When Demetrius was overthrown Jonathan's brother, Simeon, was appointed Governor of the coastal strip from Tyre to the border with

Beth Horon: site of the first battle between the Maccabeans and the Seleucids. (Photograph: Z. Radovan, Jerusalem)

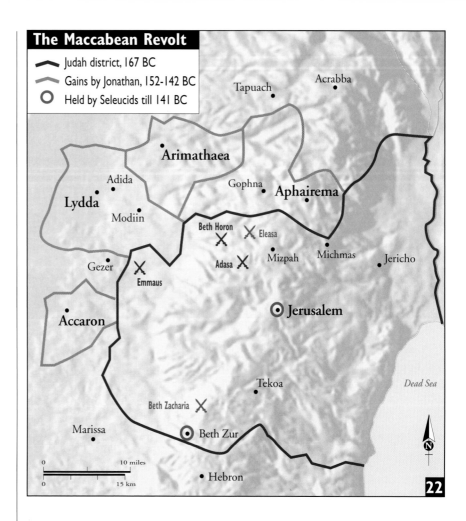

The Maccabean Revolt
- Judah district, 167 BC
- Gains by Jonathan, 152-142 BC
- ○ Held by Seleucids till 141 BC

Egypt. Demetrius continued his resistance and sent an army to punish Jonathan which he defeated close to Hazor. Another army was despatched which Jonathan went out to meet in Hamath, north of the Lebanese mountains. Demetrius's force withdrew and Jonathan was unable to bring them to battle.

Jonathan's success now alarmed Tryphon who saw him as a distinct threat and so he marched south with an army, meeting the Maccabeans at Scythopolis (Bet Shean). Tryphon, recognizing Jonathan's superior strength, withdrew, made peace, and invited Jonathan to Ptolemais (Acre), where he treacherously took him prisoner. Simeon now took charge, re-fortifying Jerusalem and capturing Joppa (Jaffa). As expected, Tryphon advanced again, bringing Jonathan with him; he met Simeon's army at Adida (between Joppa and Jerusalem) and offered to release Jonathan in return for payment. This Simeon made but Jonathan was not released. Tryphon attempted to approach Jerusalem from the south but his path was blocked by a heavy snowstorm and he retreated to Syria where he murdered Jonathan.

Naturally Simeon sided with Demetrius in the Seleucid civil war and Judah was rewarded by being granted, in 142, immunity from taxation. Simeon occupied Gazara (Gezer), starved the garrison in Jerusalem into

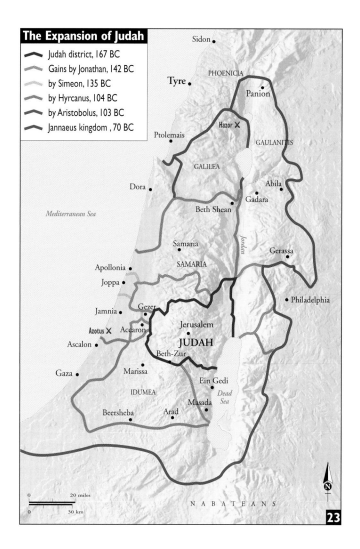

The Expansion of Judah

- Judah district, 167 BC
- Gains by Jonathan, 142 BC
- by Simeon, 135 BC
- by Hyrcanus, 104 BC
- by Aristobolus, 103 BC
- Jannaeus kingdom , 70 BC

surrender, and renewed diplomatic relations with the Romans. Antiochus VII, Demetrius's brother, demanded back Seleucid territory and unsuccessfully attacked Simeon. In 134 he besieged Hyrcanus, Simeon's son, in Jerusalem, withdrawing only after receiving tribute and hostages. The Seleucid threat to Judah ended with the death of Antiochus while he was fighting the Parthians; Judah was now independent again and ruled solely by Jewish kings of the Hasmonean monarchy. The next fifty years saw the expansion of Judah as Hyrcanus, followed by Aristobulus and Alexander Jannaeus, enlarged the Hasmonean territory. Between 126 and 76 BC the Hasmoneans conquered the coastal strip from Mount Carmel to Rhinocolura (El Arish); in the north Samaria, Galilee, southern Oturaea, and a number of cities in Gaulanitis (Golan Heights); to the east Ammon and Moab; and in the south Idumea.

After the death of Jannaeus in 76 his widow Alexandra reigned until 67 when her two sons fought each other until the Romans under Pompey intervened.

THE ROMANS TO THE CRUSADERS

This section covers nearly 1,200 years of history from the time of the Roman invasion of the Middle East until just before the Crusaders came from Europe to recover the Holy Land for Christ. It is an extremely important era for the Holy Land as it saw the birth of both Christianity and Islam and their spread across the world; their rival claims to the Holy Land added greatly to the suffering of the region.

The Romans came to the Holy Land in 64 BC and ruled it, except during the time of the two Jewish Revolts, until the Byzantines, who had split from Rome, were driven out by the Muslim Ummayids in AD 637. This section describes the following events: the Roman invasion; the First Jewish Revolt, which ended with the siege of Masada; the Second or Bar Kochba Revolt; the birth of Mohammed and the Ummayid Conquest; the take-over of Muslim power by the Abbasid dynasty; and the break-up of central Muslim power, which saw first the Fatimids and next the Seldjuks rule the Holy Land. The behaviour of the latter towards the Christians led to the Crusades.

The Emperor Diocletian decided that the Roman Empire had grown too large and unwieldy to be governed by a single ruler and so, in AD 286, he appointed Maximian as joint emperor to govern the western part of the Empire. At the same time two 'Caesars' were appointed both to be 'Emperors in Waiting' and to rule parts of the Empire. This system continued until 312 when Constantine, after a civil war, became Emperor of the European Roman Empire. At the same time, following a divine vision before the battle of Milvian Bridge (Ponte Milvio over the Tiber), he became a supporter of (but not a convert to) Christianity. Hostilities between the two emperors broke out more than once and finally Constantine defeated Licinius at the battle of Chrysopolis (Scutari) in September 323 and assumed control of the whole Empire. He also declared that, although paganism would be allowed, Christianity was to be the official religion of the Empire. Constantine moved the Roman capital to Byzantium. Roman rule of the Holy Land continued until the death of Emperor Theodosius in 395 when the Empire was split between his two sons into Rome and Byzantium, with the Holy Land forming part of the Byzantine Empire.

Heraclius became the Emperor of Byzantium in October 610 and inherited a difficult situation; to the west Slavs and Avars had overrun the Balkans virtually to the gates of Constantinople, and to the east the Persians were just across the Bosphorus at Chalcedon. Worse was to

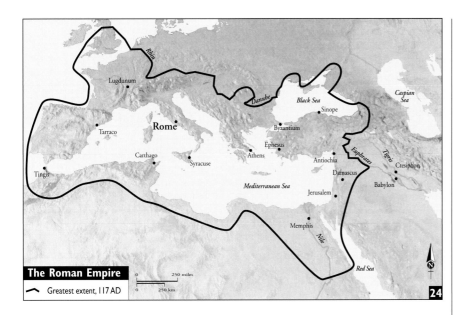

The Roman Empire
Greatest extent, 117 AD

follow; the Persian general Shahr-Baraz took Antioch in 611, Damascus in 613 and Jerusalem in 614. Here a Persian garrison was stationed and for a month relations with the local population had been tranquil when the Christians, without warning, rose up and killed every Persian and Jew. Shahr-Baraz immediately returned to Jerusalem and his army massacred the Christians, burnt the Church of the Holy Sepulchre, and removed the True Cross and other sacred relics. Jews were allowed to govern Jerusalem for three years until the Persians retook control after fighting the Jews led by Nehemiah.

In 617 the Persians had captured Egypt and without its corn (and that from Thrace) the Romans faced starvation. By 622 Heraclius was ready to launch a campaign against the Persians and, surprising them by not sailing into the Black Sea as they had expected, landed an army at the Bay of Issus. After spending the summer training his troops, Heraclius's Roman army marched north, encountered the Persian army in Cappadocia and put them to flight. It took the Romans a further five years of war before the Persians were finally defeated, a peace treaty agreed, and all captured lands returned. The True Cross was brought to Constantinople and was returned to Jerusalem by Heraclius in the spring of 629. Within ten years Jerusalem was to be captured by Islam.

THE ROMAN CONQUEST

The Hasmonean rule came to an end shortly after the death, in 67 BC, of Alexandra, widow of Jannaeus, when civil war broke out between her two sons, Hyrcanus and Aristobulus. Although Hyrcanus was the heir to the throne Aristobulus was the stronger character and before the death of his mother he managed to gain control of the major strongholds and raised an army of mercenaries. The two brothers fought for the kingdom in a battle near Jericho where most of Hyrcanus's army changed sides; Aristobulus became king. Antipater, son of the Idumaean Governor, persuaded

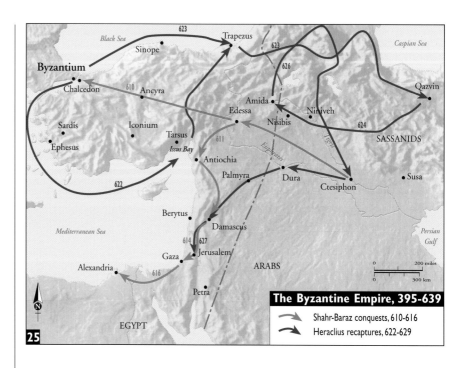

The Byzantine Empire, 395-639

⟶ Shahr-Baraz conquests, 610-616
⟶ Heraclius recaptures, 622-629

25

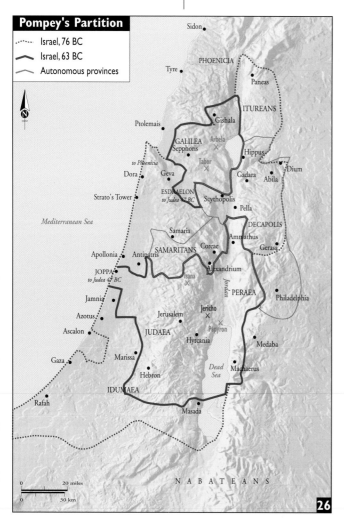

Pompey's Partition

······· Israel, 76 BC
⟶ Israel, 63 BC
⟋ Autonomous provinces

26

Hyrcanus to enlist the support of the Nabataeans under Aretas, King of Arabia, who assembled a large army and forced Aristobulus to retreat into Jerusalem where he was besieged.

Since 167 BC the Romans had been taking control of the Hellenistic world, first in Macedonia and then in Asia Minor. The Roman general Pompey had been given special powers by the Senate and had driven Mithridates, King of Pontus (northern Turkey), out of Asia Minor, forced Tigranes of Armenia to submit, and had sent, in 64 BC, one of his commanders, Scaurus, to take Damascus. Scaurus, on discovering the situation in Judaea, moved swiftly and on entering Judaea was approached by delegations from both brothers seeking his support. The size of Aristobulus's bribe won the day and Scaurus ordered Hyrcanus to break off the siege or face Pompey's army. Scaurus returned to Damascus while Aristobulus pursued Hyrcanus (who had been deserted by his Nabataean allies), and defeated him in a battle at Papyron (unlocated but close to the Jordan).

Pompey arrived in Damascus at the same time as Hyrcanus sought Roman protection. The Romans marched on Judaea and, on

The cliffs of Arbel where Jews hid from the Romans. (Photograph: Z. Radovan, Jerusalem)

arriving at Coreae (north of Alexandrium), found that Aristobulus had retired to his stronghold at Alexandrium (Sartaba, close to Massu'a) in the hills overlooking the Jordan. Lengthy negotiations were held until finally Aristobulus was forced to order the evacuation of all his forts; he withdrew with his army to Jerusalem and prepared for war. Pompey promptly marched to Jerusalem where Aristobulus promised to hand over the city and pay a ransom but his troops prevented the Romans from collecting it. Pompey held Aristobulus prisoner and advanced to the city walls. While Pompey decided on his plan of attack fighting broke out in the city between the rival supporters of the two brothers. The supporters of Hyrcanus opened the city gates to the Romans, who occupied the Upper City, while those of Aristobulus retired into the Temple, destroying the bridge connecting it to the city.

The Romans constructed a dyke around the inner walls to prevent escape and then began to fill in the low ground north of the Temple mound. Once the ravine had been filled a ramp with towers armed with battering rams and catapults was constructed close to the Baris citadel (later to become the Antonia Fortress), and another ramp was built near the destroyed bridge. The Jews did what they could to interrupt the work which took nearly three months. Finally, on a Sabbath, the walls and tower were breached and the Romans assaulted the Temple. Josephus records that 12,000 people were killed. Aristobulus and his family were taken to captivity in Rome.

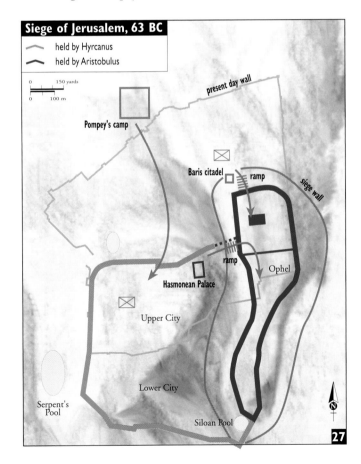

Siege of Jerusalem, 63 BC

— held by Hyrcanus
— held by Aristobulus

0   150 yards
0   100 m

Pompey's camp

present day wall

Baris citadel — ramp

siege wall

ramp — Ophel

Hasmonean Palace

Upper City

Lower City

Serpent's Pool

Siloan Pool

27

Pompey broke up the Hasmonean kingdom and installed Gabinius as pro-consul in Damascus. Israel was reduced to Judaea, Galilea, Idumaea and, on the east of the Jordan, Perea. A small Samaritan province was reformed and the main cities east of the Jordan, together with Scythopolis (Bet Shean), were joined into a 'League of Ten Cities' or Decapolis. The Carmel mountains were returned to the Phoenicians and the area of the Golan and the Jordan valley north of Galilee handed over to the Itureans. The south and south-east of the country was handed over to the Nabataeans. The former Greek cities on the coastal plain were given their independence. Hyrcanus was appointed High Priest with Antipater as Chief Administrator.

Pompey then returned to Rome leaving Scaurus with two legions. Scaurus went on to invade Arabia but was halted by difficult terrain at Pella and soon ran out of supplies despite taking all he could from the surrounding countryside. Hyrcanus sent Antipater with supplies and he negotiated with Aretas for the withdrawal of the Romans in return for a payment.

The Jewish civil war re-erupted when Aristobulus's son Alexander escaped while being taken to Rome; he raised an army and began overrunning Judaea until Gabinius set out to halt him. Mark Anthony had been sent on with an advance guard and he was joined by Jewish troops under Antipater. Alexander was forced to withdraw and in a battle near Jerusalem he lost some 6,000 of his men; he and the survivors fled to the relative safety of Alexandrium. There Alexander refused to surrender and was besieged while Gabinius organized the recovery and recolonization of the cities that Alexander had sacked. When the siege of Alexandrium was intensified Alexander was forced to surrender and this fortress and the remaining strongholds at Hyrcania (between Mar Saba and Qumran) and Machaerus (east of the Dead Sea, south-west of Medaba) were destroyed so that they could not be used again.

Aristobulus managed to escape from Rome and, after gaining Jewish support, attempted to refortify Alexandrium. When Gabinius's army approached, he abandoned all but some 8,000 soldiers and headed for Machaerus. Aristobulus was forced to fight the Romans before reaching the city and lost 5,000 men. He managed, with about 1,000 men, to fight his way to Machaerus but was recaptured there and sent back to Rome. Gabinius then had to deal with the Parthian threat but his expedition was interrupted by the need to restore Ptolemy to the Egyptian throne; in this he was greatly aided by Hyrcanus and Antipater. In his absence uprisings broke out in Syria, while Alexander, who had been allowed to return to Judaea, raised another Jewish army and began to attack the Romans. Gabinius hurried back, fought and defeated Alexander in a battle close to Mount Tabor, then turned on and defeated the Nabataeans.

In Rome Pompey and Julius Caesar had clashed, the former fleeing to the east and the latter releasing Aristobulus and sending him with two legions to win Syria and Judaea to his side. Pompey had Aristobulus poisoned and Alexander executed. Antipater then changed sides and fought for Caesar with Mithridates, first at Pelusium (near Romani) and then relieving Caesar who had been besieged in Alexandria. As a reward Caesar returned Joppa (Jaffa) and the plain of Esdraelon (Yizreel) to Judaea where Antipater appointed his sons Phasael and Herod as Governors of Jerusalem and Galilea respectively.

The assassination of Julius Caesar in 44 BC caused a fresh civil war during which Antipater maintained his rule of Judaea while submitting to various Roman pro-consuls. After the murder of Antipater, Phasael and Herod were appointed as joint rulers of Judaea. In 40 BC Syria was invaded by the Parthians, supported by Aristobulus' son Antigonus, which led to many Jews revolting against Phasael and Herod. Phasael was captured while Herod escaped to the south, finally reaching Rome. The Parthians withdrew leaving Antigonus as King in Jerusalem. In Rome Herod was appointed King of the Jews; Idumaea, west of the Dead Sea, and the Samaritan province were later added to his realm although the whole area was still in fact controlled by Antigonus.

Herod landed at Ptolemais (Akko) in 39 BC and set about recovering his kingdom, first in Galilea, then taking Joppa, before relieving his family who had been under siege at Masada, and finally laying siege to Jerusalem. This last had to be broken off when the Roman troops withdrew to winter quarters on the coast. Herod returned to Galilea, captured Sepphoris (Zippori) and pursued the Jews who escaped to Arbela (Arbel). In the battle that followed Herod's left wing was put to flight; Herod with his right wing halted the retreat, attacked the enemy and pursued them to the Jordan, inflicting heavy casualties. A number escaped to fortified caves in the cliffs below the Horns of Hattin, from which they could only be cleared by soldiers lowered in baskets to the cave entrances.

The Romans, under Macherus, returned to Herod's aid in the summer and attacked Emmaus. Herod's brother Pheroras advanced down the Jordan Valley and refortified Alexandrium. Macherus then attempted to spy on Antigonus by feigning friendship but his ruse failed and Herod was so infuriated that he set off to join Anthony who was besieging Samosata on the Euphrates. While Herod was away his brother Joseph was defeated at a battle just north of Jericho. On his return Herod followed Antigonus's general Pappus and defeated him at Isana in the Judaean hills. He then laid siege to Jerusalem and captured it in the summer of 37 BC. Herod was now the undisputed King of Judaea.

Roman catapult

THE FIRST REVOLT AND THE SIEGE OF MASADA

After the death of Herod in 4 BC the Romans ended the monarchy and split the country into three with Galilee and land east of the Jordan being detached from the main portion which was ruled by Herod's eldest son, Archelaus. He ruled for ten years but his tyranny caused the people to appeal to Rome and he was deposed and banished. Judaea then came under direct and heavy-handed rule from Rome. In AD 66 the Jews rose up against the procurator, Gessius Florus, and drove out the Roman garrison. A Roman force, sent from Syria to suppress the revolt, reached Jerusalem, but did not capture it and for some reason withdrew, only to be defeated by the Jews at the pass of Beth Horon (Beit 'Ur et Tahta). The government in Jerusalem assumed control of the whole country, with Galilee being entrusted to Josephus.

Naturally these events were unacceptable to Rome. Vespasian, a successful general, was sent to reconquer Judaea and Galilee. He invaded

Galilee in early AD 67 and, largely through the treachery of Josephus, overcame all resistance. The Romans first took Sepphoris (Zippori) which surrendered, then Garaba (Arraba), and laid siege to Jotapata (Yodefat). After its fall the Romans marched south to Caesarea and Scythopolis (Bet Shean), neither of which was held by the Jews. From there they cleared the coastal plain down to Joppa (Jaffa), and in the east took Tiberias and after a short siege Tarichae (Migdal). They then moved north and on to the Golan to take Gamala.

The Jews were split among themselves, forming three armed factions which fought each other; Vespasian conquered most of the rest of the country but left Jerusalem isolated, waiting for the internal conflict to weaken the Jews still further. When Vespasian became Emperor he left his son Titus to complete the conquest. Titus besieged Jerusalem in the spring of AD 70, broke in and destroyed the Temple in August. All resistance ended a few weeks later, other than along the western shore of the Dead Sea and around Machaerus (Mukawir, Jordan) which was captured in 71 by the Governor, Lucilius Bassus.

A group of Sicarii, Jews who employed political assassination, led by Eleazar had taken refuge at Masada, Herod's mountain fort and palace overlooking the Dead Sea some 400 metres below. From there they carried out raids against the Romans, and Jews to gain supplies, for two years until the Governor, Flavius Silva, decided to eliminate this last base of Jewish resistance. Flavius marched to Masada with the Tenth Legion and several thousand prisoners as porters and labourers in late AD 72. They

Siege of Masada, 73

constructed a wall around the base of the mountain, so that none of the 960 Jews on Masada could escape, and built a number of defended camps for the Legion. The wall was some 3,500 metres long, in parts 2 metres thick, the eastern section further strengthened with twelve towers spaced at 100 metre intervals, and built on slopes which no one could negotiate. The scale of construction illustrates the Roman determination than no Jew should escape; the total annihilation of the Jews represented a major public relations victory for the Romans.

The Romans then set about constructing a massive ramp against the western wall of Masada, the only suitable site for such an approach. The ramp had to give access to the fortress walls some 150 metres above; at its base, close to the mountain wall, it was 200 metres wide and the length of the slope was about the same. A siege tower, 30 metres high and protected by iron plates, was constructed and placed at the top of the ramp. It was armed with a battering ram and with catapults for throwing darts and stones; Josephus records that stones weighing over 23 kg could be thrown about 360 metres. As these rocks were white in colour the Jews were able to see them coming and so avoid being hit until the Romans realized and darkened them.

Once the battering ram had breached the wall of Masada the Jews constructed a second wall from timber and earth which was less vulnerable to the battering ram. Flavius ordered this to be burnt, and soon a large blaze was started; Josephus records that a sudden change of wind directed the flames towards the Romans, nearly setting the siege engines alight, but another change of wind ensured that the new wall was burnt down. Flavius decided the main assault should take place the following day but he was pre-empted by the Jews. After an exhortation from Eleazar, in which he said 'let us die before we become slaves under our enemies, and let us go out of the world, together with our children and our wives, in a state of freedom', the Jews first killed their own wives and children, then were in their turn killed by ten men chosen by lot until all of them, bar two women and five children who had hidden, were dead. The siege ended in AD 73 and had lasted some six months.

THE SECOND OR BAR KOCHBA REVOLT

The Bar Kochba revolt, which began in AD 131, was the last Jewish uprising against the Romans; indeed it was the last Jewish attempt in ancient times to regain their kingdom. At the time Hadrian was the

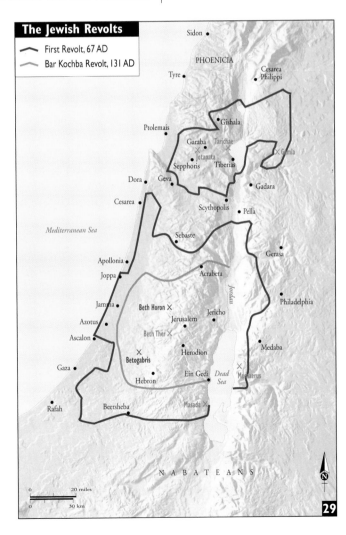

The Jewish Revolts

First Revolt, 67 AD

Bar Kochba Revolt, 131 AD

Sidon

PHOENICIA

Tyre

Cesarea Philippi

Ptolemais

Gishala

Garaba Tarichae

Jotapata

Sepphoris Tiberias

× Gamla

Dora

Geva

Gadara

Cesarea

Scythopolis Pella

Mediterranean Sea

Sebaste

Gerasa

Apollonia

Acrabeta

Joppa

Jordan

Philadelphia

Jamnia

Beth Horon ×

Jericho

Azotus

Jerusalem

Ascalon

Beth Ther ×

Medaba

Betogabris ×

Herodion

Gaza

Ein Gedi Dead Sea

× Machaerus

Hebron

Rafah

Beersheba

Masada ×

N A B A T E A N S

N

0   20 miles

0   30 km

29

Wadi Kelt – Bar Kochba country.
(Photograph: Z. Radovan,
Jerusalem)

Roman Emperor and he maintained an army of two legions in Judaea which, together with an equal number of *auxilia* troops, amounted to some 24,000 men. Even stronger forces were available close by in Egypt and Syria. Since AD 70 the Romans had expelled most of the Jewish population from the Judaean mountains and so deprived them of their traditional strongholds from which guerrilla warfare could be mounted. The other Jewish stronghold was Galilee but this was separated from the southern part of the country by the Samaritan-populated Samaria which stretched from the Jordan to the edge of the coastal plain.

The leader of the revolt was Simeon ben Kosevah, whose codename Bar Kochba means 'Son of the Star'. This revolt was not an unplanned insurrection, as the lessons of the 66–73 war had been well learnt and a great deal of preparation was carried out in the years preceding the revolt. A number of underground bases were prepared both as storage sites and as assembly areas before operations against the Romans were mounted. It has been estimated that Bar Kochba could probably mobilize up to 60,000 men but these could only be used in guerrilla fighting and could not face the Romans in a pitched battle. The Jews had also learnt the folly of retiring to strong fortresses such as Herodium and Masada where they would be bottled up by the Romans.

The revolt broke out in the autumn of AD 131, shortly after Hadrian had left the region and returned to Rome. It is thought the main causes were the banning of circumcision and rumours of plans to build a new pagan city to be called Aelia Capitolina in Jerusalem. At first the revolt

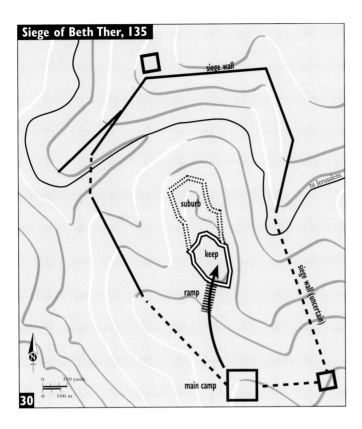

went well; by the summer of 132 most Romans had been cleared from the country and a Jewish administration had been established. Not much is known about the fighting as there was no equivalent contemporary historian such as Josephus; however, it is known that the Roman XXII Legion was totally annihilated, probably on the road to Betogabris (Bet Guvrin).

Hadrian was not ready to suppress the revolt until the spring of 133; he himself took command with Julius Severus, an extremely experienced general, as his second-in-command. Between 60,000 and 80,000 troops had been concentrated from as far away as Britain for the offensive. The attack on Galilee was launched from Acre in the west and Gerasa (Jerash) in the east. The Roman advance was slow and methodical; an advance was made along the main axis, then the area passed was sealed off and the enemy eliminated before the next advance was made.

The second phase, the recapture of the territory south of Samaria, began with advances down the coastal plain and Jordan Valley, reinforced by Legions from across the Jordan through Jericho and Egypt via Ascalon. The column in the Jordan Valley found Jewish strongpoints established on high ground at the entrances to all the wadis running down from the hills; each had to be surrounded, starved and eliminated before the Romans moved on to the next, all the way to Jericho. The Jews were able to make raids on Roman columns and camps and a considerable amount of Roman arms and equipment has been found in those cave bases which have been discovered by archaeologists.

The Romans recaptured Jerusalem in late 134 and in the next spring besieged Bar Kochba and his army in the hilltop fortress at Beth Ther

(Khirbet el Yalud/Betar), 10 km south-west of Jerusalem. As at Masada, the Romans constructed first a siege wall and then a ramp up to the walls which they had breached by the end of the summer. In the assault Bar Kochba and his men were slaughtered. Although the revolt now petered out, small groups of survivors initially managed to evade capture and hid in caves in the Judaean desert but most were soon taken or surrounded until they starved or died of thirst.

In his report to the Roman Senate Hadrian claimed to have destroyed some 50 important outposts and razed 985 villages, and to have killed 580,000 men. However, on account of the many Roman casualties, he omitted the traditional phrase, 'I and the army are well.' Hadrian changed the name of Judaea to Palestina and Jerusalem was rebuilt, renamed Aelia Capitolina, and the Jews were expelled from the city.

THE BIRTH OF ISLAM AND THE UMMAYID CONQUEST

The prophet Mohammed was born in Mecca in AD 570. At that time the Holy Land was ruled from Byzantium while Arabia was inhabited by a number of nomadic tribes, those living on the borders of the Byzantine and Persian Empires owing allegiance to their superior neighbour and acting as a buffer zone between them and other raiding Arab tribes. The terrain of the Arabian desert precluded military operations by the two empires against each other; they only faced each other directly between the Euphrates and the Caucasus.

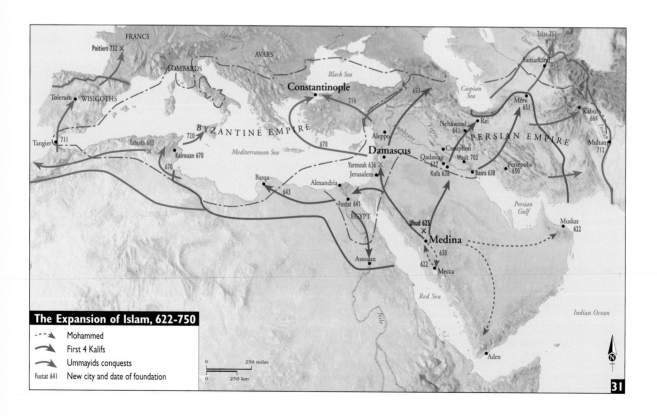

The Expansion of Islam, 622-750

- - - ▶ Mohammed
──▶ First 4 Kalifs
──▶ Ummayids conquests
Fustat 641 New city and date of foundation

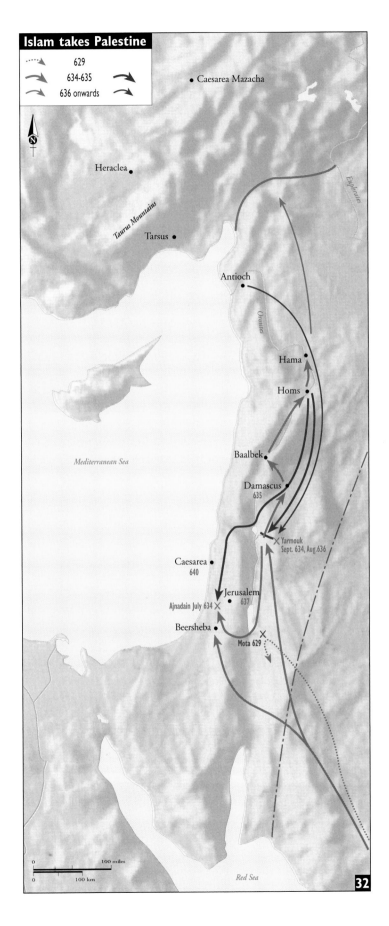

Islam takes Palestine

- ·····▶ 629
- ▬▶ 634-635
- ⟵ 636 onwards

N

Caesarea Mazacha

Heraclea

Taurus Mountains

Tarsus

Antioch

Orontes

Euphrates

Hama

Homs

Mediterranean Sea

Baalbek

Damascus
635

Caesarea
640

Yarmouk
Sept. 634, Aug.636

Ajnadain July 634 ✕ Jerusalem
637

Beersheba

✕ Mota 629

0 _____ 100 miles
0 _____ 100 km

Red Sea

32

Mohammed worked as a shepherd and as a merchant trading with Syria. After leading a caravan to Syria he married the rich widow who owned it; he now no longer needed to work and so turned increasingly to meditation. In 610, while alone in the mountains, he received a vision of the Archangel Gabriel who gave him God's instructions, and his wife convinced him he should be a prophet of the Arabs. Three years later he received instructions to start preaching; he did not start a new religion but claimed to be following the religion of Abraham which had been distorted first by the Jews and later by the Christians. He called his vision of a way of life Islam ('surrender to God') and those who followed it were Muslims ('those who had surrendered'). It was not until 620 that his teaching began to take effect when seven pilgrims from Medina visited him; two years later the number had risen to over seventy. Persecution forced Mohammed to leave Mecca and he fled to Medina (originally called Yathrib, Medinat al Nebi meaning 'the prophet's city').

In the early years the Muslims lived by raiding caravans en route between Aden and the Mediterranean, but in 625 they were nearly annihilated by the Meccans, whose livelihood they threatened, at Uhud (80 km north-west of Mecca). Mohammed built up both his military strength and his religious following from the Bedouin tribes and in 630 was able to lead 10,000 men to capture Mecca, which surrendered without resistance and the population converted to Islam. Earlier the Muslims had made their first approach to the Holy Land when a raiding force met and was defeated by the Byzantines at Mota, 8 km south of Kerak, in 629. Mohammed died in June 632.

Mohammed's successor (or Khalif), Abu Bakr, was persuaded that Syria was a tempting prize and so, in late 633, he despatched three columns to the north against the Byzantines. One entered southern Palestine, reaching Beersheba, while the other two kept to the east of the Arava and Jordan, aiming to cross the Yarmouk at Dera'a before it entered a gorge. Heraclius, the Byzantine Emperor, then at Homs, held firm at Dera'a and sent a force through Palestine to outflank the Arabs. This force met the Arabs at Ajnadain (between Ramla and Bet Guvrin) but was beaten in July 634, the Arabs having brought in reinforcements from Dera'a. The attack was resumed at Dera'a and the Yarmouk crossing was forced in September. Abu Bakr had died in August and was followed as Khalif by Umar ibn al Khattab. The Arabs next marched north and in March 635 laid siege to Damascus where the Christian bishop (who was probably opposed to orthodoxy) informed the Arabs that the walls would be only lightly guarded that night, and provided them with two ladders to scale the wall. The Governor surrendered and there was no massacre nor looting – a new development in warfare.

The Arabs marched northwards taking Baalbek, Homs and Hama; Heraclius withdrew to Antioch where he spent the next few months assembling a fresh army some 50,000 strong. When this advanced south the Arabs withdrew from their Syrian gains and retreated to Dera'a, allowing the Byzantines to hold the Yarmouk gap again. On 20 August 636 the Arabs, with 25,000 men, advanced under cover of a dust-storm which blinded the Byzantines and led to their destruction. Heraclius abandoned Syria and Palestine and withdrew to the line of the Taurus

Early Ummayid Khalifs

Abu Bakr 632–4
Umar ibn al Khattab 634–44
Othman ibn Aftan 644–56
Ali ibn abi Talib 656–61
Muawiya ibn abi Safian 661–80
Yezeed ibn Muawiya 680–3
Muawiya ibn Yezeed 683–4
Merwan ibn al Hakam 684–5
Abdul Malik ibn Merwan 685–705

Mountains, followed by the Arabs. Jerusalem held out until the winter of 636/637, the Patriarch of the city refusing to surrender except to the Khalif in person. Umar travelled to Jerusalem where he guaranteed the safety and the religious freedom of the Christians. Caesarea, supplied from the sea, held out until 640.

The next hundred years witnessed the expansion of the Muslim world as the Arab armies conquered Egypt in 641; Persia 642–652; North Africa in 682, 698 and again in 702; southern Spain in 711–712; and penetrated into Central Asia twice, first in 661 and again in 692. But there were also some setbacks. They failed in two separate campaigns to capture Constantinople; a seaborne expedition in 670 maintained a seven-year siege and in 716/717 an overland invasion was equally unsuccessful. They suffered two civil wars; the first, between 656 and 661, followed the murder of Khalif Othman ibn Affan, the first Umayyid Khalif. Muawiya ibn abi Sofian (an Umaiya), the Governor of Syria, refused to recognize Ali ibn abi Talib (a Hashemite) as Khalif. The struggle ended after Ali was assassinated, leaving Muawiya as sole Khalif. The second war, brought on by the rivalry between Medina and Damascus and between the Beni Hashim and Beni Umaiya tribes, began with the death of Muawiya in 680 and lasted for twelve years. It ended after Abdul Malik ibn Merwan (an Umaiya) invaded Iraq and marched to Mecca, taking it after an eight-month siege; Abdul Malik was accepted as sole Khalif on 3 October 692. The Umayyid dynasty was to last for a further fifty-eight years before it was overthrown by the Abbasids.

THE ABBASID CONQUEST

Both the Arab and the Muslim worlds were suffering from splits and rivalries. The Muslims were divided between the Arabs and non-Arabs, a situation worsened by the requirement for non-Arabs to pay the same poll-tax as non-Muslims. The Arabs were divided not only by the tribal rivalry between the Umaiya and the Hashim, but also by the differing forms of Islam. One sect, followed by the descendants of Khalif Ali ibn abi Talib, were known as Shiites and the other, by descendants of the Umaiya, were Sunnis. The religious dissension was further complicated by the Kharijites, a puritan sect formed by ex-soldiers disaffected by inter-Arab rivalries. Originating in Iraq, the Kharijite beliefs were adopted by the Berbers and spread throughout North Africa. Another split within the Arab people was that between the Qaisites, the traditional inhabitants of northern Arabia, and the Yemenis; over the years the Yemenis had migrated northwards and had taken part in the Arab conquests but still the rivalry remained. The Ummayids had ruled the Muslim world for over a hundred years but their power declined in 743 with Khalif Waleed II, a drunkard and blasphemer who was overthrown by Yezeed II. When he died after only six months as Khalif, power was seized by the former commander-in-chief, Merwan ibn Muhammad.

Muhammad ibn Ali, the head of the Abbasid clan, descendants of Hashim's grandson Abbas, began a campaign to undermine the Umaiya leadership, stressing their devoutlessness. His strategy was most successful

Later Ummayid Khalifs

Waleed ibn abdul Malik 705–15
Sulamain ibn abdul Malik 715–17
Umar ibn abdul Azeez 717–20
Yezeed ibn abdul Malik 720–4
Hisham ibn abdul Malik 724–43
Waleed ibn Yezeed 743–4
Yezeed ibn Waleed 744
Merwan ibn Muhammed 744–50

Abbasid Khalifs

(descended from Mohammed's uncle Abbas)
Abdulla al Saffah 750–4
Mansoor (Abu Jafer) 754–75
Mehedi 775–85
Musa al Hadi 785–6
Haroon al Rashid 786–809
Ameen 809–13
Mamoon 813–33

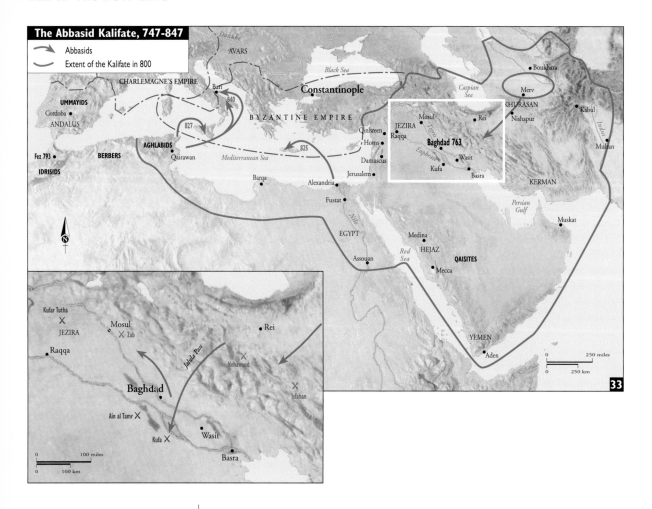

in Yemen, and with the Shiites, particularly in Khurasan. The Khajirites took advantage of the situation to launch a revolt, seizing Kufa in Iraq; those in Yemen invaded the Hejaz and occupied Mecca and Medina. Merwan suppressed the revolt in Syria and marched to Raqqa in Iraq; he was accompanied by Sulaiman, son of Hisham, who had sworn loyalty to Merwan. Returning from Raqqa Sulaiman met on the way a 10,000-strong force sent to reinforce Merwan; he managed to persuade them to join him and, breaking his pledge to Merwan, proclaimed himself Khalif. Merwan immediately marched back to Syria and laid siege to Homs where Sulaiman had taken refuge. The siege lasted a year but Sulaiman escaped and joined the Khajirites in Iraq who had, in September 746, captured Mosul.

Merwan, after taking Homs, marched eastwards, meeting the Kharijite army at Kufar Tutha (some 480 km west of Mosul), where he defeated them. They then withdrew to Mosul which Merwan besieged. During the siege Merwan despatched a force which moved southwards and defeated a Kharijite force at Ain al Tamr and, in June 747, went on to take Kufa, 120 km further south. The Kharijites abandoned Mosul and withdrew into the mountains, allowing Merwan to turn his attention to the Hejaz and Yemen where he won three victories and regained Mecca and Medina.

It was at about this time that the Abbasids took a hand. The then head of the movement, Ibrahim the Imam, after being advised of the situation,

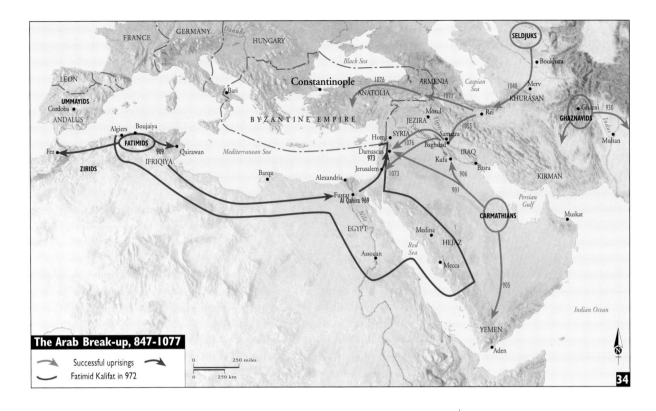

The Arab Break-up, 847-1077

Successful uprisings

Fatimid Kalifat in 972

0   250 miles
0   250 km

34

appointed Abu Muslim to lead the revolt. Abu Muslim, although a Persian, had been prominent in organizing the Abbasid underground movement in Khurasan; it proved successful in gaining support from a people desperate for peace. Abu Muslim was able to win the support both of Persians who were not committed Muslims and of the Shiites. The revolt began in June 747 while the siege of Mosul was still in progress. At the same time a civil war between the Qaisites and the Yemenis had broken out. Eventually Abu Muslim gave his support to the Yemenis who then forced the Governor of Khurasan to flee to Rei, but in the battle the Yemeni leader was killed. Abu Muslim proclaimed himself Governor in March 748 and set about taking control of the region. Once the conquest of Khurasan was complete, the Abbasid army under Qahtabe ibn Shabeeb advanced to the west, taking Nisapur in June and Rei in August. In the spring of 748 the Ummayids were defeated at the battle of Isfahan and in May at Nehawand. Qahtabe next outflanked the army from Kufa who held the pass at Jalula, and, crossing both the Tigris and the Euphrates, advanced on Kufa. Qahtabe was killed in a night action on the Euphrates but the Abbasids took Kufa in August 749. Also in August Ibrahim the Imam, who had been arrested by Merwan in early 748, was executed and his brother Abdulla Saffah ('the Blood Shedder') became the first Abbasid Khalif. A second Abbasid army was despatched to take Mosul. When the news of the capture of Kufa reached Merwan he decided to confront the Abbasids who had sent troops from Kufa to reinforce their northern army, now commanded by Abdulla's uncle, Abdulla ibn Ali.

Merwan reached Mosul first while the Abbasid army deployed on the River Zab some 130 km south of Mosul. On 25 January the Ummayids were decisively defeated in a battle about which few details are known other than that elements of the Ummayids, notably the Yemenis, were reluctant to fight. Poor morale was another factor. In the retreat, many soldiers were drowned in the River Zab, which Merwan had crossed before the battle. Merwan found the gates of Mosul closed to him and, hotly pursued, continued his flight through Syria and Palestine into Egypt where he was finally caught and killed on 5 August 750. Only Damascus, the Ummayid capital, resisted the Abbasid advance but fighting between those wishing to surrender and those who would not led to the city's fall in June 750.

The Abbasids did not complete their conquest for some months as they had to put down uprisings in Qinisreen, Homs, and Palmyra and, once the army had moved north, in Damascus; the uprising was crushed in July 751. Another revolt took place in Jezira and took some months to quell. Finally the Ummayid Governor of Iraq, who had fled from Kufa across the Euphrates to Wasit, had to be eliminated. He surrendered after a year's siege when promised safe conduct but was executed on the specific orders of the Khalif. The Abbasids ruled the Holy Land from their capital Baghdad, which was built in 763, until they were forced out by the Fatimids in 972.

THE BREAK-UP OF ARAB SOLIDARITY

Fatimid Khalifs (Qairawan)

Ubaidullah 910–34
Qaim 934–46
Ismail 946–53
Muizz 953–72

The Abbasid dynasty was the last to be able to claim total control of the Arab world and of the Muslim faith. Arab solidarity began to break up when the Ummayids in Andalus (or Spain) became independent in 763; next to follow suit in 800 was Ifriqiya (Tunisia and eastern Algeria). In the east Khurasan and Trans-Oxiana also gained virtual independence. During this time the Abbasid army changed in character. It had relied over-heavily on Khurasan for recruits and this dependence on Persians to control the Arab Empire alienated the Arab tribes. After Khurasan obtained its autonomy, the Abbasids turned to the Turkmen tribes for recruits; these soldiers were still heathen and could not even speak Arabic and so were even more hated. The transfer of the capital from Baghdad to Samarra further increased the gulf between the Khalif and his people who viewed him more and more as a despot. After the murder of Mutawakkil in 861 by his Turkmen soldiers, known as Mamelukes, the Khalifs became puppets and power was wielded by the army commanders.

The further break-up of the Abbasid Empire continued with revolts and invasions, and provinces gaining temporary autonomy. The most serious revolts were that of the Zenj, negro slaves, in 863 in southern Iraq, which cut off trade from the Persian Gulf, and that of the Carmathians (Shia in Arabia) in 900 who at one time had taken Syria and Yemen. Invasions were mounted by the Byzantines in 879 which laid waste to Jezira, and by the Dailamites from south of the Caspian Sea who occupied western Persia in 913 and took Baghdad in 945.

The origins of the Fatimids, who claimed to be descendants of Fatima, Mohammed's daughter, stem from the work of an Ismaili missionary, Abu Abdulla, who converted and came to lead the Ketama, a martial Berber tribe that lived south of Boujaiya (Bejaia, 260 km east of Algiers). The Ketama revolted against the Aghlabid Ameer and captured Qairawan (Qairouane, 130 km south of Tunis). Abu Abdulla summoned a Shiite claimant to the Imamate from Syria who assumed the name Ubaidullah and became the first Fatimid Khalif. Ubaidullah failed twice, in 913 and again in 920, to capture Egypt. In the intervening years his army fought the Berbers of the Atlas Mountains who were supported by the Ummayid regime in Andalus (Spain). In 958 the fourth Fatimid Khalif, Al Muizz li Deen Allah, felt strong enough to attempt to conquer Egypt but first he swept westwards, capturing Fez and forcing the Ummayids back into Andalus. In August 969 the Fatimid army marched into Egypt unopposed; the commander, Johar, constructed a new city called Al Qahira, 'the Victorious' (Cairo), which Khalif Muizz entered in July 972. Johar then went on to occupy Palestine and Syria.

At the same time as the Fatimids were defeating the Abbasids in Egypt and Syria there had been a revival of Byzantine military strength. Byzantine Asia Minor had long suffered from Arab raids until in 867 the new Emperor, Basil I, realized that these could be prevented if the passes through the Taurus mountains could be blocked. Basil captured the passes from the Arabs and fortified them; he then sent an army into Jezira (northern Iraq) to ravage the country and take slaves. There was then a peaceful interlude during the reign of Leo VI but his successor, Constantine VII, resumed the offensive, opposed only by the Ameer of Aleppo. When the Ameer died in 967 there was no further opposition to the Byzantines who sacked Homs and Hama in 968 (they had recaptured Cyprus in 964). In 975 the Byzantines invaded Syria again and took Damascus, Sidon and Beirut, and in Palestine they captured Caesarea, Nazareth and Tiberias; however, there were insufficient troops to hold these gains and the Byzantines returned to the Taurus passes. The Emperor, John Tzimisces, died suddenly in January 976 and the campaign was not renewed.

Fatimid Khalifs (Cairo) 972–1100

Muizz 972–5
Azeez 975–6
Hakim 976–1021
Dhahir 1021–35
Mustansir 1035–94
Mustaali 1094–1101

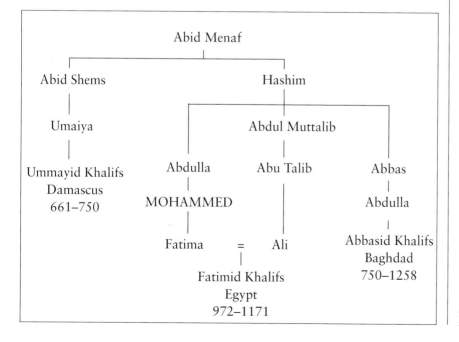

Descendants of the Prophet Mohammed.

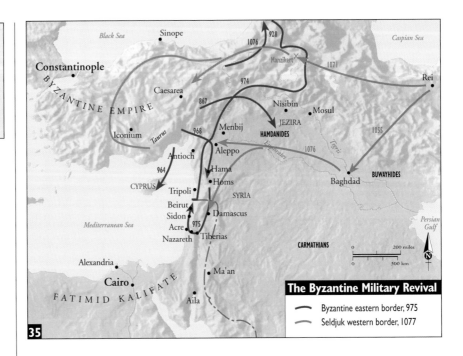

The Byzantine Military Revival
— Byzantine eastern border, 975
— Seldjuk western border, 1077

Another development was the arrival of the Seldjuks. The Seldjuk family were the leaders of a Turkmen tribe called the Ghuzz, who migrated to Bokhara at the end of the tenth century after being displaced by other migrations into Jaxartes; they were marauders rather than an organized army. They settled and embraced Islam. In 1037, under Tughril Beg and his brother Chagri, they marched into Khurasan and defeated the Ghaznavid dynasty which then ruled the province. They soon took the rest of eastern Persia, turned to western Persia, and in 1055 captured Baghdad. In 1071, led by Alp Aslan, the Seldjuks broke through the Byzantine defences in Armenia and had soon overrun most of Asia Minor. The Seldjuks also invaded Palestine and captured Jerusalem, after a siege, in 1073. The Fatimids recovered Jerusalem in 1076 but were driven out after another siege. After the death of Malikshah, the third Great Sultan, in 1092 civil war broke out which resulted in a number of kingdoms – Kirman, Iraq, Syria and Anatolia – gaining virtual independence from the Great Sultan who still held Khurasan. It was at this stage, with a fragmented Muslim world, that the Crusaders entered the scene.

THE CRUSADES

The origins of the Crusades lay in the wars against the Muslims in Spain which had acquired the status of 'Holy Wars'. They were in effect armed pilgrimages. The First Crusade was sparked off when the Byzantine Emperor Alexius appealed to Pope Urban for help against the Turks. The situation was exacerbated by the growing difficulty and danger in making pilgrimages to Jerusalem following the Seldjuk occupation of much of Asia Minor. Pope Urban called for a Holy War to recover Jerusalem at the end of the Council of Clermont in November 1095.

Before the official Crusade could be organized a mass of peasants led by a monk known as Peter the Hermit set off for Constantinople in the spring of 1096. On their way they, or more likely criminal hangers-on, set about murdering the Jews living along their route. At Semlin in Hungary, where members of an advance party of Frenchmen had previously been caught robbing the bazaar, an incident led to the sacking of the town. Peter's horde moved on to Belgrade which had been deserted by its inhabitants and, after looting the city, they burnt it down. After being given supplies at Nish the columns moved on towards Sofia; trouble broke out again and the rearguard was attacked by local troops. The fighting escalated into a full-scale battle and the Crusaders were scattered; when they managed to reassemble it was found that over a quarter had been killed or taken prisoner. From Sofia they were escorted and fed by the Byzantine army. To avoid further trouble they were quickly taken to Constantinople and transported over the Bosphorus.

Although warned not to advance further until the arrival of the main Crusader armies, the horde moved to Civetot (between Yalova and Karamursel) where they set up camp after pillaging the surrounding area. The French element made a profitable raid up to the gates of Nicaea (Iznik), killing many of the Christian inhabitants. The Germans in their turn went beyond Nicaea and managed to capture the castle at Xerigordon where they were besieged by a Turkish force. Lack of water forced them to surrender; all were either killed or sent into captivity. Peter himself was still in Constantinople when the Turks advanced on Civetot; it was decided that a stand must be made but, shortly after leaving camp, the Crusaders were ambushed, pursued back to Civetot and with few exceptions massacred. So ended the so-called 'People's Crusade'.

The progress of the First Crusade is described in detail under the headings: the March to Antioch; the Fighting at Antioch; and the March to Jerusalem. After the capture of Jerusalem the Crusaders had to decide who should rule their new possessions. The throne was offered first to Raymond, but he declined it as he could not be king in Christ's kingdom; the only other candidate, Godfrey de Bouillon, accepted the post but refused the title of king. The new kingdom soon faced a new threat as the Egyptian army, led by the Vizier al-Afdal, advanced towards Ascalon (Ashkelon).

Godfrey ordered intelligence to be collected and soon learnt from captured Egyptian scouts the size and deployment of the Egyptian forces. He concluded that al-Afdal was not planning an immediate attack but was waiting for supplies to be delivered by sea; nor was he expecting a Crusader attack. Godfrey, with Robert of Flanders, marched out from Jerusalem on 9 August 1099 to be joined by Raymond and Robert of Normandy once their own scouts had confirmed the situation. Concentrating at Ibelin (Yavne) the Crusaders deployed on the plain of Ascalon on the 12th; the Egyptians, taken by surprise, were completely defeated. The Muslims in Ascalon would only surrender to Raymond; the other Crusader leaders would not accept this and withdrew their forces, leaving Raymond with insufficient men to assault the town.

There were now three Crusader provinces: the Kingdom of Jerusalem and the principalities of Antioch and Edessa. Robert of Normandy and Robert of Flanders were returning to Europe leaving Raymond as the only Crusader leader without his own territory. These three marched northwards; reaching Lattakieh, which was still held by Byzantium, they found it besieged by Bohemond and the newly arrived Papal legate, Daimbert, Archbishop of Pisa, who had brought with him a Pisan fleet. The Crusader leaders remonstrated with Daimbert who withdrew the fleet, leaving Bohemond unable to continue his siege. Lattakieh opened its gates to Raymond, and the Byzantines provided sea transport for the two Roberts to reach Constantinople. Meanwhile Tancred and his small force of knights had entered Galilee, which the Egyptians had captured but had not had time to reoccupy after their defeat at Ascalon, and then went on to take Tiberias, Nazareth and Beisan (Bet Shean) for the Crusaders.

Godfrey died in July 1100 and his brother Baldwin was summoned from Edessa to take the throne. Daimbert opposed this and attempted to persuade Bohemond to prevent Baldwin reaching Jerusalem, but by then Bohemond had himself been captured by the Turks while he was campaigning on the Euphrates. Baldwin was crowned by Daimbert in Bethlehem in December.

The news of the Crusader conquests and the continued preaching for crusade encouraged a new wave of Crusaders to set out for the Holy Land. First, in 1100, a large army of Lombards crossed the Bosphorus with the aim of releasing Bohemond from the Turks. Although advised not to invade northern Anatolia, the Lombards went ahead only to be destroyed at a battle near Mersivan. Next came an army from eastern France led by William, Count of Nevers; this was destroyed at Heraclea (Karapina). Finally a third army, consisting mainly of Germans, was also destroyed at Heraclea after being ambushed by the Turks.

For the next forty years the Crusaders were continually at war, either against the various Muslim states on their borders or against the Byzantine Empire. They were also split among themselves and from time to time

---

Crusader Battles 1100–9

Capture of Haifa July 1100

Defeat of Bohemond at Malatia August 1100

Destruction of Lombards at Merzitun July 1101

Destruction of William of Nevers at Heraclea August 1101

Destruction of Franco-Bavarians at Heraclea August 1101

1st Battle of Ramla won September 1101

2nd Battle of Ramla lost May 1102

Battle of Harran lost May 1104

3rd Battle of Ramla won August 1105

Surrender of Tripoli July 1109

their internal rivalry led to Crusader/Muslim alliances being formed. However, overall Crusader-held territory expanded. They now held the whole coastline from Alexandretta in the north as far south as (but not including) Ascalon. To the east the Kingdom of Jerusalem had penetrated on to the Golan and across the Jordan where the Crusaders built fortresses along their eastern border as far south as Aila (Aqaba). In 1144 Imad ad-Din Zengi, ruler of Mosul and Aleppo, attacked Edessa and, on Christmas Eve, following a four-week siege, he broke into and captured the city. The loss of Edessa led to the despatch of the Second Crusade from Europe.

Although it was the Pope who called for the Second Crusade it was Bernard, Abbot of Clairvaux, who was the driving force in recruiting it. The German contingent, led by Conrad III, set off in May 1147, a month ahead of the French contingent led by Louis VII. Conrad reached Nicaea without incident and from there sent his non-combatants by the coastal route while he and the fighting portion of the army took the shorter but more dangerous route through Anatolia. A large Turkish army ambushed them at Dorylaeum (Eskisehir) at the end of October and won a convincing victory. Conrad's men lost control and suffered many casualties as they struggled back to Nicaea, from where the majority of the survivors returned home.

The French reached Constantinople in October 1147; here they argued whether they should proceed on their way into Asia Minor or attack the Byzantines whose alliance with the Seldjuk Sultan of Iconium (Konya) had horrified them. They were persuaded to go on their way by reports, spread by the Byzantine Emperor, of a German victory, and therefore the prospect of there being no booty left for them. After taking the coast route to Ephesus the French turned inland, only to be defeated by the Turks at Laodicea (Denizli). The survivors fought their way to Attalia where Louis with his court and some knights were taken by Byzantine ships to Antioch. Those for whom there was no room marched eastwards but were soon dispersed by the Turks. Louis marched south from Antioch to join Conrad who had arrived by sea in April 1148. A meeting was held with Baldwin III and the leading Crusader nobles at which it was decided that Damascus should be attacked. The army reached Damascus but the siege was broken off soon after. The Second Crusade had achieved nothing.

The next four years were dominated by the split between the young king, Baldwin III, and his mother, Melisende the Regent. In 1152 the kingdom was officially partitioned between them but within weeks Baldwin captured Nablus and Jerusalem and his mother took no further part in government other than to rule Samaria from Nablus. In 1150 Baldwin had built a castle at Gaza blocking the Fatimid route to Ascalon; in January 1153 every effort was made to take this last foothold of the Fatimids in the Kingdom of Jerusalem and it fell in August. At the same time the death of Zengi had led to the division of his kingdom in two: Mosul, which defended the eastern flank, and Aleppo, where Nur ed-Din could concentrate on capturing Damascus and defeating the Crusaders. Nur ed-Din retained Edessa, took most of the Principality of Antioch east of the Orontes, and in 1149 he besieged the fortress of Inab where he routed a relief force. In 1154 Damascus was his. In 1159 the Byzantine Emperor entered Antioch and concluded a treaty with Nur ed-Din which

Defence against Egypt: castles built 1136–49

Gibeln (Bet Guvrin)
Ibelin (Yavne)
Blanche Garde (Qiryat Malakhi)
Gaza

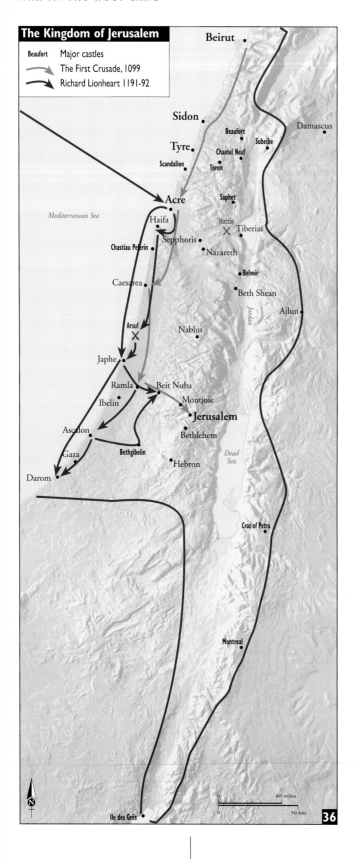

The Kingdom of Jerusalem

Beaufort   Major castles

The First Crusade, 1099

Richard Lionheart 1191-92

Beirut

Sidon

Tyre

Scandalion

Beaufort

Chastel Neuf

Subeibe

Damascus

Toron

Acre

Haifa

Saphet

Mediterranean Sea

Sepphoris

Hattin

Tiberias

Chastiau Pelerin

Nazareth

Caesarea

Belvoir

Beth Shean

Ajlun

Arsuf

Nablus

Japhe

Ramla

Beit Nuba

Montjoie

Ibelin

Jerusalem

Ascalon

Bethlehem

Gaza

Bethgibelin

Dead Sea

Darom

Hebron

Crac of Petra

Montreal

0   40 miles

0   50 km

36

Ile des Grès

led to his turning away from the Crusaders in order to fight the Seldjuks in Anatolia.

Attention now turned to Egypt which had been split by rival Viziers; Dirgham had expelled Shawar who appealed to Nur ed-Din for help; he sent in an army under the Kurdish general, Shirkuh. Shawar was reinstated but then quarrelled with Shirkuh and found a new ally in Amalric, now King of Jerusalem. While Amalric besieged Shirkuh at Bilbeis, Nur ed-Din launched a major offensive against the Crusaders in the north. He defeated the joint army of Tripoli and Antioch at Artah in August 1164, capturing both their rulers. He recaptured Harenc (Jisr el Hadid Horim), and advanced to the Orontes; further south he captured Banyas and the castle of Subeibe (Nimrod). Almaric and Shirkuh agreed terms and both withdrew from Egypt.

Amalric then married the niece of the Byzantine Emperor and concluded an alliance with him; not waiting for the Byzantine fleet to mount a blockade, he invaded Egypt. Shawar called on Shirkuh for help and, although no battle was fought, the Crusaders withdrew from Egypt, leaving Shirkur to kill Shawar and proclaim himself Vizier. Two months later Shirkuh died and was succeeded by his nephew Saladin, who secured his position by defeating a joint Egyptian/Sudanese army. In 1169 he repulsed a joint Crusader/Byzantine attack on Damietta; he then regained Gaza and took Aila on the Red Sea. After Nur ed-Din's death Saladin occupied Damascus and his sovereignty over Egypt and Syria was recognized by the Caliph. His next objective was Jerusalem, and by mid-1187 he was ready to move. Saladin's defeat of the Crusaders at the battle of Hattin and his occupation of Jerusalem are described on pages 72–5, together with a description of the Third Crusade sent to recover the Holy Land in 1189 (see pages 75–9).

The Kingdom of Jerusalem survived for another hundred years; for the first half of this period it managed to expand as a result of treaties made with the Muslims, but then came a series of withdrawals as the major cities were

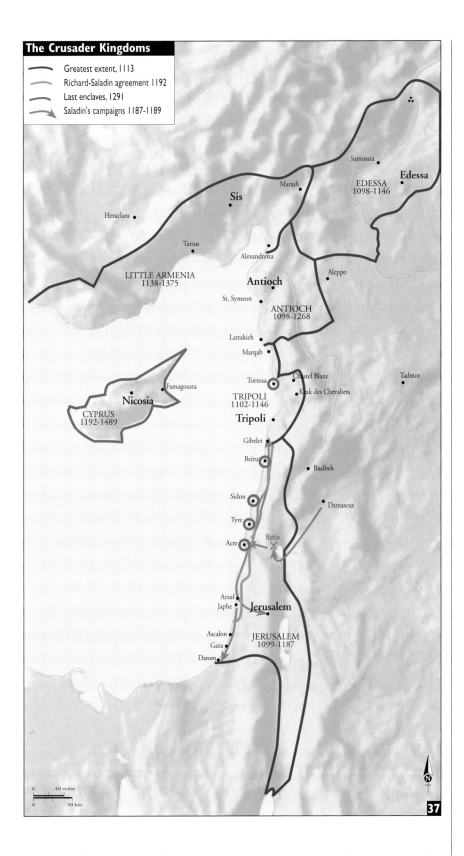

The Crusader Kingdoms

- Greatest extent, 1113
- Richard-Saladin agreement 1192
- Last enclaves, 1291
- Saladin's campaigns 1187-1189

Samosata

Edessa

EDESSA
1098-1146

Marash

Sis

Heraclaea

Tarsus

Alexandretta

Aleppo

LITTLE ARMENIA
1138-1375

Antioch

St. Symeon

ANTIOCH
1098-1268

Lattakieh

Marqab

Tadmor

Tortosa

Chastel Blanc

Krak des Chevaliers

TRIPOLI
1102-1146

Famagousta

Nicosia

CYPRUS
1192-1489

Tripoli

Gibelet

Beirut

Baalbek

Sidon

Damascus

Tyre

Acre

Hattin

Arsuf

Japhe

Jerusalem

Ascalon

Gaza

JERUSALEM
1099-1187

Darom

0   40 miles
0   50 km

N

37

lost one after another. The first treaty to be signed was between Amalric of Cyprus, who was given the throne of Jerusalem following the death of Henry in 1197, and Saladin's son al Malik al Afdal. It was necessitated by the fighting which had taken place after Amalric had taken Sidon and Beirut, and after the unsuccessful operations of the German Crusade. The Germans had attacked Toron (Latrun) but had broken off their siege on the arrival of an Egyptian army and on the news of the death of the Emperor Henry.

Pope Innocent III then organized a fresh Crusade which became known either as the Fourth or as the Crusade against the Christians. The only transport that could be found was Venetian and by June 1202 the army had assembled in Venice – but the money to pay for the shipping had not been raised. The Venetians said payment could be delayed if the Crusaders would, en route, divert to recover Zara in Dalmatia which had recently been captured by the Hungarians. This was agreed, and after capturing and pillaging Zara the Crusaders spent the winter there. Early in 1203 they were persuaded to support a campaign to place Alexius, the brother-in-law of Philip of Sabia, one of the leaders of the Crusade, on the throne of Byzantium. After lengthy political manoeuvring and several changes of Emperor, the Venetians persuaded the Crusaders to take the city. Their first attack, on 6 April, was unsuccessful, but on the 12th they landed from the Golden Horn and broke into the City. There was little resistance and the Crusaders were given three days to pillage Constantinople. Some time before this any thought of reaching the Holy Land had been abandoned.

The next Crusade to be launched, the Fifth (not counting the disastrous 'Crusade of the Children'), was instigated by Pope Innocent III. It took several years to assemble and even then the army set out for its objective, Damietta in northern Egypt, in successive groups. The first Crusaders arrived off Damietta on 27 May 1218; by the end of August they had captured a fort and chain across the river blocking the way to Damietta, and the siege proper began. The Crusaders were not only attacked by the Muslims: they also had to endure a flood, an epidemic and a harsh winter. Despite the arrival of strong reinforcements little progress was made although there was heavy fighting in July, August and September. The Muslims now offered to hand over Jerusalem, Bethlehem and Nazareth in return for the Crusaders' withdrawal from Egypt; although the Europeans were keen to accept, the offer was turned down on religious and strategic grounds. Shortly after, on 5 November, Damietta was stormed; there was little opposition as the garrison was sick. When the Crusaders finally advanced south, the Muslims had been reinforced and the river had risen. The Crusaders were now cut off from Damietta and, realizing that they were outnumbered, began to retreat through the flooded countryside, closely pursued and harried. Eventually they sued for peace and withdrew. The Crusade, which so very nearly succeeded, had achieved nothing, mainly as the result of the internal squabbles among the Crusaders.

Frederick, the Holy Roman Emperor, now took a hand. His story is a long and convoluted one, involving his marriage to the young Queen of Jerusalem, his excommunication, and his journey to the Holy Land. There he gained little support and, as he had not brought a large army with him, he was unable to make war on the Muslims. At this time the Muslims themselves were divided and were in no position to take on the Crusaders. Negotiations were opened and a treaty was signed on 18 February 1229 which handed Jerusalem, Bethlehem (with a corridor from Jaffa), Nazareth and western Galilee to the Kingdom of Jerusalem. In Jerusalem itself the Dome of the Rock and the al-Aqsa Mosque were to remain in Muslim hands.

Frederick's treaty expired in 1239 and early the next year the Muslims reoccupied the undefended, and indefensible, city of Jerusalem. The Pope, in anticipation, had prepared another Crusade which, led by Theobald of Navarre, had reached the Holy Land shortly beforehand. The Ayyubid Empire was starting to break up and a civil war broke out between rival brothers who controlled Egypt and Damascus. The Crusaders first attacked southwards, taking Ascalon but being held before Gaza. Salih Ayub in Damascus sought terms with the Crusaders in order to be able to concentrate on defending Syria against Egypt. The new treaty allowed the Crusaders to reoccupy Jerusalem and all the land west of the Jordan that they had held in 1187. After Theobald departed for Europe, Richard, brother of Henry III of England, arrived at Acre with the backing of Frederick. He first went to Ascalon where he negotiated with the Egyptians, securing a treaty that confirmed the Crusader gains and led to an exchange of prisoners. However, the peace did not last long as the Templars raided the Muslim city of Hebron; in return the Muslims blocked the road to Jerusalem and levied tolls on pilgrims. The Templars responded by sacking Nablus.

In 1244 war broke out between Ismail of Damascus and Ayub as-Salih who ruled Egypt. The Crusaders had made an alliance with Damascus in 1243. As-Salih obtained the services of the Turkomen Khwarismian troops, who had, after their defeat by the Mongols, lived as mercenaries in Mesopotamia. He swept southwards, taking Jerusalem on the way; after joining up with the Egyptian army he defeated a Syrian/Crusader army at Gaza in October 1244. Following this defeat the Ayyubid Empire reunited and the Crusaders were driven out of eastern Galilee and Ascalon.

The last Crusade to the Middle East was that led by Louis IX of France in August 1248. He sailed for Cyprus where for the two previous years he had built up a stock of provisions. The army, said to be up to 25,000 strong, including 2,500 knights and 5,000 bowmen, wintered in Cyprus, where the plan of action was discussed. It was agreed that they should return to Egypt. Reinforced by knights from the Kingdom of Jerusalem, the force embarked in May 1249, only for the fleet to be dispersed by a storm. Louis reached the Egyptian coast on 5 June and a landing was made. For some reason, instead of withdrawing into the fortress of Damietta, the Egyptians retired as far as Mansourah; Damietta was abandoned in panic and fell to the Crusaders without opposition. Louis spent the summer at Damietta and, not wishing to repeat the mistakes made by Frederick's Crusade, refused to advance until the Nile waters had subsided. In November the army marched inland, having to cross numerous rivers and canals, until on 21 December they encamped across the main Nile tributary opposite Mansourah.

An attempt to build a earth ramp across the water was unsuccessful; however, the location of a ford was revealed by a Copt in return for a large payment. The ford was crossed at dawn on 8 February with the Count of Artois commanding the advance guard which included the

The Military Orders

Founded to combine the role of monk and knight. Originally to escort pilgrims, they became the regular units of the Crusader army being far better trained than the feudal levies. Later garrisoned a number of border fortresses. Funded from and recruited in Europe.

Order of St John (Hospitallers)
Originating in a pilgrim hostel after the capture of Jerusalem; established a hospital. Expanded by Raymond de Puy to include knights. Said to have had 500 knights and 500 light cavalry in 1168. Wore a white cross over their tunics.

Order of the Temple (Templars)
Founded by Hugh de Payens in 1118, named after their accommodation in part of the Al-Aqsa Mosque. Wore a red cross on a white background.

Order of St Mary of Teutons (Teutonic Knights)
Founded at the time of the third Crusade.

Templar knights. Ignoring the order not to attack until Louis authorized it, and believing the vital element of surprise would be lost, Artois charged the Egyptian camp and overran it. Then, determined to capture Mansourah, he overruled the advice of the Templars and led another charge, this time into the town whose gates had been left open. The Egyptians waited in the narrow streets until the knights had all penetrated the town and then fell on them where they were at a disadvantage and killed virtually the whole force. The main army had by now crossed the river and prepared to meet an Egyptian attack. The Crusaders began to build a pontoon bridge, withstanding several attacks until the bridge was complete; this allowed the bowmen, who had been left on the far side of the river to cover the crossing, to cross and force the Egyptians to break off the attack. The Egyptians attacked again on the 11th after reinforcements had arrived and a bitter and inconclusive battle was fought. Louis remained at Mansourah, expecting there to be an Egyptian revolution but the arrival of Turanshah, as-Salih's son, convinced him that he must withdraw.

During the withdrawal the Crusaders surrendered and Louis was taken prisoner. Eventually the Crusaders handed over Damietta in return for the release of Louis and the nobles; a very large ransom was to be paid for the rest of the prisoners. Louis returned to Acre. The murder of Turanshah by the Mamelukes and the capture of Damascus by Saladin's grandson, an-Nasir Yusuf, re-ignited the rivalry between Cairo and Damascus with both sides looking for support from the Crusaders. Louis refused an-Nasir's overtures until he had secured the release of all the prisoners held in Egypt; he left the Holy Land in April 1254 to return to France. The Kingdom of Jerusalem survived a further thirty-seven years with little help from Europe as the Muslims encroached and captured city after city. The end of the Crusades is covered in the next chapter.

THE FIRST CRUSADE: THE MARCH TO ANTIOCH

The First Crusade resulted from a speech given by Pope Urban at the council of Clermont in November 1095. Urban announced that he had received an appeal from the Byzantine Emperor for help against the Turkish invaders; he also described the suffering of pilgrims bound for the Holy City of Jerusalem. He called for a Holy War, or Crusade, the fundamental aim of which was the recovery of Jerusalem. The Pope spent the next eight months touring France, repeating his message and recruiting large numbers of the nobility to the cause. They were joined later by the Normans of southern Italy. It took the leaders of the Crusade some months to recruit their forces, sort out the financing of their expedition, and make arrangements for the land and possessions they were leaving behind. Nevertheless, by the autumn of 1096 the First Crusader Army had begun its journey to the Holy Land.

The Crusaders moved in six main groups, taking various routes to Constantinople. There the Byzantine Emperor, while supporting their aim of recovering the Holy Land for Christianity, was determined to ensure that his sovereignty over lost Byzantine lands would be recognized.

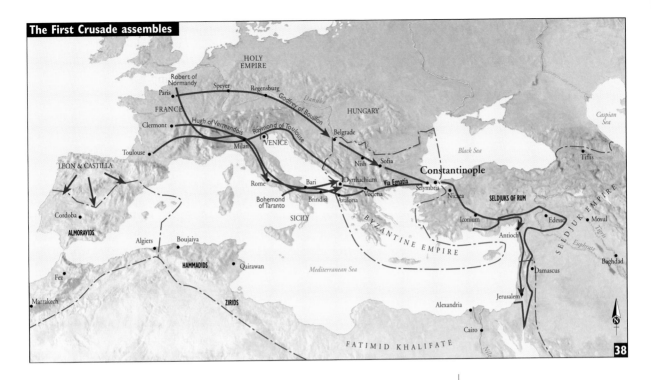

The First Crusade assembles

He prepared to welcome and feed the Crusader armies, at the same time expecting them to take an oath of loyalty to him. The first group to arrive was led by Hugh, Count of Vermandois. On his journey south he was joined first by French knights and later, in southern Italy, by Bohemond's nephew William and his Norman supporters. They crossed the Adriatic but a storm caused the dispersal of his force which made it easier for the Byzantines to keep control as the fleet approached Constantinople; on his arrival, Hugh, impressed by his reception, willingly swore an oath of loyalty to the Byzantine Emperor.

The next army to reach Constantinople was that of Godfrey of Bouillon, accompanied by his brother Baldwin. They took the overland route down the Danube and through Hungary where the king, determined to prevent a repetition of the ravages by the army of Peter the Hermit, agreed to supply Godfrey with provisions, but held Baldwin hostage until the Crusaders had left Hungarian territory. The Byzantines had prepared supplies for Godfrey's army and it reached Selymbria (Silivri), on the Sea of Marmora, on 12 December 1096, without incident; here discipline broke and the soldiers ravaged the local countryside. Once order had been restored Godfrey advanced to the walls of Constantinople. Relations first improved and then worsened until the Emperor, worried by the approach of other Crusader armies, turned his full strength on Godfrey, whose troops fled, convincing him that he should take the oath of allegiance.

Godfrey's army was shipped over the Bosphorus to make camp at Pelacanum (Gebze) just as the next Crusader contingent arrived. Again some fighting was necessary before its leaders agreed to take the oath and to join Godfrey across the Bosphorus. On 9 April 1097 Bohemond of Taranto reached Constantinople ahead of his army which had crossed the Adriatic further to the south and taken a different route across to Vodena on the Via Egnatia; some fighting with the Byzantines occurred when they crossed the River Varda but Bohemond immediately released his prisoners. Bohemond took the oath of allegiance and then asked the Emperor to appoint him commander of all forces in Asia, but Alexius distrusted him and said it was too early to make such an appointment.

Raymond, Count of Toulouse, reached Constantinople as Bohemond's army was being transported over the Bosphorus; he also expected to be appointed the overall commander of the Crusade. His expedition had crossed the Alps and then marched along the eastern Adriatic coast, being harassed en route by Slav tribes as they crossed Dalmatia. Once again the Crusaders were escorted along the Via Egnatia and once again there were clashes with Byzantine troops, during one of which the Pope's representative, the Bishop of Le Puy, was wounded. Raymond, on hearing that Bohemond and Godfrey were both at Constantinople, accepted the Emperor's invitation and went on ahead of his army, which without his control began raiding the countryside and was attacked and beaten by the Byzantines. At Constantinople Raymond proved reluctant to take the oath as he saw himself as the Pope's choice; he declared that if the Emperor led in person then he would follow him, as God was his only sovereign. After several days of pressure from the other Crusader leaders Raymond took a modified oath and two days later his army crossed the Bosphorus.

The last contingent to arrive at Constantinople was that led by Robert, Duke of Normandy, and joined en route by Robert, Count of Blois, and Robert, Count of Flanders. They had marched through Italy to Bari where Robert of Flanders crossed the Adriatic immediately while the other two wintered in Italy before reaching Constantinople in early May. Two weeks later they crossed the Bosphorus to join the other Crusader armies at Nicaea (Iznik) which they were besieging. From now on, instead of crossing the territory of Byzantium which they had been sent to help, they would be confronting hostile Turks who would not be providing them with supplies.

At Nicaea the Crusaders surrounded the walls, which stretched for 6 km, but were unable to prevent provisions reaching the city as part of it rested on Lake Ascania and the Crusaders had no boats to mount a blockade until these were provided by the Byzantines. The vanguard of the Seldjuk army now approached but was beaten off. On 21 May the main body attacked Raymond's army, which aided only by Robert of Flanders and his men, fought a desperate battle all day. The Sultan, realizing he could not defeat the Crusaders on the open battlefield, decided to abandon Nicaea and withdraw into the hills where he would have an advantage. The Seldjuk withdrawal and the success of the blockade of the lake led to the surrender of the city on 18 May, only a few hours before the planned Crusader assault was to have taken place.

The Crusaders now split their army in two and, in order to conserve supplies along the route, decided to march at one-day intervals. The first half, commanded by Bohemond, camped on the plain leading to Dorylaeum (Eskisehir) on the evening of 30 June. Early next morning the Turks, who had been lying in wait close by, charged the camp, surrounded it and subjected it to volley after volley of arrow fire. The Crusaders managed to hold out until the second half of the army appeared,

Byzantine Rulers 1095–1200
Alexius Comnenus 1081–1118
John Comnenus 1118–43
Manuel 1143–80
Alexius II 1180–3
Andronicus 1183–5
Isaac 1185–95
Alexius III 1195–1203

surprising the Turks who were forced to retreat after the Crusaders linked up and went on to the offensive. At this moment a force led by the Bishop of Le Puy, which had been guided through the mountains, appeared behind the Turks who fled to the east, leaving their camp to be captured intact. (There is some difference of opinion as to exactly where the battle took place; Steven Runciman, who has studied the various accounts and visited the area, places it on the plain of Sari-su.)

The march now took the Crusaders to Philomelium (Aksehir) and then on the southern route between the desert and the mountains to Iconium (Konya); there was virtually no water on the way and many horses died. Iconium was reached in the middle of August; it had been abandoned by the Turks but there was water and forage there. Then, carrying water with them, they marched on to Heraclea (Ereğli) where the next fertile valley lay. Here they met a Turkish army which they attacked immediately and which retired quickly to the north, abandoning the city. The choice now lay between the direct route, which required the crossing of the Cilician and the Syrian Gates, both difficult passes and easily defended, or the longer northerly route past Caesarea Mazacha (Kayseri) and then south to Marash (Maras).

The bulk of the Crusaders set off for Caesarea but Tancred and Baldwin refused to take Byzantine advice and made for the Cilician Gates. Caesarea was reached by the end of the month and the army moved straight on to Comana which they relieved from a Turkish siege. Bohemond went in pursuit of the retreating Turks while the rest of the army went on to Coxon (Guksun) where they heard a rumour that the Turks had abandoned Antioch. Raymond despatched a force of knights to occupy the city but at a castle on the Orontes they learnt that the Turks were in fact strongly reinforcing the city. The march from Coxon to Marash was a nightmare of bad weather and dangerous mountainous roads: much baggage and many horses were lost. At Marash Bohemond caught up with the main body and Baldwin appeared from Cilicia, but he then left to go east. After resting at Marash the army moved out on 15 October, and five days later reached the 'Iron Bridge', three hours' march north, and in sight, of Antioch. Four months after leaving their camps on the Bosphorus, the Crusaders were about to invade the Holy Land.

THE FIRST CRUSADE:
THE FIGHTING AT ANTIOCH

It had taken almost two years from the Council of Clermont for the First Crusade to reach the gates of Antioch (Antakya). The City occupied some 8 square km on the southern bank of the Orontes and the northern slopes of Mount Silpius, and its wall was defended by 400 towers carefully spaced so that the whole length of the wall could be covered by arrow fire. The fortifications had originally been built by the Emperor Justinian; its citadel stood 300 metres above the city. The siege began in October 1097. The Crusaders were unable to surround the city as the mountains to the south were too steep and jagged, but nor had Yaghi-Siyan, the Turkoman Governor, sufficient troops to man the walls completely. The defenders

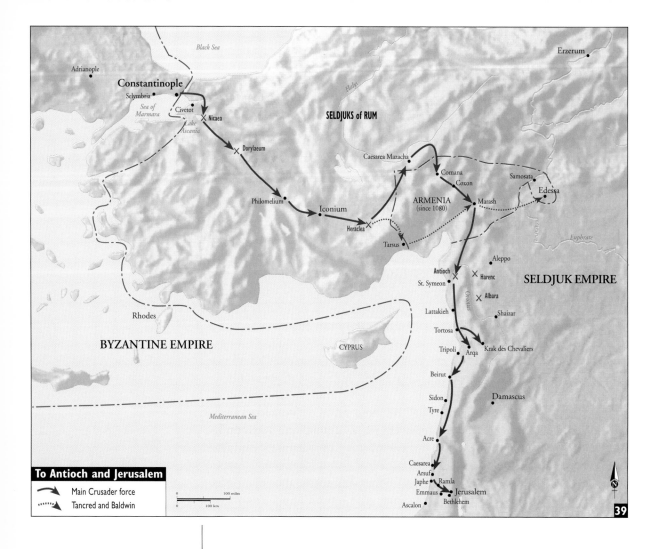

expected an immediate assault but the Crusaders decided that they could not afford to suffer the heavy casualties that would result from an assault and their troops needed to rest. Their plan was to wait and hope that the Emperor would send reinforcements and a siege train by sea. Only Raymond disagreed.

The siege did not go well for the Crusaders, who soon began to run out of food, while the Seldjuk garrison began to make forays aimed at cutting off and attacking foraging parties. However, the Crusaders were successful at Harenc (Jisr el Hadid Harim), where they lured out the garrison of the fort and destroyed it. They also managed to occupy the port of St Symeon (Samandag) when a squadron of Genoese ships bringing reinforcements arrived. At the end of December, when supplies had practically run out and men and horses were dying of starvation, Bohemond and Robert of Flanders led a major expedition to find supplies in the Orontes Valley. Raymond was left in charge of the siege of Antioch. Yaghi-Siyan made a major sortie and attacked the Crusader camp; although surprised, the Crusaders managed to beat off the attack and pursued the Turks back to the fortress gates, nearly breaking into the city. Both sides suffered heavy casualties.

A large force intended to relieve Antioch had been organized by Duqaq, Ruler of Damascus, and the Emir Ridwan of Aleppo (Halab), but when they heard of Bohemond's expedition they advanced to the village of Albara (close to Shaizir) and surprised the Crusaders there. Robert's troops bore the brunt of the attack while Bohemond waited until the Turks thought they had won and then fell on them, causing heavy casualties. Because of their casualties the Crusaders had to return to Antioch without any supplies but they had at least prevented the relief of Antioch. In February Ridwan collected another army which first recaptured the fort at Harenc and then prepared to attack the Crusaders. On Bohemond's advice, the infantry was left to defend the camp, while the remaining 700 mounted knights were despatched to take up a position between the Orontes and Lake Antioch. When the Turks advanced at dawn they were immediately charged, then the Crusaders withdrew, drawing the Turks into the narrow strip of land where they could not be outflanked. Here the Crusaders regrouped and charged again, causing the whole Turkish army to flee back to Aleppo, abandoning Harenc.

Supplies were still short, although some were being sent from Cyprus to St Symeon. On 6 March 1098 an English fleet arrived at the port, bringing a siege train provided by the Byzantine Emperor. Bohemond and Raymond set out to raise recruits from the pilgrims with the fleet and to escort the siege machinery to their camp; on the return journey they were attacked, their soldiers fled and the siege weapons were captured. Just as Godfrey was about to set out to rescue the survivors of Bohemond and Raymond's force the Turks launched an attack from Antioch on the Crusader camp so that their raiding party, now burdened with the siege machinery, could safely return to the fortress. Godfrey held the attack and, when Bohemond and Raymond appeared with what was left of their force, they drove the Turks back into Antioch. They then intercepted the returning Turkish raiders and recovered the siege train.

In May Kerbogha, the Atatabeg of Mosul, with troops from Baghdad and Persia, had set out to join Duqaq and relieve Antioch. It became essential for the Crusaders to capture the city before they were trapped between it and the approaching armies. Fortunately for them Kerbogha decided he must first neutralize the Crusaders under Baldwin who had established themselves at Edessa (Urfa). He therefore delayed there for three weeks before realizing that he would be unable to break into the fortress and should waste no more time in getting to Antioch. The delay gave Bohemond, who had established an understanding with a disaffected captain in the garrison, time to organize an attack. The assaulting force would be allowed to scale the section of wall controlled by the defector. Bohemond let the other Crusader leaders into the secret only on the evening before the attack. The Crusaders left their camp before dark on 2 June and marched eastwards to give the garrison the

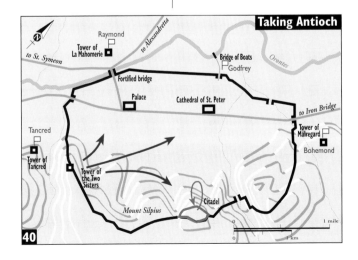

impression that they were intending to intercept Kerbogha. After dark they turned back and a party of knights climbed a ladder and were let into the Tower of the Two Sisters; from here they captured the two adjoining towers, giving the Crusaders two undefended sections of the wall to scale. By the end of the day only the citadel remained in Turkish hands.

It was now the Crusaders' turn to be besieged in Antioch. On 7 June Kerbogha's army was camped where the Crusaders had been camped for so long. First Kerbogha replaced the garrison of the citadel with fresh troops and then he attempted to break into the city from the citadel but his assault was repelled and he decided on a siege. The Crusaders hoped that the Byzantines would rescue them; by this time the Byzantine Army had reached Philomelium (Aksehir). Here the Emperor learnt not only of the Crusaders' plight but also that another Turkish army was advancing to engage him before he could reach Antioch. Deciding that the security of the Byzantine Empire was more important than saving the Crusaders, he withdrew to the west. The Crusaders never forgave Byzantium for what they saw as treachery to 'Warriors of Christ'.

What occurred next was seen by many as a miracle. First there were the visions of Peter Bartholomew which led to the discovery of the Holy Lance; used to pierce Christ's side on the cross, it was excavated under the Cathedral of St Peter. The Crusaders' morale was considerably improved while outside the walls Kerbogha's army was beginning to break up: Duqaq wanted to move south to counter Egyptian aggression; there were feuds between the Emirs; there were disagreements between the Turks and Arabs; and large numbers of soldiers were deserting. A Crusader delegation led by Peter the Hermit achieved nothing, and the Crusaders decided that their only option was a pitched battle. At dawn on 28 June, led by the Holy Lance, they marched out of Antioch. Kerbogha, though advised to attack before the Crusaders had all deployed, waited too long; then, seeing their strength, he made a belated attempt to arrange a truce. But it was too late. The Turkish archers were unable to halt the Crusader advance which is said to have been inspired by a vision of St George on a nearby hillside. Duqaq withdrew his army from the field and his example was followed by other Emirs; the Turkish army broke up and fled, hotly pursued by the Crusaders.

THE FIRST CRUSADE: THE MARCH TO JERUSALEM

Several months elapsed after the defeat of Kerbogha before the Crusaders were ready to set out for Jerusalem. The period was mainly taken up with the quarrel between Raymond and Bohemond as to the status of Antioch, with Bohemond claiming it for himself and Raymond reminding him of his oath of allegiance to the Emperor Alexius. An epidemic, possibly typhoid, caused many deaths, including that of the Bishop of Le Puy, thus depriving the Crusade of its spiritual leader and a wise adviser. A number of local conquests were made, including the town of Albara where the first Latin Bishop was appointed. The army was keen to move on to Jerusalem and eventually offered to recognize Raymond as leader of the whole Crusade if he would organize the operation. Leaving Bohemond, Godfrey and Robert of Flanders at Antioch and Baldwin at Edessa, the Crusaders marched out on 13 January 1099.

While the Crusaders had been at Antioch, changes had occurred further south; the Egyptians, observing the defeat of the Turks and realizing that the Crusaders intended to take Jerusalem, had invaded Palestine and after a forty-day siege had themselves captured Jerusalem. They then took control of the country as far north as Beirut and repaired the city's defences.

The Crusaders' strength was around 1,000 mounted knights and 5,000 infantry. Initially there was disagreement over the route to be taken, with Raymond advocating the coastal route which would make resupply much easier; Tancred pointed out that this meant they would need to capture the fortresses along the coast and said that they did not have the necessary strength. He recommended advancing directly on Jerusalem; this plan had the disadvantage of taking the Crusade through territory controlled by their enemy, Duqaq of Damascus. A compromise was agreed: they would march first to the coast north of Tripoli and avoid the coastal fortresses.

The Crusaders had two early successes: the capture of the fortress of Hosn al-Akrad (Krak des Chevaliers), which had been abandoned by its garrison, and the port of Tortosa (Tartus) where the gates were opened after the Crusader detachment fooled the Governor into believing their force was very much larger than it was by lighting a great number of camp fires. Raymond, who was laying an unsuccessful siege to Arqa, called on Godfrey and Robert to join him as there were rumours that a Muslim relief army was being assembled. Their arrival only led to renewed bickering between the Crusader leaders; the argument intensified after a letter was received from Emperor Alexius saying they were to wait until he joined them at the end of June so that he could lead them into Jerusalem. Only Raymond was in favour of waiting but he was overruled and the army resumed its march south, crossing into Fatimid-controlled territory on 19 May 1099.

The Crusaders were now without naval support as the Fatimid fleet was much stronger. At Beirut the Crusaders agreed, in return for supplies, not to ravage the neighbourhood but at Sidon the garrison attempted to attack the Crusaders, which resulted in the surrounding country being despoiled. The army paused at Tyre but the garrison there remained inside the walls; Acre was reached on the 24th where the Governor also saved the neighbourhood in return for supplies. After resting at Caesarea the army went on to Arsuf (Nof Yam) where they turned east, finding Ramla to have been deserted. Here there was a discussion as to which task took priority: the capture of Jerusalem or the defeat of the Egyptians, but the march to Jerusalem continued. At Emmaus a delegation from the Christians in Bethlehem came and asked the Crusaders to liberate them, and a group of knights immediately rode there. On 7 June the army reached Nebi Samuel (Nabi Samwil) and, at last, could see Jerusalem; they called the hill Montjoie.

The Governor of Jerusalem, on hearing of the approach of the Crusader army, took a number of steps to make a siege more difficult. He blocked up or poisoned all the wells in the immediate vicinity of the city and drove all the flocks of goats and sheep out of reach of the Crusaders. In addition he expelled all Christians from the city, greatly reducing the numbers he

Montjoie, or the Tomb of Samuel (Nabi Samwil), from where the Crusaders first saw Jerusalem.

The Old City of Jerusalem. (Photograph: Z. Radovan, Jerusalem)

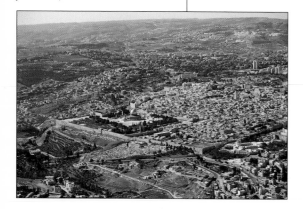

would have to feed during a siege. The Crusader army, which now numbered some 1,200 knights and about 10,000 infantry, was insufficient to surround the city completely and it concentrated its efforts between Mount Zion in the south-west round to Herod's Gate in the north. The east and south-east sectors were uncovered, and this enabled the garrison to send out parties to ambush the Crusader water supply columns which had to travel at least 10 km to find clean water.

The Crusaders also lacked the means to build siege machinery, but, after a visit to a hermit on the Mount of Olives who persuaded them that faith in God would give them victory, an abortive attack was launched on the northern wall. Although the outer defences were breached the shortage of ladders meant that insufficient troops could scale the walls and the attack was beaten off. Fortunately, soon after this, a small number of ships reached Jaffa, bringing not only much-needed supplies but also the wherewithal (other than wood) to construct siege engines. There were few trees close to Jerusalem and expeditions had to be mounted to the woods around Samaria, some 55 km away, to collect the necessary timber. Two large towers and one smaller one were built out of sight of the city.

On 6 July a priest claimed that he had had a vision of Adhemar, Bishop of Le Puy, who had given him instructions as to what the Crusaders must do to be

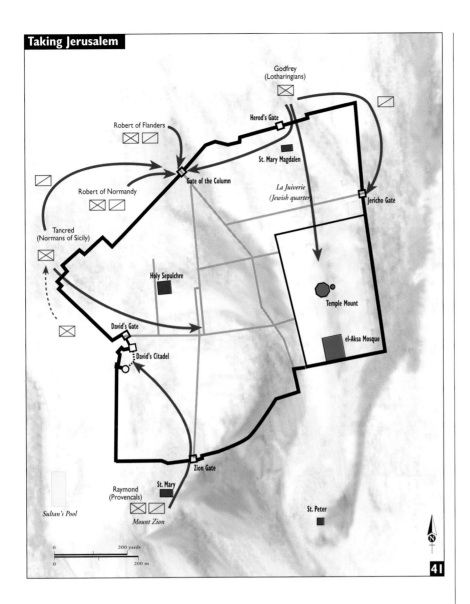

Taking Jerusalem

Godfrey
(Lotharingians)

Herod's Gate

Robert of Flanders

St. Mary Magdalen

Gate of the Column

La Juiverie
(Jewish quarter)

Robert of Normandy

Jericho Gate

Tancred
(Normans of Sicily)

Holy Sepulchre

Temple Mount

David's Gate

el-Aksa Mosque

David's Citadel

Zion Gate

St. Mary

Raymond
(Provencals)

St. Peter

Sultan's Pool

Mount Zion

N

0   200 yards

0   200 m

41

allowed to capture the city. Obeying the instructions, the Crusaders fasted for three days and then, barefoot, processed round the walls of Jerusalem before climbing the Mount of Olives to be preached to by Peter the Hermit and other priests. Two days later the towers were completed and, surprising the defenders, were brought up to the walls – one on Mount Zion and one close to Herod's Gate, with the smaller one at the north-west corner of the city where a feint attack was to be made. Before the towers could reach the walls the surrounding ditch had to be filled and this took all night of the 13th and the next day, the workers taking heavy casualties from stones and flaming liquid thrown from the walls.

By that evening Raymond, at Mount Zion, had managed to cross the ditch but was unable get on to the wall. Next morning Godfrey placed his tower close to the northern wall and by midday had built a bridge between them. The assault party of Lotharingians captured a section of the wall and the Crusaders poured in over the scaling ladders; the Gate of the Column was captured and opened to let more Crusaders in. The

Muslims retreated to the Temple Mount but this was not fortified and they surrendered. The Governor was still fighting in the southern part of the city but seeing the battle was almost lost retired into David's Citadel, which he then offered to hand over in return for his life and those of his bodyguard. Raymond accepted the terms and the Governor was escorted away; all other Muslims in the city, including those given sanctuary in the el-Aqsa Mosque, were massacred, as were the Jews who were burnt in the synagogue in which they had taken shelter.

THE BATTLE OF THE HORNS OF HATTIN

In 1185 Baldwin IV, the leper King, had died and the Regent, Raymond of Tripoli, proposed a four-year truce. Saladin agreed, seeing it as an opportunity to restore his authority without fear of Christian attack. By mid-1186 Saladin had secured his eastern borders after Mosul had acknowledged his sovereignty. He therefore rallied the Muslim armies for the *Jihad* against the Crusader state, and by June 1187 had assembled a force of over 100,000 men.

Meanwhile the Crusaders were in some disarray; following the death of the eight-year-old Baldwin V a struggle over the succession developed between Raymond and Jocelin of Courtenay, which was not resolved by the latter proclaiming Sibylla Queen and so her husband, Guy, King. At the same time Reynald of Chatillon, who backed King Guy, found the truce curtailed his plunder of caravans; however, at the end of 1186, he could no longer resist the booty offered by a caravan travelling from Cairo to Damascus, and he attacked it. That it was Reynald, who had so often broken truces, who was guilty particularly infuriated Saladin. After Saladin's envoys had been rebuffed, war seemed inevitable. The Crusaders, realizing they could not fight without Raymond, who had already confirmed the truce with Saladin, sent a group of knights to negotiate with him. This group foolishly attacked a much stronger force of Muslim cavalry which Raymond had permitted to cross his territory – and they paid the price for their rashness. Raymond was so shocked to see their heads carried on the Muslim lances that he immediately joined King Guy and swore fealty to him.

On 1 July Saladin crossed the River Jordan south of Lake Tiberias, sending part of his army into the hills to camp at Cafarsset (Kafr Sebt, probably close to Sede Ilan) where they blocked the lower road from Nazareth to the south of Lake Tiberias. He went on to attack the town of Tiberias, where the garrison and Raymond's wife, Lady Eschiva, took refuge in the castle. The bulk of Saladin's army made camp at Hattin, at the point where the upper road from Nazareth comes down to the lake just north of Tiberias.

At a council held in Acre, where the Crusaders had assembled, Raymond sensibly advised that the fierce summer heat favoured remaining on the defensive where there was plenty of water and fodder. He argued that before long Saladin's army would have to retire and that would be the moment to launch an attack. The Crusaders, with some 20,000 infantry and 1,300 cavalry, moved forward to La Safori (Zippori), a few kilometres

---

Crusader Northern Frontier Fortresses

Qal'at Shaqif (Beaufort), guarding the Litani crossing

Banias (at times the Crusaders also held Qal'at Subeibe or Nimrod), guarding Damascus to Hula Valley route

Hunin (Chastel Neuf), guarding the western exit from Hula Valley

Metsad Ateret (Le Chastelez), guarding the Bnot Ya'acov ford

Safed – the central look-out post

Habis Jaldak (Cave de Sueth), guarding the Yarmouk Valley

Belvoir v. Coquet, guarding the Jordan bridge at Naharayim

north of Nazareth where there was ample water and grazing, on 2 July. That evening a messenger, who had been allowed to pass unhindered in the hope that his news would cause the Crusaders to advance, arrived from Tiberias to tell them of the siege. Once again Raymond urged staying on the defensive, warning that there was no water between La Safori and Lake Tiberias; even though his sons begged that their mother, Raymond's wife, be saved, he argued that he would rather see Tiberias lost than the whole kingdom. The council resolved to stay at La Safori but during the night King Guy was persuaded by Reginald and the Master Templar that Raymond was not to be trusted ('how could he abandon his own wife?, and remember he had had a pact with Saladin'), and the order to advance at dawn was issued.

The next day, 3 July, was hot and windless, and the 25 km march led the Crusaders across a series of treeless hills so there was no shade for the exhausted army. Worse, throughout the march they were harried by Saladin's mounted archers who swooped in, inflicted casualties and quickly rode away unharmed. By nightfall they had reached the plateau above Tiberias and the Templars who had led the advance reported that they could go no further. Many of the barons wanted to press on until water was reached but many of the soldiers were incapable of continuing and the king ordered a halt for the night. The king himself camped at Lubia (Kibbutz Lavie) where there was a well but this was found to be dry. The plight of the soldiers was made even worse when Saladin ordered the scrub covering the hills to be set alight so that the camp was enveloped in smoke.

The Saracen army deployed during the night and at dawn the Crusaders found themselves surrounded. The infantry, whose only thought was to obtain water, made a desperate attempt to break through en masse to the lake but found they were too strongly hemmed in. Many were killed straightaway and many more taken prisoner. The mounted knights fought bravely, driving back a succession of Saracen cavalry charges. The king ordered Raymond to attempt to break out, which he did successfully as the enemy opened ranks to let them through, closing them again to allow no more to escape. Raymond had no alternative but to ride away from the battlefield, suspected by some of treachery. King Guy made his final stand on the twin-peaked hill known as the Horns of Hattin, from which the battle takes its name. The king and his barons were taken prisoner but were eventually released after a ransom had been paid, but the surviving Templar and Hospitaller Knights were all executed. Reynald of Chatillon, whom Saladin held guilty of ignoring treaties and truces, of attacking defenceless caravans, and of threatening the holy city of Mecca during his seaborne campaign in the Red Sea, was brought to justice before Saladin himself. He felled him with his sword, then he was killed by a guard.

The Crusader kingdom was now defenceless and while isolated fortresses might hold out, there was no army left to prevent Saladin occupying the land. After taking the castle at Tiberias without a fight he moved to Acre which surrendered three days later. An attack on Tyre failed and rather than wage a siege Saladin pressed on, taking Saiete (Sidon) and Baruth (Beirut) before turning south. Ascalon and Gaza fell and the Saracens reached the walls of Jerusalem on 20 September. Saladin

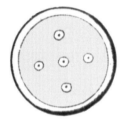

Saladin's sign

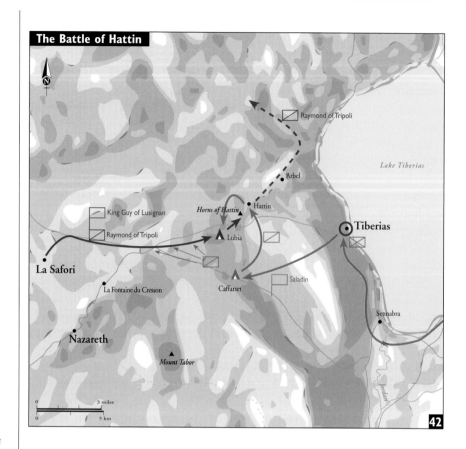

The Battle of Hattin

N

Raymond of Tripoli

Lake Tiberias

Arbel

King Guy of Lusignan

Horns of Hattin Hattin

Raymond of Tripoli

Lubia

Tiberias

La Safori

La Fontaine du Cresson

Caffarset

Saladin

Nazareth

Sennabra

Mount Tabor

Jordan

0   3 miles

0   5 km

42

The Horns of Hattin, viewed from the south. (Photograph: Z. Radovan, Jerusalem)

first attacked from the north and north-west but the sun was in his soldiers' eyes; the Saracens then moved to the Mount of Olives and began mining near the Gate of the Column. On the 29th the wall was breached and the next day the Crusaders began negotiating the terms of surrender. Saladin entered the city on 2 October (the anniversary of Mohammed's flight from Mecca and to Heaven on the 27th day of Rajab). The news of the fall of Jerusalem and the defeat at Hattin shocked Europe and immediately a new Crusade assembled, led by Richard Coeur de Lion, King of England, King Philip II of France and the German Emperor, Frederick I. However, it would not reach the Holy Land until 1191.

THE THIRD CRUSADE

By November 1187 Saladin's campaign was over, and bar a few enclaves, the Crusaders had been driven from the Middle East. In the north they still held Antioch, Tripoli and Tyre; they also held four castles at Krak des Chevaliers, Marqab (Margat), Chastel Blanc, and Tortosa (Tartus), all in the county of Tripoli and held by the military orders. The news of Saladin's victory set off a new round of recruiting for another Crusade to recover the holy places. Three armies were to be assembled and led by Richard Coeur de Lion, the son of Henry II of England; the Holy Roman Emperor, Frederick I Barbarossa; and Philip II Augustus, King of France. However, the first force to set out comprised 300 knights sent by the King of Sicily, whose arrival helped save Tripoli, where they landed, and Tyre

Krak des Chevaliers, Syria.
(Photograph: Sarah Duncan)

from capture as Saladin preferred to press on into Syria rather than lay siege to them. The first major army to set out was that of Barbarossa. It probably numbered over 100,000 men, and left in May 1189, taking the overland route through Asia Minor. Crossing Hungary without incident the army was held up when it reached Byzantine territory and only the threat of an attack on Constantinople persuaded the Emperor to give permission for the army to cross the Dardanelles. In Anatolia they were harassed along the route until they reached Iconium (Konya) where the army of Saladin's son-in-law, Qutb ad-Din, awaited them, only to be decisively defeated. In June 1190 Barbarossa himself was drowned crossing the River Calycadnus and the army began to disintegrate, with a number of knights returning to Europe; they suffered further loss when they were attacked as they crossed the Syrian Gates. What was left of the army finally reached Acre in October, able to play only an insignificant role in the Crusade.

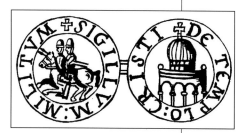

The Templars' Seal.

King Guy had been released by Saladin in July 1188; he gathered as many knights as he could as they were released from captivity and they marched on Tyre where Conrad of Monferrat had been holding out. Conrad refused to recognize Guy as King, nor would he surrender the city to him. After remaining outside the walls of Tyre for several months Guy, with the aid of a Pisan fleet which had arrived in April 1189, laid siege to Acre where he was reinforced by Crusaders, mainly Danes and Frisians, arriving from Europe. Guy's attempt to storm the city on 5 May 1190 failed and they lost all their siege engines which were burnt. Saladin, though unprepared and short of money, had to act against Guy but was unable to break the defences protecting the Crusader lines in an attack on 15 September. A Crusader attack on Saladin's camp in October was repulsed, though a feigned withdrawal by the Saracen right wing also deceived Saladin who reinforced it, allowing the Crusaders to rout his weakened centre as well as his right wing. As the Crusaders began the pursuit they were charged by Saladin and forced back to the defences of their camp. Reinforcements continued to arrive throughout the winter but without the supplies needed to feed the army.

In Europe war had broken out between England and France, which delayed the departure of their crusading armies. The war ended in July 1189, Henry II dying two days later and succeeded by Richard. With peace secured, the French and English armies began their journey on 4 July 1190. Philip marched to Genoa to embark on a Genoese fleet while Richard met an English fleet at Marseilles. The two armies sailed to Messina where they spent the winter; there the English fell out with the Sicilians and Richard took the city of Messina. The French army sailed at the end of March; ten days later Richard followed but diverted to Cyprus which he captured en route, reaching Acre on 8 June 1191. The French built siege engines and Richard had brought catapults so the siege of Acre could now be renewed in earnest. Saladin had also received reinforcements and was able, each time a breach was made in the walls and an assault attempted, to launch a counter-attack against the Crusader camp. But the Crusaders now had command of the sea and supplies could not reach the city. On 4 July the first surrender proposals were made and rejected; on

Acre and its harbour. (Photograph: Z. Radovan, Jerusalem)

the 12th, after Saladin had failed to come to the garrison's rescue, the terms of surrender were agreed. Acre had been besieged for nearly two years. Philip returned to France leaving his army under the Duke of Burgundy but with Richard in overall control.

Leaving Acre on 22 August, Richard marched south, taking the coastal route as Saladin had blocked the shorter inland road. His aim was to capture the port of Jaffa before moving on Jerusalem. Saladin engaged him at Arsuf (Tel Arshaf, Reshef) on 7 September; the Saracens made charge after charge but could not break through the line of knights and after each charge was beaten off the bowmen reformed ready for the next. Richard intended to continue these tactics until he could see the Saracens were exhausted, when he would unleash his cavalry. Eventually two knights could wait no longer and initiated a charge; Richard managed to establish control and after two further charges Saladin's army withdrew from the field. At Jaffa the Crusaders refortified the town as a base for the forthcoming march on Jerusalem. Negotiations with Saladin were opened, during which Richard offered his sister in marriage to Saladin's brother, but the talks came to nothing. Despite the rain Richard advanced on Jerusalem in mid-November, spending Christmas at Latrun and reaching Beit-Nuba, only 20 km from the city, in mid-January. Here, despite the keenness of his soldiers to continue, he was persuaded by those who knew the country better that the risks were too high and that even if they took Jerusalem they would be too weak to hold it against Saladin and the reinforcements arriving from Egypt. He waited.

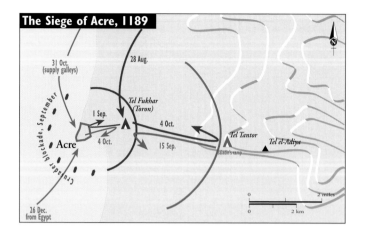

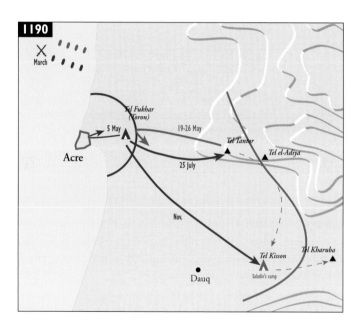

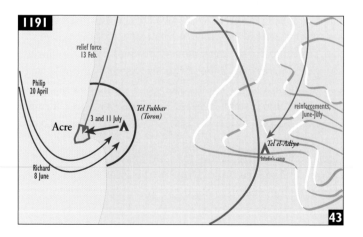

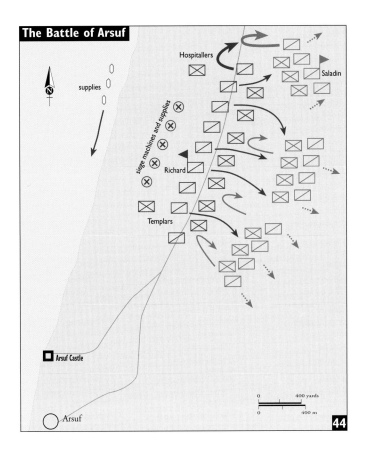

The Battle of Arsuf

Hospitallers

Saladin

supplies

siege machines and supplies

Richard

Templars

■ Arsuf Castle

0   400 yards
0   400 m

○ Arsuf

44

To keep the army occupied the soldiers were put to rebuilding the fortifications of Ascalon. Although a treaty with the Saracens had been agreed it had not been ratified, and Richard decided to capture the castle at Darom some 30 km down the coast from Ascalon. This was achieved so easily that another march on Jerusalem was attempted, the Crusaders again reaching Beit-Nuba but again deciding that they would be unable to hold Jerusalem once the European armies went home. In preparation for returning home Richard withdrew to Acre, whereupon Saladin captured Jaffa; Richard retook it in a daring seaborne landing during which he waded ashore at the head of his men. Saladin made one more attempt to take Jaffa before the main Crusader army, which had now reached Caesarea, arrived overland. The Crusaders were heavily outnumbered, being reduced to only 54 knights with 15 horses, but they managed to withstand cavalry charges throughout the day by a combination of a fence of spearmen supported by archers. In the evening Saladin withdrew to Jerusalem.

Finally, in September, Richard and Saladin reached agreement and a truce was signed. The Crusaders would retain the coastal strip from Jaffa to Tyre, but Ascalon and Gaza were to be handed over to Saladin once their fortifications had been destroyed. The Muslims remained in Jerusalem but would allow Christian pilgrims access. Richard left the Holy Land in October, only to be recognized and taken prisoner as he crossed Austria in disguise; he was released only after payment of a large ransom over one year later.

A Hospitaller's Seal.

THE MUSLIM
RECONQUEST

Having taken the Holy Land from the Fatimids who had ruled it from Cairo, the Crusaders were eventually defeated at the Horns of Hattin by the Ayyubid, Saladin, who originated in Syria but conquered Egypt and established his rule from Cairo, and they were finally evicted from the Holy Land by the Mamelukes, the military caste who superseded the Ayyubids. It is necessary therefore to start this section with a description of the overthrow of the Ayyubids, then to highlight the Mameluke era and their supersession by the Ottoman Empire. It is also necessary to mention both the Mongols and Tamerlaine; neither conquered the Holy Land but the military conquests of the former brought them into conflict with the Mamelukes, while Tamerlaine advanced as far south as Damascus. The only other attempt at conquest in this era was that of Napoleon, which is described in detail on pages 87–91. The defeat of the Ottomans (by then known as Turks) by the British in the First World War is covered in the next chapter.

THE MAMELUKES

The Mamelukes formed the professional Egyptian army. This was composed of boys of the Turkmen tribes of Central Asia who were bought, originally by the Abbasids, as slaves and were drafted into the service of a Sultan or an Ameer where they received several years of military training, principally as mounted archers. Each Sultan formed his own guard of several thousand Mamelukes; the guards of previous Sultans formed regiments in the army, known by the name of their Sultan. These units were known as Royal Mamelukes. Mamelukes were also owned by other Ameers who had to maintain a specified number and provide them for the Sultan in time of war. Legally they were freed on the completion of their military training but remained committed to serve when needed. Sons of Mamelukes could also serve in the army and were known as 'halaqa'; they were more numerous than the Mamelukes but much less respected and mainly served as garrison troops outside Egypt.

The Mamelukes were for many years renowned for their loyalty. A number of events led to the slackening of Mameluke discipline and to the loss of their respect for the Ayyubid dynasty. These included the invasion

Basis of Mameluke Efficiency

1. Long training as boys, under strict discipline, commanded by eunuchs.
2. Blind dedication to the master.
3. Unswerving loyalty to his comrades.
4. Ability the only criterion for promotion, no private influence.
5. Very slow promotion, no fast stream for the clever; experience needed to be mature soldiers.
6. Veterans treated with great respect.

from *Soldiers of Fortune*, John Glubb

of Egypt by Louis IX in 1249; the death of the Ayyubid Sultan, Al Salih Ayoub; and the murder of his eldest son Turan Shah. After the murder Shajar al Durr, Ayoub's widow, became Sultana of Egypt and married the Mameluke commander-in-chief, Izz al Deen Aibek.

Syria refused to recognize this accession and broke away, proclaiming Saladin's great-grandson Malik al Nasir Yusuf, then King of Aleppo, its king. After reaching Damascus Al Nasir attempted to take Egypt and fought the Mameluke army at Abbasa, some 45 km north of Cairo. He was beaten and withdrew across Sinai and the Ayyubid Empire was divided. A peace settlement was soon reached in which Palestine was ceded to Aibek while Al Nasir ruled Syria and Trans-Jordan as far south as Kerak. In 1257 Shajar arranged the murder of her husband but a few days later was herself murdered. After a brief power struggle another army officer, Qutuz, became the Mameluke Sultan.

In January 1256 the Mongol Great Khan, Mangu, despatched an army led by his brother, Hulagu, to conquer Mesopotamia, Syria and Egypt. In February 1258 the Mongols captured Baghdad and in January 1260 Aleppo, whereupon Al Nasir abandoned Damascus but was later captured and killed. Hulagu sent a message to the Mamelukes in Egypt demanding their surrender, but at this juncture news of the death of the Great Khan reached Hulagu and, leaving a garrison in Syria, he returned to Mongolia with the bulk of his army.

Hearing of Hulagu's departure the Mameluke Sultan Qutuz decided to fight those Mongols remaining in Syria. On 3 September 1260 the Mamelukes and Mongols fought at Ayn Jalud (the well of Harod, Gidona), 18 km south-east of Nazareth. At first the speed of the Mongol assault broke through the Mameluke advance guard but when they came up to the main body they found themselves outnumbered and enveloped from both flanks. After a fierce fight the Mongols were decisively beaten and withdrew. The Crusaders from Acre supplied the Mamelukes and allowed them to cross their territory but did not take part in the fighting. Both Qutuz and the Mongol commander, Kitbugha, showed great bravery and leadership throughout the battle; the latter was executed after his capture. The Mamelukes entered Damascus and proclaimed the union of Egypt and Syria. On the march back to Cairo Qutuz was murdered by Baybers, the Bunduqdari, who succeeded as Sultan. He created the Mameluke Empire which was to last for some three hundred years.

As the Mongols were now occupied with internal battles over their succession, Baybers decided that he would take on the Crusaders before they could re-invade Syria. At this time the Crusaders were both weak and split; there were two states: the Kingdom of Jerusalem (which no longer included Jerusalem) and the combined province of Tripoli and Antioch, two narrow strips of territory along the Mediterranean coast. The northern state had been an ally of the Mongols while Jerusalem sided with the Egyptians. In a series of campaigns between 1265 and 1268, Baybers captured Jaffa, Zefat and Antioch, leaving Jerusalem as only a small state stretching from Haifa to Beirut, while in the north Bohemond retained only Tripoli. In 1277 Qalaun, first as regent and then as Sultan, succeeded Baybers who had accidentally drunk the poison intended for an Ayyubid prince.

Mameluke Sultans 1250–1382

Al-Muizz Aibek 1250–7
Al-Mudhaffar Qutuz 1259–60
Baybers Bunduqdari 1260–77
Al Mansoor Qalaun 1279–90
Al-Ashraf Khalil 1291–3
Al-Nasir Muhammad 1293–4 (also 1298–1308, 1310–41)
Al-Nasir Hasan 1347–51 (also 1354–61)
Al-Ashraf Shaaban 1363–77
Al-Salih Hajji 1381–2

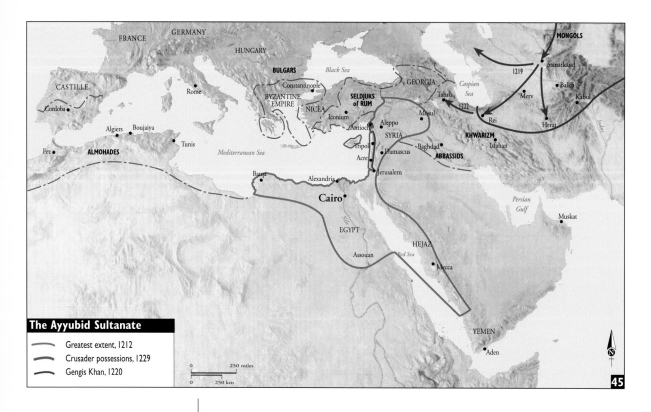

The Mongols invaded Syria again in 1280, after the viceroy of Damascus, who had revolted against the Mamelukes, called for Mongol support. After taking Aleppo they withdrew but then decided to occupy Syria. A pitched battle was fought near Homs on 30 October 1281 and, although the Mameluke left wing fled, the Mongols were eventually routed; but only after the Mamelukes had suffered such heavy casualties that they were unable to pursue the Mongol survivors.

Qalaun decided to take advantage of the Crusaders' internal disputes; he warned them against siding with the Mongols by ordering, in April 1285, and in breach of the truce reached in 1281, the capture of the Hospitaller fortress of Marqab (Margat, just south of Baniyas on the Syrian coast). After a month's siege the garrison negotiated its safe passage to Tripoli and vacated the fort. Then in March 1289 Qalaun attacked Tripoli, bombarding the walls with stone-throwing siege-engines (mangonels) and driving mines under the walls. The Crusaders began to withdraw by sea, but the walls were breached, and the city taken on 26 April 1289; the inhabitants were massacred and the city and its harbour destroyed.

In 1291, outraged by a massacre perpetrated outside Acre by newly arrived and undisciplined Crusader reinforcements from Venice, Qalaun turned his attention to the Kingdom of Jerusalem, but he died before the campaign could begin. His son, Khalil, laid siege to Acre with the strongest siege-train ever assembled, said to include ninety-two mangonels. The Crusaders attempted a couple of sorties but neither was successful, nor did they manage to destroy any of the siege equipment. Much effort was devoted to mining under the four towers and on 15 May a stretch of the

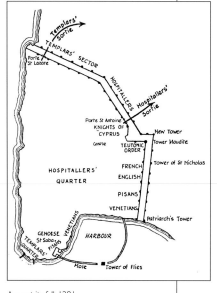

Acre at its fall, 1291.

The Valley of Yizreel by Ain Jalud where the Mamelukes halted the Mongol advance. (Photograph: Z. Radovan, Jerusalem)

outer wall near the New Tower collapsed and the Mamelukes took the tower next morning. On 18 May a dawn assault, employing flame-throwers and accompanied by the beating of 300 drums, was made along the whole eastern wall of the city from the Patriarch's Tower to the New Tower; the defenders held out until the afternoon when the Mamelukes poured into Acre. The Templars' castle at the south-western corner held out for a further ten days before it was destroyed. All the defenders, said to number some 1,000 cavalry and 14,000 foot soldiers, and as many as 40,000 inhabitants were slain and the walls and towers totally demolished. The siege had lasted six weeks. Following the fall of Acre, their capital, the Crusaders decided to evacuate the Holy Land and by mid-August they had gone; the last to leave was the garrison of Chateau Pèllerin (Atlit).

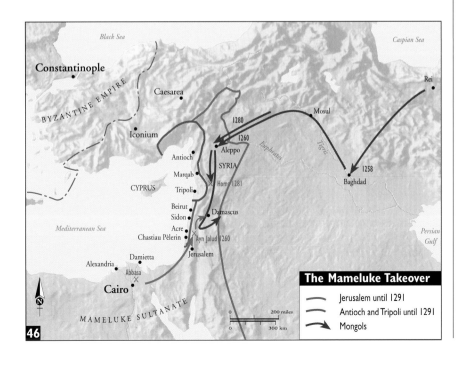

The Mamelukes now ruled a region stretching from southern Egypt and Arabia as far south as Mecca, to south-eastern Anatolia and to the Euphrates. Mameluke power waned following the death of Malik Al Nasir Mohammed, the greatest of the Mameluke Ameers, who had ruled from 1310 to 1341. There were no fewer than twelve Ameers in the next forty years, a period that witnessed several epidemics of plague and a failed attempt by the Crusaders, now based in Cyprus, to capture Alexandria and negotiate its return in exchange for Jerusalem. In November 1382 the last of the Al Nasir dynasty was overthrown and a Circassian, Malik al Dhahir Barqooq, became Ameer.

To the north-east a new figure had emerged: a bandit leader named Timur the Lame (later corrupted to Tamerlaine), who by 1370 had taken control of Trans-Oxiana. In fewer than twenty years he had conquered Central Asia, Georgia, Persia and India. On his return from India he learnt of the death of the Mameluke Barqooq whose son, Faraj, was still a child. In October 1399 Tamerlaine marched from Samarkand to Tabriz, laid waste to Georgia again, took the Ottoman town of Sivas, and then turned south. He sacked Aleppo in October 1400 and Hama in northern Syria in November; on 26 December an inconclusive action between Tamerlaine and the Mamelukes took place close to Damascus. On hearing a rumour of a planned *coup d'état* in Cairo, the young Sultan and his senior officers returned to Cairo, and the Mameluke army, deserted by its leaders, melted away. To avoid a siege of Damascus, Tamerlaine sent a message to the city saying that it would be spared; but when the gates were opened the army entered and immediately sacked the city. Tamerlaine did not move further into the Holy Land but turned north to Mosul, then, after a six-week siege, he sacked Baghdad; he next invaded and conquered Asia Minor before returning to Samarkand.

The Mameluke Empire continued to control Egypt, Palestine and Syria for another hundred years but under Circassian rulers the army continued to deteriorate. The Mameluke military strength was based on their superior cavalry but the invention of gunpowder and the introduction of firearms and artillery spelt their death knell, particularly as the Mamelukes considered the use of gunpowder to be dishonourable and so refused to introduce the new weaponry into their forces. The Ottomans, on the other hand, were among the first to make good use of gunpowder and this led to their defeat of the Mamelukes by 1517.

THE OTTOMAN EMPIRE

The Seldjuk dynasty came to an end in 1300 and Asia Minor was divided between a score or more of Turkish Ameers. One was Othman, leader of a Turkman tribe which had migrated in 1220 from Khurasan, in eastern Persia between the Hindu Kush and the Salt Desert, to escape the Mongols. They settled at Sugut, some 140 km south-east of Constantinople, on the Seldjuk–Byzantine border. Under Othman, the Othmanlis (later corrupted to Ottomans) converted to Islam. He also increased their armed strength from 400 to 4,000 men. In 1326 Othman took the town of Brusa only 80 km from Constantinople; his son and

Mameluke (Circassian) Sultans (1382–1517)
Al-Dhahir Barqooq 1382–9 (also 1390–9)
Al-Nasir Faraj 1399–1412
Al Muaiyad Shaikh 1412–21
Al Ashraf Barsbai 1422–38
Al-Dhahir Jaqmaq 1438–52
Al-Ashraf Inal 1453–61
Al-Dhahir Khushqadam 1461–7
Al-Ashraf Qaitbai 1468–96
Al Ashraf Qansuh 1501–16

successor, Orkhan, extended Ottoman control to Nicaea (Iznik), the shoreline opposite Gallipoli and, in 1337, to Nicomedia (Izmit).

Orkhan created the Ottoman army in which only Muslims could serve and which included a number of mercenaries. His successor recruited large numbers of orthodox Christians into the army and started the Janissaries, who were converted Christian boys, trained in the same way as the Mamelukes; the brightest of them became administrators rather than soldiers. The Ottomans had the best army in the Levant but it was never exposed to serious risk; territory was acquired step-by-step, to be followed by colonization and the construction of forts. The Ottoman entry into Europe was at the request of the ailing Byzantine Empire which sought their help first against the Serbs in Macedonia, and later in Thrace during the Byzantine civil war.

Orkhan died in 1359 at the age of seventy-two, and was succeeded by his second son Murad. Murad immediately began to expand Ottoman territory in Europe, first taking Corlu (74 km west of Constantinople) in 1360 and Adrianople (Edirne) and Philippopolis (Stamboliyski) the next year. The Hungarian king organized a force that included Serbs and Bosnians to oppose the Ottomans' westward advance but this was defeated in a surprise night attack at the River Maritsa (probably close to today's Purvomay). The Ottomans were renowned for taking large numbers of wives and concubines from the territories they captured and over the years acquired the blood of many races of eastern Europe, the Transcaucasus and Middle East. Over the next twenty years they consolidated their hold over south-eastern Europe until in 1389 the Serbs assembled an army to fight the Ottomans at Kosovo; the Serbian defeat and subsequent establishment of Islam there has bedevilled the Serbs to this day.

Accounts differ, but Bayazid succeeded Murad, who was killed at the time of the battle of Kosovo; it seems Bayazid strangled his brother to ensure his claim. Between 1390 and 1393 Bayazid turned to the east and conquered the other ameerites of Asia Minor leaving only Smyrna in the hands of the Hospitallers. In 1395 another Crusade was assembled under the King of Hungary and in September 1396 it had reached Nicopolis (Nikopol) on the Danube in northern Bulgaria. Bayazid outnumbered the Crusaders but the battle was thrown away by the French and Hungarian knights who followed different plans of action. The French knights charged the Ottoman irregular cavalry who scattered, but they were then held up by an obstacle of pointed stakes, from behind which the Ottoman archers inflicted heavy casualties before they were cut down. The French were then confronted by the main Ottoman force which had remained hidden behind a ridge. The Ottoman cavalry first destroyed the surviving French knights and then charged the Hungarian infantry who were finally broken after a charge by Bayazid's Serbian allies.

In 1402 Tamerlaine invaded Asia Minor and defeated the Ottomans at the battle of Anqara in July and then ravaged the whole of Asia Minor before returning to Samarkand. The Ottoman Empire barely survived but from 1413 it began to recover its strength, unhindered by the equally weakened Mamelukes or by Tamerlaine's successors. Sultan Muhammed, in 1453, captured Constantinople, the last remaining part of the Byzantine

The Othmanli Dynasty

Othman 1288–1326
Orkhan 1326–59
Murad I 1359–89
Bayazid 1389–1402
Sulaiman 1402–10
Muhammad I 1402–21
Murad II 1421–51
Muhammad II 1451–81

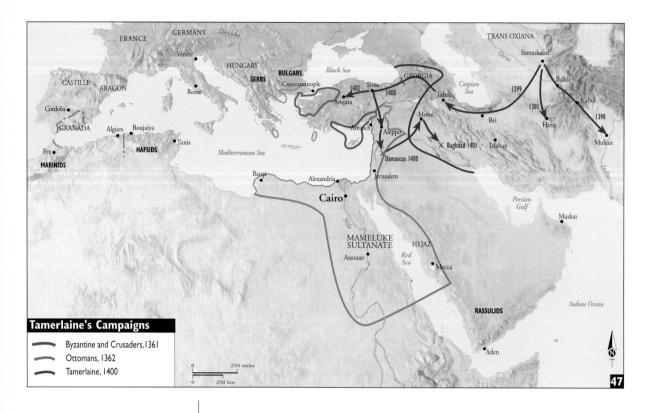

Tamerlaine's Campaigns

- ∼ Byzantine and Crusaders, 1361
- ∼ Ottomans, 1362
- ∼ Tamerlaine, 1400

47

Empire, employing a large quantity of artillery, then a newly invented weapon.

Sultan Saleem attacked and defeated the Persians at Chaldiran (halfway between Tabriz and the Turkish border) in 1515; again artillery won the day because the Persians had none. Saleem then turned on the Mamelukes and defeated their army at Marj Dabiq (near Ein Tab, north of Aleppo) on 24 August 1516; he went on to occupy Damascus in October. On 1 December 1516 Saleem reached Jerusalem. There was no opposition – the 'ulama' went out to hand over the keys of the Dome of the Rock and the El Aqsa Mosque. So the Ottoman rule of the Holy Land began, and it would continue until the British defeated the Turks in the First World War. Saleem marched on to Egypt, defeating the Mamelukes outside Cairo on 22 January 1517.

Although the Ottoman Empire lasted over 400 years it was not a peaceful period, with wars to the west, north and east of the empire. In the west Sulaiman defeated the Hungarians at Mohac in 1526 and occupied most of their territory; however, he failed on two occasions to reach Vienna. To the north there were constant wars with Russia from the time of Catherine the Great in 1762 until the First World War. To the east there were many campaigns against the Persians, and Baghdad changed hands regularly; it was held by the Ottomans from 1534 to 1619, 1638 to 1704 and from 1831 until 1919. The Persians ruled it from 1508 to 1534 and 1619 to 1638, and the Mamelukes controlled it from 1638 to 1704. In Egypt power was recovered by the Mamelukes by 1700 although there was still an Ottoman Governor and a pretence of Ottoman sovereignty.

Virtually none of these conflicts, other than Napoleon's attempt to capture Acre, affected the Holy Land which was split between two Vilyats.

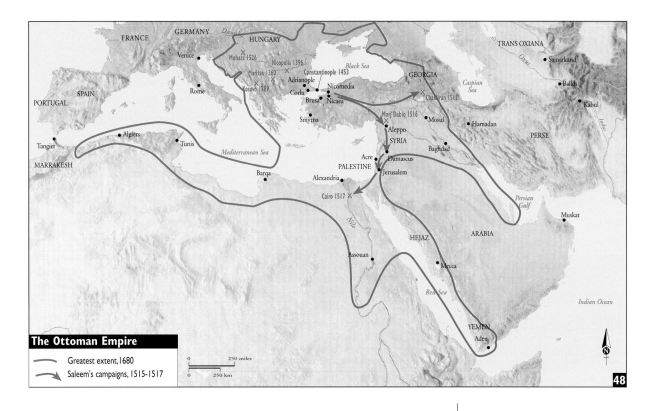

The Ottoman Empire

⌒ Greatest extent, 1680

➤ Saleem's campaigns, 1515-1517

0   250 miles

0   250 km

48

One, with its capital at Acre, controlled a region from the coast as far south as today's Hadera across to Al Hamma (Hammat Gader) on the Yarmouk, then northwards on the eastern side of Lake Tiberias to Banias and on into Lebanon. The remainder of Palestine was administered from Damascus. In the north various local leaders attempted to create autonomous princedoms; the most successful was Ahmed al Jazzar who, when the Ottomans failed to crush him, was appointed Governor of Syria; it was he who defended Acre against Napoleon.

NAPOLEON'S CAMPAIGN AND THE SIEGE OF ACRE

Napoleon's invasion of Palestine, then more often referred to as Syria, was not an offensive move to capture the Holy Land but rather a defensive move against the Turkish forces being assembled to retake Egypt. Napoleon, who was then the Commander-in-Chief of the French Army, arrived at Alexandria on 1 July 1798, having set sail with an army of 35,000 men from Toulon on 19 May. The invasion of Britain being then impracticable, his aim was to attack Britain's trade by capturing Egypt and excluding the British 'from all their possessions in the East to which the general can come'. Napoleon had a vision of repeating the conquests of Alexander the Great, taking back India for France and then turning to overthrow the Turks and 'take Europe in the rear'. He was lucky: Nelson, who was searching the Mediterranean for him, had been at Alexandria only two days before. The disembarkation began immediately. Alexandria fell with little resistance and, after a series of night marches, Napoleon's army came in sight of Cairo on 21 July. Here it was attacked by the Mameluke cavalry, some 5,000 men strong, but the attack failed and Napoleon's troops entered the Cairo Citadel on the 22nd. On 13 August Napoleon received the news that his fleet had been destroyed by Nelson at the battle of Aboukir Bay and that Alexandria was blockaded by the British navy.

By mid-December the news had filtered through to Napoleon that Turkey had declared war on France and was assembling two armies, one in Syria and another on the island of Rhodes; the latter force was preparing to land on the Egyptian coast. The Turkish commander, Achmed Pasha, was known as 'Dgezzar' ('butcher') on account of his cruelty. Napoleon decided not to allow the Turks time to put their plan for a combined attack into action and he immediately advanced into Palestine, aiming to take the ports of Jaffa and Acre in order to deny them to the British and Turks. The French army for this operation was only 13,000 strong, with four divisions of infantry, each of 2,500 men, supported by 3,000 cavalry, artillery and engineers. On 9 February 1799 Reynier's division reached El Arish and captured the village which had been obstinately defended by some 2,000 men, 500 of whom were killed, the remainder retreating into the fort. Both sides received reinforcements but the Turks were surprised on the night of the 14th and were routed, and the fort surrendered on the 20th. Gaza fell next, the Turks withdrawing as the French advanced. Jaffa was reached on 3 March and was besieged although the French siege artillery was still at sea. The garrison held out, making a couple of unsuccessful sorties, until the 7th when Jaffa was stormed after a breach was made in the walls. Many Turks were slain and some 2,000 prisoners were taken; because no troops could be spared to guard them, they were ordered to be shot two days later.

The army started its march north on 14 March, reaching Acre on the 17th. Here Napoleon took up a position on the reverse slope of a ridge with his line extended to the sea on both sides of the town. To give warning of any Turkish reinforcing movement, observation posts were established at Haifa, Nazareth, Safed (Zefat) and south of Tyre. In early March Acre received some welcome support from a British naval squadron commanded by Sir Sydney Smith which had, on 15 March, captured seven French ships carrying Napoleon's siege train. These guns were soon unloaded and stationed on the ramparts, replacing the small and largely unserviceable Turkish guns. Napoleon directed the siege from an area of high ground known then as Richard Coeur de Lion's Mound and today as Napoleon's Hill; nine assaults were launched at breaches made by the field artillery but each time the French were repulsed by the Turks and the British marines and sailors, supported by the guns of two frigates.

By the beginning of April Turkish reinforcements began to approach, crossing the Jordan both north and south of Lake Tiberias. The French General Junot first encountered these at Loubieh (Kibbutz Lavie), halfway between Nazareth and Tiberias. Napoleon sent Kleber's division to link up with Junot and on 11 April, while moving forward to Loubieh, they encountered beyond Cana (Kafr Kanna) a force of some 4,000 Turkish

---

Napoleon's Syrian Campaign: Order of Battle

Kleber's Division:
25 & 75 Demi-Brigade of the Line
part of two light infantry demi-brigades
Reynier's Division:
9 & 85 Demi-Brigade of the Line
Lannes' Division:
13 & 59 Demi-Brigade of the Line
part of 22 Demi-Brigade of Light Infantry

Bon's Division:
18 & 22 Demi-Brigade of the Line
part of 4 Demi-Brigade of Light Infantry
Murat's Cavalry: 900 men, 4 guns
Cafferelli's Engineers: 340 men
Daumartin's artillery: 1,400 men; 8 three pounders; 15 eight pounders; 4 twelve pounders; 15 six inch howitzers; 3 six inch mortars
Guides: 400 men

cavalry and pushed them back to the Jordan. Wary of having to engage the whole Turkish force, the French then withdrew to Nazareth. Meanwhile the main Turkish force advanced from the southern end of Lake Tiberias to the plain of Esdrelon (Emeq Yizreel) with a detachment crossing Jacob's Bridge (Bnot Ya'acov) and advancing to Safed. Napoleon sent Murat to the Bridge to cut off the northern detachment and set off with Bon's division to join Kleber and engage the Turks; however, Kleber had already moved to get between the Turks and the Jordan. Before daybreak on 16 April, Kleber, who had camped at Saphorie (Zippori), set out to attack the Turks. However, difficulties on the night march meant that, having gone round the eastern side of Mount Tabor, he only reached the plain after dawn when he found himself with Turkish forces ahead and behind him. The 4,000 Turkish infantry were in position at Foulieh (Afula) but the cavalry, warned of the French approach, had managed to move round to the north of Kleber. The French division formed two squares and held off attacks from 25,000 cavalry. Napoleon, arriving on the heights west of Nazareth, sent General Rampon with half his force to Kleber's support and the other half, under General Vial, to try to force the Turks back towards the Jordan and to cut them off from Jenin where they had established a base. Informed of Napoleon's arrival, Kleber immediately attacked, took Foulieh and then turned on the Turkish cavalry who were also under attack from Rampon's column from the west. Vial cut off their retreat. The Turks broke up in disorder and during the night the survivors crossed the Jordan south of Lake Tiberias. The Turks lost over 5,000 men and large quantities of supplies which the French eagerly claimed.

At Acre a large mine had been dug under the tower at the north-east corner of the city but when this was blown on 24 April it failed to create a breach. The bombardment continued and another attack on the 25th was repulsed. The French artillery was reinforced on 30 April by nine heavy guns landed from frigates at Tantourah (10 km south of Atlit) and these concentrated their fire on the wall to the east of the tower. An attack launched on 1 May was unsuccessful but a sortie by the garrison was counter-attacked by two companies of Grenadiers, resulting in about 500 Turks and British sailors being killed or wounded. On 6 May the garrison's counter-mining managed to reach the main French mine, which could not be exploded through lack of gunpowder, and the mine was destroyed. Next day the sails of thirty Turkish ships bringing reinforcements and supplies from Rhodes were visible on the horizon. The French redoubled their efforts to break into the city and that night another attack by two demi-brigades was launched but it too was thrown back with heavy losses on both sides. On the night of 7 May the French managed to occupy the Tower but could get no further. By the time of the next assault, launched the following day, Turkish reinforcements, led by Hassan Bey, had arrived. The attack, led by General Lannes, penetrated into the garden of the Seraglio where Lannes was seriously wounded and General Rimbaud killed. Dgezzar Pasha was loath to allow any but his own troops to enter the garden but as only two hundred of them remained he was persuaded to send in a newly arrived battalion (the Chifflick Regiment). The garrison next made a sortie from the main gates; they were forced back, but the French were halted by two

Napoleon's Proclamation at Acre, 17 May 1799

Soldiers
You have traversed the desert which separates Africa from Asia with the rapidity of an Arab Force. The Army which was on its march to invade Egypt is destroyed. You have taken its General, its field artillery, camels and its baggage; you have taken all the fortified posts which secure the wells of the desert ... during three months, in the heat of the sun, taken 40 pieces of cannon, 50 stands of colours, taken 6,000 prisoners and razed or destroyed the fortifications of Gaza, Jaffa, Haifa, and of Acre ... the castle of Acre is not worth the loss of those brave soldiers who must fall in the time.

Acre, showing the Ottoman defences. (Photograph: Z. Radovan, Jerusalem)

Siege of Acre, March–May 1799

XX Lannes

XX Reynier

mine

Seraglio

mosque

Napoleon's Hill

lighthouse

N

0 400 yards
0 400 m

"Tigre"

49

58-pounder guns from the frigate *Tigre* which had been mounted at the gates. Napoleon made one more attempt to take the city shortly before sunset. This time the attackers were allowed through the breach into the garden where they were cut to pieces in savage hand-to-hand fighting which cost the French 200 dead and 500 wounded, including General Bon who later died of his wounds. The last French attack on Acre took place on 10 May; this also failed, with reports that some battalions had refused to advance over the dead bodies of their comrades.

By now the French Army was seriously afflicted by the plague; in total they had lost 5,000 men killed or wounded, and to sickness. Receiving news of insurrection in Egypt, Napoleon decided to raise the siege and march back to Egypt. The evacuation of the sick and wounded began on the night of 17 May, and withdrawal continued until the rearguard left on the night of the 20th. The army had reached Jaffa by 24 May and rested there for three days, occupied in destroying the fortifications and punishing the nearby villagers who had attacked and looted French supply convoys. As many of the sick and wounded as possible were taken off by sea. The French left Jaffa on the 28th and 29th, burning all the villages that lay in their path before reaching El Arish on 2 June and Cairo on the 14th. On 25 July the French defeated a Turkish force which had landed at Aboukir Bay, claiming that some 10,000 Turks were forced into the sea. (A British account suggests these figures are exaggerated, as the Turkish force numbered only 8,000, of which nearly 2,000 were taken off by boats.) On the night of 22 August Napoleon took advantage of an unseasonable south-east wind and set sail for France, taking with him many of his commanders and staff including Berthier, Lannes and Murat, all later to become Marshals of France.

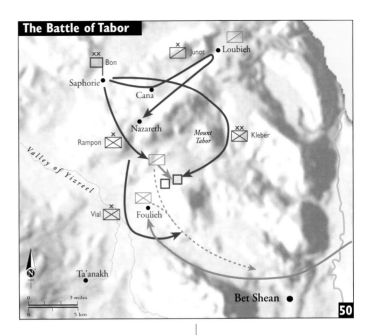

The Battle of Tabor

Mount Tabor, scene of Napoleon's defeat of the Turks in April 1799. (Photograph: Z. Radovan, Jerusalem)

FIRST WORLD WAR

OVERVIEW OF THE WAR AGAINST THE TURKS

The purpose of this section is to describe in outline the conduct of operations in Sinai and Palestine, and military operations in other parts of the Middle East. The Battles of Gaza, Beersheba and Megiddo are described in detail following this introduction, as is the surrender of Jerusalem.

The First World War started in August 1914 and Britain declared war on Turkey on 5 November that year. Turkey's entry into the war opened a number of new war fronts: Egypt, Mesopotamia, the Caucasus and, later, Gallipoli. Britain's main concern in the area was maintaining the Suez Canal for communications with the Indian Empire; at that time Egypt was still nominally part of the Ottoman Empire but had been in reality independent but with British protection. Turkish forces were in position to threaten British interests in Egypt and the Canal from Palestine and from eastern Libya where Senussi tribesmen had limited Turkish artillery and machine-gun support. The Turks also threatened the important coaling station at Aden and British interests and oil in the Persian Gulf. Various plans were made to replace the small regular army garrison in Egypt which was needed in France; by November a Territorial Army division and several yeomanry regiments had reached Egypt, elements of Indian Army units en route to France could be borrowed and Australian and New Zealand troops were to move to Egypt for training before deploying to France.

The German-backed Turkish plan of operations was first to attack the Russians in the Caucasus with a force of 200,000 men and cut off the vital supply of oil, and secondly to concentrate a force of 140,000 men at Damascus and then to threaten the Suez Canal. A third objective was to advance from Baghdad to Basra to seize the oil-wells and pipelines of the Anglo-Persian Oil Company and so deny the Royal Navy that source of oil; initially only one division was allocated to this task. The Turks had for some time been attempting to stir up trouble for the British on the Indian north-west frontier but this had little effect other than alerting the authorities in India, who, basing their opinion on their relations with the semi-independent Arab rulers of the Gulf, foresaw the possibility of a Turkish offensive there. In the middle of October a brigade of the 6th Indian Division embarked for the Gulf, reaching Bahrain on 23 October. It first took the Turkish fort of Fao and then proceeded up the Shatt-el-Arab to land on the western bank opposite Abadan to protect the Anglo-Persian oil refinery. Additional troops arrived from India before Turkish reinforcements could be sent from Baghdad, 800 km away, to strengthen Basra, and the town fell to the British on 22 November.

The first Turkish attack on the Suez Canal took place in February 1915 when it was defended by Indian Army brigades. The Turks, advised by the German colonels Kress von Kressenstein and von Frankenberg und Proschlitz, avoided the coastal approaches, either along the Mediterranean coast or the southern route from Ma'an through Aqaba to Suez because both could be threatened from the sea. Instead they advanced from Beersheba across central Sinai via Bir Gifgafa towards Ismailia on the Canal, bringing with them heavy artillery and bridging pontoons. The attack on the night of 2/3 February was hindered by a sandstorm but some small parties of Turks managed to cross the Canal, only to be eliminated. A second attack was launched in daylight but was equally unsuccessful and the Turks decided to withdraw. The consequence of this attack was that the Turks realized they could tie down substantial British forces, which could have been better used elsewhere, so long as they threatened the Canal. The British eventually decided that the Canal could be more economically defended from a position across Sinai. The Turks withdrew to Beersheba, leaving a small force in Sinai, but the British did not move forward to El Arish until mid-1916.

In the northern Mediterranean the unsuccessful attempt to force the Dardanelles took place in March 1915, followed by the landings on Gallipoli at Helles in April and at Suvla Bay in August. Since the first naval bombardment in November 1914 the Turks had worked hard to fortify both Gallipoli and the Dardanelles and the landings never achieved their aim of taking the whole peninsula. After months of bitter fighting and heavy casualties on both sides it was decided to withdraw. In October the Salonika campaign began, with the aim of backing Greek support for the Serbs who were under attack from both the Austro-Hungarians and the Bulgarians. The evacuation of Gallipoli was completed in January 1916 with the force withdrawing to Egypt. In January 1916 General Sir Archibald Murray was sent to Egypt, initially to take control of all Mediterranean operations including Salonika, the defence of the Suez Canal and the formation of an Imperial strategic reserve, although not of operations in the Western Desert nor internal security in Egypt. This concept was soon altered when the French took command of operations in Salonika, Murray now being responsible only for its administration until September when the Salonikan army became totally independent. A further change was made in March when it was decided that it was unwise to have two major commands and commanders based in the same area and so Murray assumed command of Egypt and the Western Desert as well.

With the troops released from defending Gallipoli, the Turks now planned a major assault on Egypt but the plan was interrupted and delayed by the Russian attack on and capture of Erzerum in north-east Turkey in February 1916. At this time nine infantry divisions were deployed in Egypt with three more Australian and New Zealand divisions in the process of being formed; however, this situation did not last long as

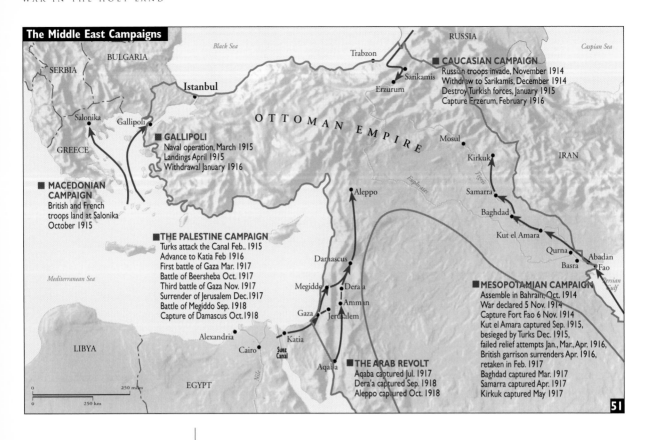

The Middle East Campaigns

CAUCASIAN CAMPAIGN
Russian troops invade, November 1914
Withdraw to Sarikamis, December 1914
Destroy Turkish forces, January 1915
Capture Erzerum, February 1916

GALLIPOLI
Naval operation, March 1915
Landings April 1915
Withdrawal January 1916

MACEDONIAN CAMPAIGN
British and French troops land at Salonika October 1915

THE PALESTINE CAMPAIGN
Turks attack the Canal Feb.. 1915
Advance to Katia Feb 1916
First battle of Gaza Mar. 1917
Battle of Beersheba Oct. 1917
Third battle of Gaza Nov. 1917
Surrender of Jerusalem Dec.1917
Battle of Megiddo Sep. 1918
Capture of Damascus Oct.1918

MESOPOTAMIAN CAMPAIGN
Assemble in Bahrain, Oct. 1914
War declared 5 Nov. 1914
Capture Fort Fao 6 Nov. 1914
Kut el Amara captured Sep. 1915,
besieged by Turks Dec. 1915,
failed relief attempts Jan., Mar., Apr. 1916,
British garrison surrenders Apr. 1916,
retaken in Feb. 1917
Baghdad captured Mar. 1917
Samarra captured Apr. 1917
Kirkuk captured May 1917

THE ARAB REVOLT
Aqaba captured Jul. 1917
Dera'a captured Sep. 1918
Aleppo captured Oct. 1918

51

one division was sent to Mesopotamia in February, and seven to France between February and April, with three more going in June. The security of the Canal now rested on a strong defensive line constructed some 11,000 metres to the east of the canal so that it was out of artillery range, but this line required more troops to hold it than were likely to be available. General Murray appreciated that the defence of Egypt could best be insured by holding a line across Sinai from El Arish to Quseima and he was authorized to advance in the first instance to Katia, some 40 km east of the Canal. As the advance across Sinai progressed a railway and pipeline would be constructed so that the force could be supplied and, more importantly, watered.

The departure of the divisions from Egypt led the Turks, despite the delay to the arrival of their own reinforcements, to mount a small operation towards the Canal. The yeomanry screen was surprised 6 km east of Katia on 23 April 1916 and the Turks pressed on to Katia and took it. Relief efforts were unsuccessful at first but Katia was retaken two days later. The Turks' German commander, Kress von Kressenstein, awaiting the arrival of German machine-gun, anti-aircraft and artillery units, made no further move for three months, by which time the British position at Romani had been greatly strengthened. Once the railway line reached Romani, the 52nd Division was deployed there in support of the ANZAC Mounted Division which had been protecting the construction of the railway. It was anticipated that the Turks would attack the British right, as the left was protected by the sea, and would try to cut the railway west of Romani; this would mean attacking through an area of soft sand and high

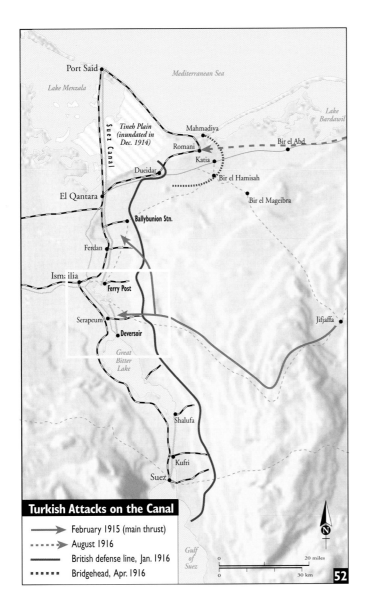

Turkish Attacks on the Canal

➡ February 1915 (main thrust)
▸▸▸ August 1916
— British defense line, Jan. 1916
▪▪▪ Bridgehead, Apr. 1916

52

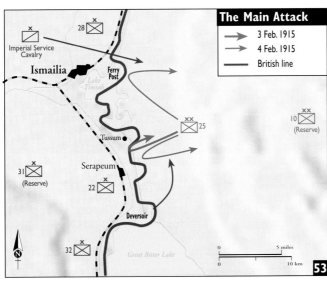

The Main Attack

➡ 3 Feb. 1915
➡ 4 Feb. 1915
— British line

53

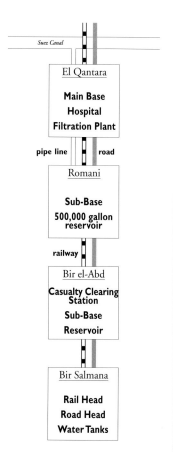

Suez Canal

El Qantara

Main Base

Hospital

Filtration Plant

pipe line   road

Romani

Sub-Base

**500,000 gallon
reservoir**

railway

Bir el-Abd

**Casualty Clearing
Station**

Sub-Base

Reservoir

Bir Salmana

Rail Head

Road Head

Water Tanks

*The Logistics Chain, November
1916.*

dunes. On 24 July the Turks advanced to within 15 km of Romani but then halted for ten days, and the British prepared to advance if the Turks did not attack. The Turks began their attack on 3 August, closely following up 2 Australian Light Horse Brigade (2 LHB) as it retired after a routine day's reconnaissance, but they failed to establish themselves on the ridge held by the British. By late afternoon on 4 August the Turks were in the sand dunes, as the British had expected, and were tired and dispirited. The British plan was to destroy the Turkish force but the infantry were unable to cope with the heat and the heavy going and the Turks managed to withdraw; however, they lost some 4,000 men prisoner and probably another 4,000 dead and wounded.

The Arab revolt began in June 1916 following unsuccessful attempts by the Germans and Turks to initiate a Jihad, or holy war, throughout the Muslim world, and the successful efforts of the British in persuading the Amir of Mecca, Sherif Hussein, to rise against the Turks and gain Arab independence. Having quickly captured Mecca, Hussein also wanted to take Medina which was much more heavily garrisoned but he was dissuaded from this by Captain T.E. Lawrence and instead made a 400 km flanking march to threaten the Turkish lines of communication. The threat to Mecca was removed as the Turks were forced to disperse their troops to protect the Hejaz railway.

The British advance into Palestine began unsuccessfully with the failure to take Gaza in the first two battles of March and April 1917. Gaza was not taken until November, after the arrival of General Allenby and the capture of Beersheba at the end of October. Allenby's next objective was Jerusalem but before he could move against it the Desert Mounted Corps (DMC), with the 60th Division, were despatched to attack the retreating Turks. The Turkish rearguard prevented the cutting off of any large force and progress on 7 and 8 November was slow; on the 9th only one division could move forward owing to lack of water. The Turks now prepared to make a stand to protect the junction of the railway with the branch line to Jerusalem but their orders to the Turkish 7th Army to launch a counter-attack from Hebron were intercepted. General Allenby disregarded this threat, considering the Turks too disorganized; in the event they made a demonstration on the 10th and then withdrew to Beit Jibrin (Bet Guvrin). On 13 November an attack on Junction Station (Nahal Soreq) was launched by XXI Corps and the DMC, the latter with one division protecting the right flank while the rest of the DMC operated on the left. The main defensive features were two villages on high ground, Katrah (north Gedera) and 2 km to the north El Maghar, and the narrow ridge which ran north-eastwards from El Maghar. Here the 52nd Division was held up until a charge by the 6th Mounted Brigade captured the ridge and the 8th Mounted Brigade captured two other villages to the north. When they saw the cavalry on the ridge the infantry renewed their attack and took both Katrah and El Maghar. The Turks retreated to Aqir (Eqron).

The Turks were withdrawing to a line Jaffa–Lydda (Lod), with detachments covering Ramla and Latrun, and to a position near Khulda (Hulda) on the Junction Station–Latrun road. The DMC advanced up to these positions, encountering strong resistance at Sarafand (Zerifin) and Nes Ziyona; both were taken by the New Zealand Mounted Rifle Brigade which also repulsed several Turkish counter-attacks. The ridge between Abu Shushe and Sidun was taken by the Yeomanry Division in another spirited cavalry action. On 15 November the ANZAC Mounted Division entered Ramla and Lydda without opposition. The New Zealanders continued northwards, finding Jaffa undefended and the Turks holding a line along the Nahr el Auja (Nahal Yarqon), while to the east the Yeomanry found Amwas strongly defended. All this time the railway from Egypt was being extended, with a gauge change at Deir Sneid (Netiv ha Asara), and it was now joined to the Turkish line at Junction Station. By 5 December the line was open to Ramla and Lydda.

The advance on Jerusalem now began but was severely hampered by stout Turkish resistance, the very hilly terrain and difficult going, the lack of roads suitable for bringing up artillery, and the onset of winter weather. After three weeks of fighting XXI Corps was relieved by XX Corps but it was not until 9 December that the road to Nablus, north of Jerusalem, was cut. By then the demoralized Turks had decided to withdraw and the Mayor of Jerusalem set out to surrender the city; on 11 December General Allenby made his formal entry into Jerusalem. The capture of the city came at an opportune moment for the Allies as Russia had just collapsed, the Italians had been beaten at Caporetto and the Germans had launched a counter-offensive at Cambrai.

As both Jerusalem and Jaffa remained within range of Turkish artillery, the next task was to push further north with XXI Corps in the coastal plain and XX Corps north and east of Jerusalem. XXI Corps had to cross the Nahr el Auja, a rather more impressive obstacle then than it is today, being 36 metres wide at its mouth and 12 metres wide at Hadra, 5 km inland; the attack was to take place between the two. The 52nd Division made the assault crossing on the night of 20 December without any preliminary bombardment. They crossed at three places: the ford close to the beach where the water was only a metre deep; at a crossing roughly half a kilometre inland; and at a third site 1 km west of the destroyed bridge at Hadra (where Route 4 now crosses the Yarqon). The first crossing took place at 8 pm at the middle site, where some of the bridging rafts were holed and the troops had to be towed across on the rafts. This was a slow process, but by 11 pm two battalions were across. The battalion from 157 Brigade sent a company to cover the ford while the battalion attacked the trenches 1 km to the north. The 156 Brigade battalion attacked the farm 1 km west of Sheikh Muwannis. By midnight a footbridge had been constructed, 156 Brigade had completed their crossing and two battalions took Muwannis and the trenches to its south. At the easternmost crossing, delays in constructing a bridge led to the infantry being rafted across. At 3.30 am two battalions attacked and took Khan Hadra, the farm and a hill to its north-east. There was little Turkish opposition north of the river and by nightfall on 22 December XXI Corps had established itself on a line running from Arsuf (Nof Yam) on the coast south-east through Sheikh Balluta (Hadar Ramatayim) and Fajja (Givat HaShalosha) to Rantye (Rinnatya).

On 27 December the Turks attempted a counter-attack on Jerusalem. They pressed hard and managed to capture some forward positions but the defensive line held. The Turkish attack had been so confidently

---

Air Support

Palestine Brigade
Royal Flying Corps

5th (Corps Artillery) Wing
14 Squadron: 16 BE 2e aircraft
113 Squadron: 8 BE 2e, 5 RE 5 aircraft

40th (Army) Wing
67 Australian Squadron: 6 Bristol Fighters; 3 Vickers Bullets; 3 DH 2s; 2 Bristol Monoplanes; 1 Bristol Scout
111 Squadron: 7 BE 2cs and 2es; 5 RE 8s; 5 BE 12cs; 1 Martinsyde

21 Balloon Company

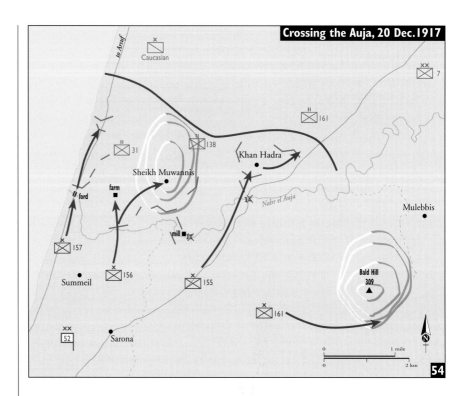

Crossing the Auja, 20 Dec. 1917

expected that a counter-stroke made by the 10th Division had been planned for the morning of the 27th and this successfully took its first objectives and a general advance began on the 28th; Ramallah was taken the next day by a brigade of the 74th Division. By dawn on 30 December the British line ran from Janiya, crossed the Nablus road 1.5 km north of Ramallah, to Beitin (Bethel) and then south to Anata.

In the aftermath of the Third Battle of Ypres General Allenby came under severe pressure from London to knock Turkey out of the war. It was suggested that he should start by advancing to Aleppo; Allenby responded that he would need at least sixteen infantry divisions to do so. He was also facing severe administrative problems, made worse by heavy rain which had caused flooding in the coastal plain. In February General Smuts was sent out to review the situation and he recommended that either Palestine or Mesopotamia should make the offensive and that for logistic reasons it should be Palestine. Allenby's plan was first to advance to the River Jordan to protect his right flank and to then concentrate on destroying the Hejaz railway and isolating the Turks south of Ma'an. Then he would advance to Haifa and Tiberias, his main force remaining on the coast, with a smaller force moving on Damascus in conjunction with the Arab forces. To administer and supply this force he would need large quantities of railway lines (620 km) to build a double-track to Haifa, with additional construction units and even more coal than the 6,000 tonnes a month already being consumed.

In February Jericho was captured by the 60th Division and the ANZAC Mounted Division exploited to the Jordan River. Next a general advance involving both XX and XXI Corps was made to improve the position in Judea and the Jordan valley; after four days' fighting the objectives were

AUSTRALIAN
COMMONWEALTH
MILITARY FORCES
(General Service Badge)

taken and the line now ran from Ras el Ain (Antipatris), Madjal Yaba (Rosh ha' Ayin), Nabi Saleh, Sinjil and Kefar Malik to El Musallabe (8 km north-west of El Auja). Next there was a raid on Amman, planned as a swift mounted operation. However, the weather caused the Jordan to rise, making crossing difficult. The element of surprise was lost and the Turks were able to reinforce Amman. The force reached the outskirts of Amman on 27 March but was unable, despite four days of hard fighting, to take it. A withdrawal began and the force was back over the Jordan with a thousand prisoners by the evening of 2 April. The raid, although not as successful as had been hoped, did have a positive result in that Turkish forces here were strengthened at the expense of those west of the river.

Events in Europe, notably the German breakthrough in Picardy, now ended any chance of a spring offensive as Allenby had to send two divisions plus yeomanry, siege artillery, machine-gun companies and extra infantry to France. These seasoned troops were replaced gradually by far less experienced Indian units. A second raid across the Jordan, this time to capture Salt, was made in April; again it was not completely successful but the intention of causing further Turkish redeployment east of the Jordan was realized. Allenby maintained a show of interest on his right by keeping two cavalry divisions in the Jordan Valley throughout the summer. By August the Indian replacements had arrived and had been incorporated into the weakened British divisions and Allenby was ready to launch his final offensive.

The Battle of Megiddo began on 16 September. By the 21st, Nazareth, Beisan (Bet She'an) and Nablus had been captured and the two Turkish armies west of the Jordan were broken. On 23 September the 5th Cavalry Division took Acre and Haifa, whose port was immediately brought into service. Chaytor Force in the Jordan Valley was watching the Turkish Fourth Army which made no move until 22 September when news of the defeat at Megiddo was received and it began to withdraw. Chaytor Force moved north up the valley taking the bridge at Jis et Damiya (the Adam Bridge) and by 25 September had captured both Salt and Amman; they were then ordered to block the retreat of the II Corps from Ma'an. The Turks surrendered once they knew the British force was strong enough to protect them from the Arab forces that had surrounded them.

The advance on Damascus was made by the 4th Cavalry Division via Irbid and Dera'a, a 220 km route, and by the Australian and 5th Cavalry Divisions which crossed the Jordan north of Lake Tiberias and followed the ancient caravan route through Quneitra (140 km). 4 Division encountered rear-guards at Semakh (Deganya), where Von Sanders had positioned German machine-gunners, at Irbid, where the Turks held off the attack until after dark, and at Er Remte. When they entered Dera'a on the 28th they found the town had already been captured by Feisal's Arabs who had been harrying the Turkish retreat from Amman. On the 27th the Arabs had taken many prisoners at Sheikh Saad and, after the Turks had massacred the inhabitants of a village, they destroyed the column responsible. The Australians met resistance at the Jisr Benat Yakub (Bnot Ya'acov Bridge) but cavalry managed to cross the Jordan both north and south of the destroyed bridge and the Turkish rear-guard withdrew that night. The terrain on the Golan was rough and the cavalry had advanced

Aircraft Capability
BE 2e Reconnaissance
Engine: 90hp
Speed: 82mph at 6,500ft
Endurance: 3¼ hours
Max Height: 11,000ft
DH2 Fighter
Engine: 100hp
Speed: 86mph
Endurance: 2¾ hours
Max Height: 14,000ft
BE 8 Reconnaissance
Engine: 150hp
Speed: 102mph
Endurance: 4¼ hours
Max Height: 13,000ft

no further than Quneitra by dusk on the 28th; they continued the advance on the afternoon of the 29th and met another rear-guard at Sa'sa where the ground was particularly difficult to cross. On the 30th the last Turkish rear-guards were met at Kaukaba on the Quneitra road and at Kiswe on the Dera'a road; at the former the Turks fled as the Australians charged and at Kiswe the Turks were cut off by troops of the 5th Division and most were captured. The Australians attempted to pass Damascus to the north and to cut the Beirut and Homs roads but were blocked by the Barada Gorge through which the Turks were fleeing; there they could only be engaged by machine-gun but this turned them back to Damascus.

Permission to enter Damascus was not given until 1 October and a brigade of Australians hurried through the city to continue the pursuit on the Homs road, taking 750 prisoners that day and 1,500 the next. Another 12,000 prisoners were taken in Damascus where the administration was handed over to the Arabs. London now urged Allenby to occupy Aleppo, over 300 km away, and the rest of Syria, but although there would be little or no resistance the problems of resupply dictated a cautious approach. An infantry division was despatched up the coast to Beirut but this had already been reached by the French navy and by armoured cars sent from Rayak and Zahle which had been taken by the 4th and 5th Cavalry Divisions. As the 4th was suffering from a serious outbreak of malaria, the 5th Division proceeded alone, reaching Homs, already occupied by the Arabs, on 16 October, and then linking up with the cavalry that had advanced up the coast to Tripoli. Although some 20,000 Turkish troops were estimated to be in the Aleppo area, 4th Cavalry Division, much reduced in strength, was ordered forward, getting close enough to Aleppo on 23 October to demand the surrender of the city; this was refused. Reconnaissance sorties took place on the 24th and 25th and an attack was planned for the 26th. However, the Arabs managed to enter the city on the evening of the 25th and forced the garrison to withdraw. The cavalry was too weak to continue the pursuit but this was of little consequence as Turkey had now agreed to an armistice. In this final phase of the war some 75,000 Turkish troops were taken prisoner, of whom nearly 4,000 were in fact Germans; Allenby's army, which had advanced some 560 km, had suffered 5,666 casualties.

The war was now drawing to a close. As early as 4 October the Germans had sent proposals for an armistice to the American President, following the breaking of the Hindenburg line in late September; after the Battle of Vittorio Veneto the Austrians sought an armistice with the Italians on 27 October. The main cause for the Turkish surrender was not the victory in Palestine and Syria, though this played a part, but rather the Allied success in Macedonia and the armistice accepted by Bulgaria. As early as 12 October the British Naval Commander-in-Chief, Admiral Calthorpe, had been sent to Lemnos to prepare the armistice terms; he was joined on the 20th by General Townshend, who had been captured at Kut, with the news that the Turks were ready for a peace separate from Germany. The Turkish envoys reached Lemnos on the 26th and the armistice signed on board HMS *Agamemnon* on the 30th came into effect at noon on the 31st.

Transport Animal Efficiency			
	Max Load (lb)	Water Daily	Feed Daily (lb)
Camel	400	once	24
Horse	310	twice	20
Mule	200	twice	16

THE BATTLES FOR GAZA

In February 1917 the Allies decided to launch a series of offensive operations that spring. The British captured Baghdad on 11 March, an offensive was begun in Macedonia, and in April both the French and British began offensives on the Western Front. While General Murray had been instructed not to attempt to capture Jerusalem before the autumn he was not discouraged from attacking Gaza as his contribution to the overall offensive plan.

The plan of attack, which was to be accomplished by the Desert Column, was for the two mounted divisions to encircle the town and prevent any escape. The 53rd Division would assault the town from the south and south-west, having formed up on the El Sire Ridge. The 54th Division was to protect the attacking troops from any Turkish counter-attack from the east by taking up positions at Sheikh Abbas. Before the attack could be launched an approach march involving the crossing of Wadi Ghazze had to be made. At that time of year the Wadi was dry but it had been cut wide and deep by years of storm waters and so had steep banks and many vertical cliffs.

The advance from Rafah, where the bulk of the force was positioned close to the railhead and the water pipeline, began on 21 March, with movement mainly at night, and was completed by midnight on the 25th. On the 26th the cavalry moved off at 2.30 am and crossed the Wadi Ghazze at Um Jerrar. The 53rd Division had started out at 1 am, crossing the wadi near El Breij, its two leading brigades then advancing along the parallel ridges of El Sire and Burjabye. At 4 am a thick fog unexpectedly rolled in from the sea, reducing visibility to 20 metres and causing a delay of several hours. Nevertheless, it was decided that the attack would continue as planned. The cavalry managed to cross the wadi in thick fog and advanced on a compass bearing, reaching Sheikh Abbas at 8 am. As the fog was lifting they encountered a Turkish patrol and were attacked by two aircraft. The encirclement of Gaza was completed by 11 am, when a detachment reached the sea. 161 Brigade of the 54th Division, which was in reserve, was ordered to move to El Burjabye from where it could support either of the infantry divisions.

Both leading brigades of the 53rd Division had reached their assembly areas by 8.30 am and both decided, despite the fog, to press forward; the 158th reached Mansura and the 160th Esh Sheluf. Further delay then occurred as the Divisional Commander, General Dallas, decided to carry out a reconnaissance and then to discuss the plan with his brigade commanders; this meant the attack could not take place until noon. The artillery bombardment began at noon, directed by forward observers and airborne spotters; the brigades, some 4 km from their objectives, then began to advance. At about the same time 159 Brigade reached Mansura and manoeuvred so as to take up a position to the right of 158 Brigade. Also at this time General Chetwode, fearful that the attack might not succeed by nightfall, decided that the cavalry should attack Gaza from the north and north-west; this necessitated a repositioning of the flank protection force. By dusk the three brigades of the ANZAC Mounted Division had reached the outskirts of Gaza. The 53rd Division spent the

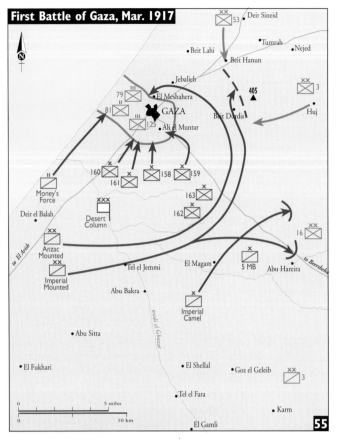

First Battle of Gaza, Mar. 1917

55

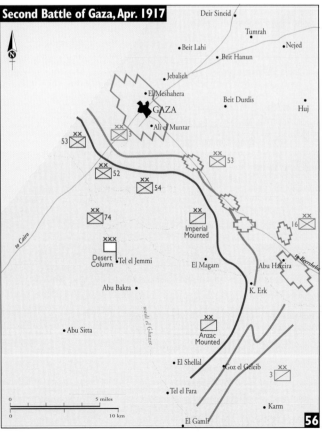

Second Battle of Gaza, Apr. 1917

56

afternoon fighting through the forward Turkish positions, hampered by machine-gun and artillery fire and by the extensive Turkish trenches and the thick cactus hedges. By 6.30 pm the whole Turkish line of trenches south and west of Gaza between the El Arish and Beersheba roads had been captured.

During the afternoon Turkish reinforcements began to approach the area; from the north an infantry regiment in three columns was reported past Deir Sineid (south of Yad Mordechai), while from the north-east an estimated 3,000 infantry with two squadrons of cavalry were approaching 6 Mounted Brigade's screen; they forced their outpost from Hill 405 and from Jemmameh (Ruhama). A third force was advancing on the 5th Brigade from Beersheba. As the cavalry had not been watered since crossing Wadi Ghazze General Chetwode concluded that their extrication was more important than continuing the attack and just after 6 pm he ordered them to retire behind Wadi Ghazze, a difficult operation given the wide dispersion of the units and the distance some men were from their horses. All went well until 3 Light Horse Brigade was strongly attacked at dawn, as it crossed the Gaza–Beersheba road; fortunately a light car patrol appeared which covered the withdrawal of the brigade and caused heavy Turkish casualties with its machine-gun fire.

At about 5.30 pm General Dobell ordered the 54th Division to pull back some 3 km to the Burjabye ridge, with its left flank to be just over a kilometre north of Mansura where it would link up with the 53rd Division; however, the news of this redeployment never reached the 53rd Division. At about 7 pm General Chetwode warned the commander of the 53rd Division of the cavalry's withdrawal and advised him to pull back far enough to make contact with the 54th Division. General Dallas objected to abandoning his hard-won gains and asked for more troops to bridge the gap between the two divisions. Additional troops were not available and he therefore ordered his division to withdraw, with its left at the Tel el Ujul caves just north of Wadi Ghazze and its right close to Sheikh Abbas. It was not until midnight that the misunderstanding was discovered, when elements of the 54th Division were found to be at Mansura. By this time it was too late to reverse the orders. At 5 am General Chetwode finally realized that the 53rd Division had abandoned all the positions it had taken the day before; he immediately ordered that patrols should be sent to find out whether the Turks had reoccupied their trenches. Ali Muntar and Green Hill were unoccupied and 161 Brigade re-occupied them but were counter-attacked shortly afterwards and the positions were temporarily lost before being retaken. Next a Turkish force, which had come from Beersheba, reached the now unoccupied Sheikh Abbas feature and began shelling the 53rd Division's headquarters, reserves, medical units and camel transport. General Dallas, whose division was now directly under command of General Dobell, reported that the position of both the 53rd and 54th Divisions would be untenable unless fresh troops took Sheikh Abbas. Before any decision could be reached Ali Muntar was recaptured by the Turks and Green Hill was virtually surrounded; orders were therefore given for both divisions to withdraw south of Wadi Ghazze. The

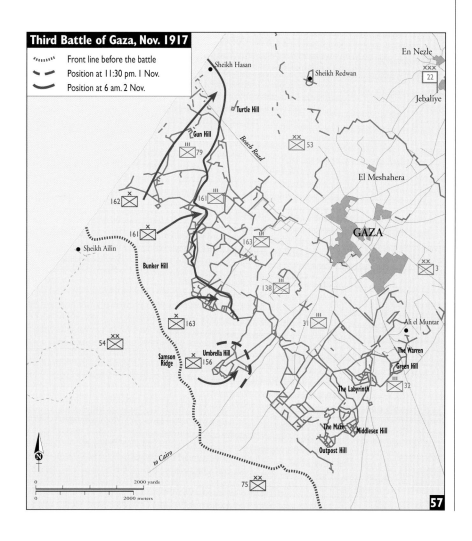

withdrawal took place that night and was completed without Turkish interference by 4 am on 28 March. So ended the first Battle of Gaza.

The battle cost the British 423 killed, 2,012 wounded and 512 missing, while the Turkish losses numbered 201 killed, 1,085 wounded and 1,061 missing. (The British took 837 prisoners including the commander and staff of the 53rd Turkish Division.) Several reasons have been put forward to explain the British defeat. The command and staff arrangements meant that commanders were too far from the battlefield and so orders and, more importantly, situation reports took far too long to reach their destinations, causing for instance the unnecessary withdrawal of the 53rd Division. The unexpected fog caused less delay than the time spent in bringing the brigade commanders to meet General Dallas. The force was sadly lacking in artillery, as one of both the 53rd and 54th Division's three artillery brigades (each having twelve 18-pounders and four 4.5-inch howitzers) had been left with the Suez Canal defences. However, the battle plan, which was well conceived, and the conduct of the troops who fought bravely and professionally under adverse conditions of heat and lack of concealment against a strongly entrenched and determined enemy, cannot be blamed.

Earlier in March British forces had captured Baghdad, and it was thought, wrongly, that the Russian Revolution would lead to greater Russian efforts, particularly in the Caucasus. The Prime Minister, Lloyd George, therefore considered that, if the Turkish forces were swept out of Mesopotamia and a major advance was made into Palestine, Turkey might sue for peace. On 30 March General Murray received instructions to attack and capture Jerusalem immediately. Murray's protests that he had insufficient forces for the operation were overruled by the War Office which considered that he had a 50 per cent advantage in infantry and artillery strength, and an overwhelming superiority in cavalry, as well as having better quality troops. General Murray had no alternative but to order another attack on Gaza.

The situation was much changed from that before the first battle: the Gaza garrison had been reinforced, Turkish trenches had been dug just north-west of Mansura and a series of redoubts created along the Gaza–Beersheba road as far east as Wadi Esh Sheria. Turkish reserves were encamped at Tel El Sheria, Khan Kufiye and Khan el Bir. The total Turkish strength was estimated to be 34 battalions and 100 guns. For their part the British had extended the railway to within 8 km of Wadi Ghazze, developed water supplies and storage, and brought up the artillery that had been left on the Suez Canal. The newly formed 74th Division was brought forward, as were the fourth brigades of the two cavalry divisions. Additional fire support would be given by the Royal Navy.

The second Battle of Gaza began on 16 April when three infantry divisions (the 52nd, 53rd and 54th) crossed Wadi Ghazze to take up overnight positions 4 to 5 km closer to Gaza while the cavalry divisions demonstrated at Abu Hureira and surprised the outpost at Khan Erk. On 18 April the day was spent in bombarding the Turkish positions and in bringing up ammunition and water. The attack began on the 19th at 7.30 am after a two-hour bombardment. Progress was slow and casualties heavy; some positions were taken but most were then lost to counter-attacks. By nightfall the reserve brigades had been committed and artillery ammunition was getting low, and the infantry was ordered to halt and consolidate their positions. They were preparing to renew the attack the next day but this order was rescinded when the casualty figures and ammunition shortages were revealed. The British had lost 500 killed, 4,360 wounded and some 1,570 missing, though the Turks only captured 270, mostly wounded, prisoners. Turkish losses were far fewer: 400 killed, 1,370 wounded and 240 missing.

A number of important developments took place before the Third, and final, Battle of Gaza was fought in October 1917. In June General Sir Edmund Allenby replaced General Murray as Commander-in-Chief and immediately revitalized the Eastern Force. Allenby called for reinforcements and, although he did not receive as many as he had wanted, he was able to field six infantry and three cavalry divisions (as opposed to the four and two which had taken part in the Second Battle of Gaza). Most importantly he received a considerable amount of artillery: divisional artillery units were now up to establishment in 18-pounders, and in heavy artillery Allenby now had a total of 88 guns compared with the 16 in the earlier battle. The Eastern Force and the Desert Column were discontinued and replaced by three corps (two infantry and one cavalry) under GHQ which moved to Rafah. Finally, before launching the assault on Gaza, Allenby captured Beersheba and turned the Turkish left flank.

The final attack on Gaza began on the night of 1/2 November, after an artillery bombardment that had opened on 27 October, supported by the Navy, which included five monitors and a cruiser, on the 29th. The first phase was to capture the extensive Turkish strongpoint known as Umbrella Hill, which lay some 650 metres ahead of the main trench line; this was captured at 11.30 pm, 30 minutes after H-Hour. The next phase was to take the forward trench lines from a point north-west of Umbrella Hill running in a north-westerly direction until they reached the second trench line running across the sand dunes to the sea. Two brigades of the 53rd Division with one from the 52nd Division (which had also captured Umbrella Hill) were given this task. In the third phase they were to press forward towards the town, and in the fourth phase the third brigade of the 53rd Division was to continue up the sand dunes until it had taken Sheikh Hasan. The second phase began at 3 am on the 2nd when, as had been expected, Turkish artillery fire following the capture of Umbrella Hill had died down. The second and third phases were not completely successful as some units attacked the wrong objectives; this led to follow-up units, seeing their objectives being attacked, thinking they had gone wrong and so also attacking the wrong objectives. The fourth phase was completed shortly after 6 am. Although not all the objectives had been reached the overall situation was good and, apart from a 1,000-metre sector running north–south just over a kilometre south of Sheikh Hasan, the whole of the Turkish first line of trenches had been occupied. In this battle the Turks lost over 1,000 dead and 450 men captured; British losses were 360 killed, 1,960 wounded and 370 missing.

Several counter-attacks were attempted on Sheikh Hasan but they were broken up by artillery and naval gunfire. The next three days were spent consolidating the positions gained and preparing for the next advance.

Turkish Order of Battle, October 1917
Eighth Army
Gen. Kress von Kressenstein
XXII Corps
Gen. Refet Bey
3rd Division
53rd Division
7th Division (Army reserve)
XX Corps
Gen. Ali Fuad Bey
16th Division
26th Division
54th Division
24th Division (in reserve)
19th Division (Yilderim reserve)
III Corps
Gen. Ismet Bey
3rd Cavalry Division
27th Division

On the night of 6 November the 75th Division was ordered forward; finding that the majority of the Turks had slipped away the troops quickly overran the trench systems to the south and south-east of Gaza, reaching Ali Muntar at 7 am on the 7th. The 54th Division, sensing the enemy had fled, pushed out patrols and reached the trench lines north of Gaza and at Sheikh Redwan by 4.30 am. With the capture of Gaza and Beersheba, Allenby was now able to turn to the objective given him by London – the capture of Jerusalem and the expulsion of the Turks from Palestine.

THE BATTLE OF BEERSHEBA

On his arrival in the Middle East General Allenby decided to adopt the plan prepared by General Chetwode to first capture Beersheba and the water wells there before attacking the weakest part of the Turkish line, its left. It was hoped that the Turks could be deceived into thinking that the attack on their left was only a feint while the main attack would be made directly against Gaza. The outline plan was to assemble, as secretly as possible, a force consisting of the four divisions from XX Corps and two divisions of the Desert Mounted Corps (DMC) for a combined assault on 31 October. The approach march began as early as the 21st, with movement taking place only at night and the troops remaining hidden by day. The camps at Rafah where they had been waiting were left standing and lit up at night; the Royal Flying Corps and anti-aircraft fire kept Turkish spotter planes at a height which made observation difficult.

Beersheba was held by the Turkish III Corps, which formed part of the 7th Army. At the time of the battle it had one cavalry division, two infantry divisions (one of which had only two regiments, both of Arab soldiers), and one regiment from a division not in the Corps under its command, a total force of roughly 5,000 men, 60 machine-guns and 28 artillery pieces. The main trench defences, held by 27 Division, lay in an arc between the railway lines running north-west and south from Beersheba and some 6 to 7 km from the centre of the town. In the town was one regiment of 24 Division, the remainder being in position at

The Imperial Camel Corps. (Alain Roth Archive)

Kauwukah (Eshel Ha Nasi) 20 km to the west. The closest reinforcements were the reserve division of the Turkish XX Corps at Jemmameh (Ruhama) and the 8th Army reserve division 40 km north at Iraq el Menshiye (Qiryat Gat).

The approach march went forward uninterrupted except for an attack on an outpost north of El Baqqar (halfway between Hazerim and Ze'elim) in the line held by the 8th Mounted Brigade. The post held out against a much superior force for seven hours until it was finally overrun by a cavalry charge leaving only three survivors; the commander, Major A.M. Lafone, was awarded the Victoria Cross posthumously. The Turks withdrew as elements of the 53rd Division approached; had the Turks managed to remain on the line of the outposts the construction of the railway line from Shellal (Gevulot) would have been delayed. By 29 October the DMC had reached Khalasa (Revivim) and Asluj (Mash'abbe Sade), where the engineers were digging out the wells, and on the night of 30/31 October took up positions to the east of Beersheba on an arc from the Beersheba–Asluj track to Wadi Saba about 8 km from the town. That same night the two assaulting divisions, the 60th and the 74th, moved forward 12 km across country to within 2 km of the Turkish trenches between the Wadi Saba and the Beersheba–Khalasa track. The 53rd and 70th Divisions were already holding a line protecting the left flank of the Corps.

The preliminary bombardment began on Point 1070, the highest point in the trench line, at 5.55 am on the 31st; because there was not a breath of wind the target was soon obscured by clouds of dust and the

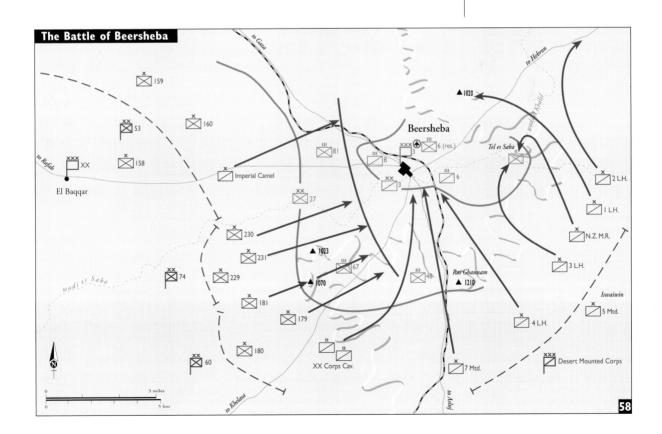

bombardment and attack were delayed for 45 minutes. At 8.30 am, after a 45 minute bombardment, the attack was launched and Point 1070 was soon captured; this was the signal for the artillery to engage the remainder of the objective and at 12.15 pm the main attack went in, taking all its objectives by 1.30 pm. The infantry advanced no further than 2,000 metres beyond the trenches as the plan was for the cavalry to capture Beersheba with a rapid charge that might prevent the Turks from destroying the wells; it was essential that they were captured intact in order to water the horses. On the right the DMC had begun its advance at 6 pm on the 30th; the leading brigades of the ANZAC Mounted Division were the 2nd Light Horse (LHB), ordered to block the Beersheba–Hebron road, and the New Zealand Mounted Rifles (NZMR), ordered to occupy Tel es Saba (Tel Sheva), which commanded all the ground to the east. The tel was held by a Turkish battalion and a machine-gun company and the New Zealanders made slow progress until 3 LHB was ordered to assist by enveloping the Tel from the south. The fire of their artillery battery allowed the NZMR's battery to advance to within 1,200 metres of the tel

from where they could fire more effectively. At 1.30 pm the Corps Commander directed 1 LHB of the Australian Mounted Division to move round to the right of the NZMR; this move became unnecessary as a New Zealand regiment had crossed Wadi el Khalil and was engaging the tel from the north. Soon after an assault was made and the tel was taken by 3 pm whereupon it was shelled by the Turks and attacked from the air. 1 LHB were sent to take Point 1020 north-east of Beersheba.

Turkish trenches at Beersheba. (Alain Roth Archive)

General Allenby, who had come forward to XX Corps' Headquarters at El Baqqar, ordered General Chauvel to capture the town by nightfall. It took some time to concentrate 4 LHB but shortly after 4.30 pm they began their attack, first at the trot and then at the gallop, astride the Iswaiwin–Beersheba track and armed only with bayonets as they had no swords. The attack came under machine-gun fire from Turks on Ras Ghannam but they were quickly driven from their positions by the brigade's artillery battery. The trenches encountered during the charge mainly faced south and the first were quickly swept through but at the second there was more opposition and so, while the 12th Light Horse Regiment, followed by the 11th, carried on into the town, the 4th dismounted and fought the defenders with rifle and bayonet. The 12th and the 11th regiments, despite capturing several hundred prisoners, pushed through the town and took up a line of outposts to the north-west, joining the line formed by the ANZAC Division.

British casualties had been relatively light. In XX Corps, 136 men had been killed and 1,010 wounded (two-thirds of these casualties were suffered by two battalions of the Royal Welch Fusiliers which met fierce resistance at Point 1023). The DMC lost 53 killed and 144 wounded; of these, 31 killed and 32 wounded were suffered by the 4 LHB during the charge on Beersheba. Over 2,000 Turks were taken prisoner, half of these being captured during 4 LHB's charge. No attempt was made on the 31st to send reinforcements to Beersheba, the German Commander of the 8th Army, General Kress von Kressenstein, still believing the attack was a feint, as the bombardment of Gaza had begun. British plans to roll up the Turkish left were severely hampered by the shortage of water; the supplies available in Beersheba were far less than had been anticipated. The next fighting was concentrated on two features some 16 km north of Beersheba: Tel el Khuweilfe, which the 53rd Division was unable to capture, and Ras el Naqb, to its east, from which the Turks were unable to dislodge successive cavalry brigades. The attack by XX Corps on the Turkish positions at Sheria took place on 6 November, the three divisions involved having to swing through 90 degrees to attack in a westerly direction along the lines of the trenches which faced south. The attack was completely successful and orders were given for the next objectives, which were all taken on the 7th. Meanwhile the 53rd Division launched an attack on Tel el Khuweilfe which was held up and bitter fighting continued all day until on the 8th the Turks began to withdraw. This marked the end of the Battle of Beersheba, and the pursuit of the Turks now began.

British casualties, 3 Nov.–15 Dec. 1917
Killed 2,509
Wounded 14,698
Missing 1,721

Turkish casualties, 31 Oct.–31 Dec. 1917
Killed 1,568
Wounded 9,415
Prisoners 12,000
Missing 3,450

THE SURRENDER OF JERUSALEM TO ALLENBY

On the evening of 19 November 1917 Allenby's troops were spread out, with the Desert Mounted Corps (DMC) holding a line from the coast just south of Nahr el Auja (Nahal Yarqon) and running south-east to Tahta (Tira), XXI Corps facing north and east some 20 km west of Jerusalem, and XX Corps remaining around Gaza. A wedge had been driven between the two Turkish armies with the 7th in the east now cut off from rail support. Although Allenby's supply lines were strained and his progress would soon be impeded by the winter rains, he decided to take advantage of the Turks' disorganization and advance on Jerusalem at once. The plan finally adopted was for XXI Corps to move forward astride the Jaffa–Jerusalem road with the Yeomanry Division on its left, aiming to cross the Jerusalem–Nablus road at Bireh (Bira) 16 km north of the city. One cavalry brigade was to follow the railway line on the right flank, and on approaching Jerusalem it would swing to the left, thereby cutting off the Turks who would be forced to withdraw from Jerusalem. No fighting was to take place within 10 km of the city. Progress was slow and the going extremely difficult, with few routes passable by wheels. Artillery was confined to the line of the main road. When Allenby ordered a halt on 24 November the 75th Division had captured the strategic hill of Nabi Samweil (Nabi Samwil) but had been unable to take El Jib, while the Yeomanry, which had been forced back from the Zeitun Ridge, had not yet reached the Nablus road. The troops were exhausted after three weeks' marching and fighting; they had suffered heavy casualties and endured extremes of weather; the Turks were too strongly entrenched to be pushed back until fresh troops were available.

The XXI Corps was in the process of being

General Allenby enters Jerusalem on 11 December 1917. (Alain Roth Archive)

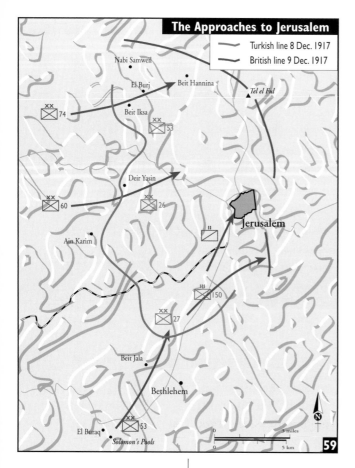

The Approaches to Jerusalem

— Turkish line 8 Dec. 1917
— British line 9 Dec. 1917

relieved by XX Corps; one brigade of the 60th Division had relieved the 75th Division and on the 26th a second brigade had taken over the positions of a brigade of the 52nd Division on Nabi Samweil. The remainder of the 60th Division was ordered to complete the relief of the 52nd Division by dawn on the 28th. The left of the XXI Corps line was held by the Yeomanry Division with its left held by 22 Brigade between Beit Ur el Foqa and Beit Ur et Tahta. From there to the right of the 54th Division, which was holding a line in the coastal plain, there was a gap of about 8 km. At this moment the Turks made a number of small counter-attacks whose intensity increased on the 28th as they sought to exploit the gap between the Yeomanry and the 54th Division. A stout defence limited Turkish gains until the arrival of the Australian Mounted Division which, together with 7th Mounted Brigade and a brigade of the 52nd Division, restored the situation. By 1 December the relief of XXI Corps and the Yeomanry Division by XX Corps was complete and preparations for the capture of Jerusalem could begin in earnest.

On 8 December the attack began, with the 60th Division on the right and the 74th Division on the left, along a front running from south-east of Ain Karim to Nabi Samweil, with the 53rd Division advancing up the road from Hebron. The 60th Division took its first objectives, defences east of Ain Karim, Deir Yassin and the trenches west of Beit Iksa, by 7 am; they then had to halt as progress by the 53rd Division had been slow and their right flank would be exposed if they continued forward. The 74th Division captured Beit Iksa but not until 11 am as the going was particularly hard and steep; further advance on Khirbet el Burj, which required the crossing of a deep gully, was postponed until the next day. The 53rd Division had reached Solomon's Pools south of Bethlehem on 7 December but on the 8th came under heavy and accurate fire from Bethlehem. The Divisional Commander was not prepared to engage these guns as he had been given orders not to violate Bethlehem and he had great difficulty in communicating with the Corps Commander who was pressing for a swift advance. Two battalions had managed to make some progress towards Beit Jala under accurate artillery fire but they did not receive orders to capture the feature until 4 pm and then met no opposition as the Turks were pulling out.

By now the Turks were seriously demoralized and the commander of the Turkish XX Corps, deciding further resistance was hopeless, ordered a general withdrawal, leaving Jerusalem unoccupied by dawn. The Mayor then set out to surrender the keys of the city but encountered only low-ranking soldiers (two cooks who had lost their way, next two sergeants on outpost duty and then two artillery officers who promised to return to their battery and telephone the news), all of whom felt unable to accept the surrender. Eventually more senior officers became involved: first to arrive was the commander of 303 Artillery Brigade, who was carrying out a reconnaissance; he was then joined by the commander of 180 Brigade of the 60th Division. When they reached the Jaffa gate they were joined by Major-General Shea, Commander of the 60th Division, who formally accepted the surrender of the city. This was the thirty-fourth occasion on which it had been captured or recaptured. No troops were allowed into the Old City until General Allenby entered the city on foot on 11 December.

On the 9th, the 60th and 74th Divisions, after receiving reports from patrols that the Turks had withdrawn, resumed their advance, finding no resistance until the rearguard on Mount Scopus was reached but this was soon driven back. By 2 pm Tel el Ful (Newe Ya'acov), a commanding hill 5 km north of Jerusalem, was taken by the 60th Division. The 74th Division, without fighting, established a line running from Tel el Ful to Wadi ed Dumm then north of Beit Hannina to Nabi Samweil.

THE BATTLE OF MEGIDDO

General Allenby had spent the summer of 1918 reorganizing and retraining his army and improving his lines of communications; the Turks also took advantage from the halt to British offensive operations to bring up reinforcements and strengthen their defences against the expected autumn offensive. The Turkish defences stretched from the coast 3 km north of Arsuf (Nof Yam) through Jaljulye (Jaljulya) and Kufr Qasim, from where the trenches running east were far less developed than those to the west, to Jisr el Damiye (Adam Bridge) on the Jordan and on to Salt and Tel Nimrin. There were three Turkish armies, two to the west of the Jordan with their junction at Furkah (Farkha), and one to the east of the Jordan; all told they numbered 32,000 infantry, 2,000 cavalry, and 400 guns. Allenby outnumbered them by roughly two to one, having 57,000 infantry, 12,000 cavalry and 540 guns. His plan was to break through the Turkish lines in the coastal plain with XXI Corps while XX Corps advanced astride the Jerusalem–Nablus road, and to send the Desert Mounted Corps (DMC) through the gap to take the railway junction at El Affule (Afula), Beisan (Bet Shean) and the bridge over the Jordan at Jisr el Mejamie (Naharayim). A detachment was to be sent in an attempt to capture the German commander, Liman von Sanders, whose headquarters were at Nazareth. A small force under General Chaytor was to operate in the Jordan Valley to protect the right flank, acting as if it were the DMC, and would appear to threaten an attack on Amman. The Arab army was to threaten, if not take, the railway junction at Dera'a and to cut the line north and west of Dera'a to prevent reinforcement from the north and, it was hoped, to draw off Turkish reserves located in the Plain of Esdraelon (Emeq Yizreel). The fight for Megiddo was more of a campaign than an isolated battle and involved all the British troops based between the Mediterranean and the Jordan River.

Formation signs of the Australian Light Horse

1st Brigade

2nd Brigade

3rd Brigade

4th Brigade

5th Brigade

1st Regt/1st Brigade

2nd Regt/1st Brigade

3rd Regt/2nd Brigade

Machine Gun/5th Brigade

and other combinations

Wadi Ara and the Musmus Pass crossed by the 4th Cavalry Division. (Photograph: Z. Radovan, Jerusalem)

The concentration for the attack began on 16 August when the DMC, which was then holding the right of the British line, moved westwards to its assembly area between Arsuf and Jaffa, with every measure being taken to convince the Turks that it still lay on the right flank. All movement took place at night, camps were left standing, dummy horses were set up to replace the horse lines, sleds towed by donkeys created dust to represent activity, wireless traffic continued and the two West Indian battalions of Chaytor's force marched each day from Jerusalem to the Jordan, being ferried back at night by motor transport. Chaytor's force also included two Jewish-manned battalions of the Royal Fusiliers.

The battle began on 16 September. There were air attacks on Dera'a and the railway line to the south was cut by Lawrence's Arabs; the line north of Dera'a was cut on the 17th. Some Turkish reserves were immediately despatched from Haifa. Chaytor Force began its operations in the Jordan valley on 17 September. Next the 53rd Division attacked along an 8 km front on the eastern side of the Jerusalem–Nablus road, starting shortly before 10 pm on the 18th. The main attack began at 4.45 am on

Australian light cavalry. (Alain Roth Archive)

19 September, preceded by an intense artillery bombardment lasting only 15 minutes. Surprise was complete and there was little real opposition. By nightfall the divisions of XXI Corps had reached a line stretching south from Tulkarm, through Et Taiyibe (Taiyiba), Felamiye (Falama), Bidya (Biddya) and Ra-fat (Rafat).

The DMC moved forward during the night ready to begin their advance early in the morning; by 8.30 am 5 Cavalry Division had crossed the Nahr el Falik (Nahal Poleg) and shortly after 11 am reached Liktera (Hadera). Here, after their 40 km advance, the men rested and watered the horses, and prepared to continue the advance at 6.15 am. The brigades of 4 Cavalry Division reached Tel edh Dhrur (Sede Yizhaq), Jelame (Lahavot Haviva) and Jett (Jatt) during the late afternoon. There was water at the first two villages and the horses were watered but there was little at Jett and 10 Brigade rode on to Kerkur (Karkur) at the western end of the Musmus Pass (Wadi Ara). The 2nd Lancers were sent on a further 8 km to Kh'ara about one-third of the way through the pass. The division closed up on Kerkur by 10 pm and the commander ordered the 2nd Lancers to advance through the pass to El Lajjun (Zomet Megiddo) which they reached at 3.30 am on the 20th and where they were joined by 12 Brigade at 4.00 am. The 2nd Lancers pressed on to El Affule but encountered a Turkish force sent, too late, to block the Musmus Pass. The cavalry charged and, although under machine-gun fire, lost only a single man wounded and 12 horses killed, while killing 46 Turks and capturing 470. Meanwhile, 5 Cavalry Division had continued their advance late on the 19th and crossed the southern end of the Carmel Mountains following first Wadi Qudrah and then Wadi el Fuwar. They crossed the watershed at 1 am on the 20th and reached Abu Shuse (Mishmar Ha Emeq) on the Haifa–Megiddo road at 2.15 am. One brigade proceeded to Nazareth, but failed to capture the German Commander although they completely broke up his headquarters, while a regiment of 14 Brigade moved south, took El Affule station and

General Allenby with French General Baillout. (Alain Roth Archive)

linked up with 4 Division; this then moved on to Beisan where it was concentrated by 6 pm; by then the Division had covered some 110 km in thirty-four hours. The third division of the DMC, the Australian Mounted Division, less two brigades, crossed the Musmus Pass on the 20th and was then ordered to ride on to Jenin where they surprised the Turks and by the next morning had taken some 8,000 prisoners.

In XX Corps area the attack by the 53rd Division had taken all its objectives bar one by dawn on the 20th; but this single failure meant that the Turkish- and British-built supply routes could not be linked and the artillery could not move forward. Two further attacks in daylight also failed and the position was not taken until after dark on the 19th. With a

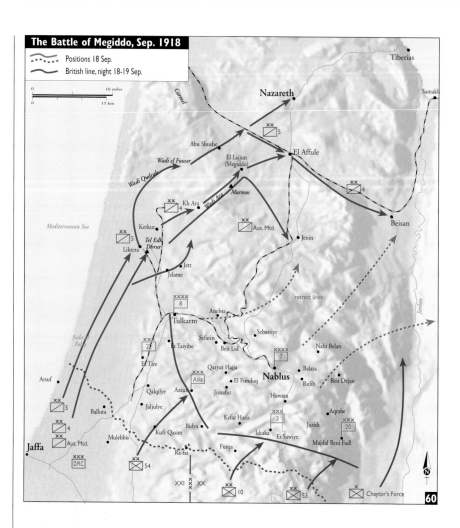

The Battle of Megiddo, Sep. 1918

Artillery ammunition planned expenditure: Rounds per day for sixteen days	
Field, Mountain artillery	150
4.5 inch howitzers	120
60 pounder guns	90
6 inch howitzers	90
8 inch guns	60
6 inch VIII guns	60

division each side of the Nablus road, XX Corps was to attack and take the line Kefar Haris–Jemma'in–Aqrabe but the timing of the attack depended on the progress made by XXI Corps. The Corps was ordered to move forward at 7.45 pm on the 19th after 15 minutes' artillery bombardment and by dawn on the 20th 10 Division, on the west of the road, had advanced over halfway to its objectives, meeting opposition only here and there. The 53rd Division met stiffer resistance and made slow progress, managing to advance only 3 km along its front. The Corps cavalry regiment advanced up the road and reached Es Sawiya by evening; the road was repaired, and two batteries of heavy artillery were brought forward. The 10th Division now faced a strong defence on the line Iskaka–Haris where the Turks had positioned a good number of machine-guns and four artillery batteries but, after some heavy fighting, had taken the Turkish line by nightfall. In the expectation that the Turks would break once they heard that the DMC had broken into their rear area, the 53rd Division was directed to press forward and attempt to cut the road running east from Nablus to the Jordan crossing at Jisr ed Damiye. The 10th Division was to move directly on Nablus. By 1 am elements of the 53rd Division had taken Khan Birket el Qusr without opposition; shortly before dawn the division had reached the crossroads west of Madjal Bani Fadl and had taken Jurish, to find that the Turks were withdrawing in haste. Aqrabe was taken by mid-morning and Beit Dejan by evening. The 53rd Division was then halted as there was now no need to block the road east from Nablus as it was under artillery fire and air attack. The 10th Division resumed its attack shortly before midnight, and although the road was in a bad state, Quza was reached by 5.30 am and Huwara by 7 am. Rujib was held in strength but when outflanked from the east the Turks fled, only to be cut off by the cavalry and captured. A battalion of 30 Brigade had occupied Nabi Belan (Mizpe Kabbir), 8 km east of Nablus, by 5 pm while 29 Brigade occupied Balata, 1,500 metres east of the town, at 1 pm. Finally 5 Australian Light Horse Brigade moved down the Tulkarm road, defeated the last resistance and captured Nablus. The road to the Jordan was found to be choked with transport and equipment abandoned by the Turks in their flight and over a hundred guns were recovered. All told XX Corps had taken close on 7,000 prisoners for the loss of 225 killed and 1,362 wounded.

On 20 September XXI Corps continued to advance in a north-easterly direction. On the left of the Corps the 60th Division took Anebta at 11.20 am, cutting both the Nablus–Tulkarm road and the railway; to its right the 7th Indian Division, aiming for Sabastiya, met heavy opposition and could not initially break through between Sefarin and Beit Lid as 19 Brigade's artillery had not got forward. The troops were in need of water but there were supplies at Beit Lid and an attack with covering fire from machine-guns failed after getting within 200 metres of the village. 21 Brigade was brought up and it attacked and took Kh. ed Deir and now with artillery support the 19th took Beit Lid at 6.15 pm. At 9.30 pm the third brigade of the division passed through to advance on Sabastiya and the railway station at Massudiye which it captured at 3 am on the 21st. The 3rd Indian Division advanced eastwards with all three brigades forward, and the 7th Brigade had soon taken Azzun which had been the Asia Corps Headquarters (a predominantly German formation), but progress in the wadi to the south of the village by 8 Brigade was held up by a group of Germans who could not be displaced until a single howitzer was brought dangerously far forward and could at last engage them. After this the advance continued without opposition until Jinsafat was reached that evening. 9 Brigade on the left met little opposition but encountered very hard going and were short of water; its artillery was soon engaging the Turks fleeing eastwards from Baqa, and by mid-afternoon the brigade had captured prisoners some 3 km north-east of El Funduq and at Qaryat Hajja. The operations of XXI Corps had cost 446 killed and 2,932 wounded but it had captured up to 12,000 men and 149 guns.

The battle of Megiddo had broken the two Turkish armies west of the River Jordan and although Liman von Sanders had planned to hold a new line on the River Yarmouk, the Sea of Galilee and Lake Huleh this became impossible given the degree of disintegration among the Turkish troops. Only occasional rearguard actions, usually by German troops, hindered the advance on Damascus which Allenby had ordered as the battle of Megiddo was ending.

Egyptian Expeditionary Force Order of Battle, September 1918

Gen. Sir Edmund Allenby

Desert Mounted Corps
Lt-Gen. Sir Harry Chauvel
4th Cavalry Division
5th Cavalry Division
Australian Mounted Division

XX Corps
Lt-Gen. Sir Philip Chetwoode
10th Division
53rd Division Artillery: one gun, one heavy, two mountain, one siege batteries

XXI Corps
Lt-Gen. Bulfin
3rd (Lahore) Division
7th (Meerut) Division
54th Division
60th Division
75th Division Detachment Francaise de Palestine Artillery: five heavy, thirteen siege, six mountain batteries

Chaytor Force
Maj.-Gen. Chaytor
ANZAC Mounted Division
20th Indian Brigade
two Jewish battalions Royal Fusiliers
two battalions West Indies Regt

Note: Brigades in 10, 53, 60 and 75 Divisions each had one British and three Indian battalions.

THE ISRAELI WAR OF INDEPENDENCE

This section covers the Jewish struggle for the independence of Israel. A number of battles are described in detail; in chronological order these are: the struggle for control of the road from the coast to Jerusalem; the fighting that divided Jerusalem; the delay imposed on the Egyptians by the defence of Kibbutz Yad Mordechai; Operation 'Yoav', which opened the way to the Negev and trapped an Egyptian force at Faluja, and Operation 'Horev' which was to isolate the Egyptian forces on the coast from those on the Hebron road; and Operation 'Uvda', the capture of Um Rashrash (Elat) and the advance to the Red Sea. This introduction describes the background to Israel's independence and highlights the other fighting which took place both before and during the War of Independence.

The State of Israel received its independence on 15 May 1948, on the implementation of the United Nations General Assembly Resolution of 29 November 1947 to establish Arab and Jewish states in a partitioned Palestine. The international recognition of Israel was the signal for six Arab armies to invade Palestine, but this was not the real start of the War of Independence, as fighting between Arabs and Jews had occurred some years before this. Indeed, it is hard to know when to start the story; the war certainly escalated with the passing of the UN Resolution in November 1947 but there had been fighting before then.

The Jewish repopulation of Palestine began in 1882 mainly as a result of the pogroms in Russia in 1881 and the persecution of Jews in Poland and Romania. In the 'first *Aliyah*', some 25,000 Jews emigrated to Palestine to join the 24,000 already living there; the 'second *Aliyah*' took place between 1904 and 1914 when 40,000 Jews arrived from Europe and the Yemen. In 1907 a small secret group called *Bar-Giora* was formed to protect Jewish settlements; this force soon expanded into a more open force, the *Hashomer* ('Watchmen'). At much the same time international Jewish political activity began in Europe when the Zionist Organization was founded at the first Zionist Congress in 1897. The Zionist aim was to gain agreement from the Ottoman authorities for political autonomy in Palestine and the right of Jewish settlement; it also raised money to fund the acquisition of land.

At the 1919 Peace Conference the principle of a British Mandate for Palestine was agreed to and this was welcomed by Jewry and approved by Feisal, the moderate Arab leader who had been promised independence for

Iraq, Lebanon and Syria. In 1922 the League of Nations confirmed the terms of the British Mandate which included the principles of the Balfour Declaration. The Balfour Declaration, made by the British Foreign Secretary, George Balfour, in November 1917, stated the British policy of support for the establishment of a national home for the Jewish people in Palestine. The homeland was to be established without prejudicing the rights of the Palestinian population.

In 1920 the Arabs attacked the northern Jewish settlement at Tel Hai and overran it; three other settlements in the north had to be abandoned. Jews were killed in Jerusalem and Haifa. This led to the formation, by the Jewish Labour Movement, of the *Haganah* to replace the *Hashomer*; as Jews were forbidden to bear arms the *Haganah* began as an underground organization. There was serious anti-Jewish rioting in 1921 by Arabs opposed to Jewish immigration, and this led to the *Haganah* seeking aid from Jews elsewhere, including the supply of men, finance and arms, and the provision for military training abroad. Worse rioting broke out in 1929; between 23 and 26 August, 133 Jews were killed and over 300 wounded across the country and seven settlements had to be abandoned. The worst atrocities took place in Hebron where fifty-nine Jews, including women and children, were killed. After this the *Haganah* was reorganized and expanded; in 1934 its constitution was changed and it ceased to be a popular militia but became the precursor of a national defence force. In 1931 a group broke away from the *Haganah* and formed the *Irgun Zvai Leumi* (IZL), or 'National Military Organization', which was to take a far harder line both against Arab attack and, after the publication of the severe restrictions on Jewish immigration in 1939, the British authority.

The Arab Revolt of May 1936 was aimed as much at British authority as at the Jewish population. However, the British government, influenced by fears that the whole Middle East would turn against it, took little action to begin with and it was only in the second month that firm measures started to be taken. The revolt ended in October; 80 Jews had been killed while the British Army had killed over 100 Arabs and destroyed several hundred homes in their operations to suppress the rebellion. Once again the *Haganah* was strengthened, and many of its members joined the British-officered and -armed Supernumerary Police force, formed to protect Jewish settlements. One British officer, Captain Orde Wingate, later the Chindit leader, instituted and trained the 'night squads' which took the offensive, mounting raids and setting ambushes. Arab/Jewish clashes continued throughout 1937 and 1938, as did those between Arabs and the British forces.

After the 1936 revolt the British Government appointed a commission headed by Lord Peel to examine the future of the British Mandate for Palestine. In July 1937 the commission recommended partitioning Palestine into Jewish and Arab states with a British-controlled sector running from (and including) Jaffa to Jerusalem. Other partition plans were designed by the Morrison-Grady Commission, the Jewish Agency, and lastly, in 1947, the United Nations.

In the Second World War the *Haganah* joined the British against the Axis forces and by 1941 had formed nine companies of commandos (*Plugot Mahatz*), which became known as the *Palmach*, to be ready for

---

Balfour Declaration

Foreign Office, 2 November 1917

Dear Lord Rothschild
I have much pleasure in conveying to you on behalf of His Majesty's Government the following declaration of sympathy with the Jewish Zionist aspirations, which has been submitted to and approved by the Cabinet: 'His Majesty's Government view with favour the establishment in Palestine of a National Home for the Jewish people, and will use their best endeavours to facilitate the achievement of this object, it being clearly understood that nothing shall be done which may prejudice the civil and religious rights of existing non-Jewish communities in Palestine or of the rights and status of Jews in any other country.' I should be grateful if you would bring this declaration to the knowledge of the Zionist Federation.
yours sincerely

Arthur James Balfour

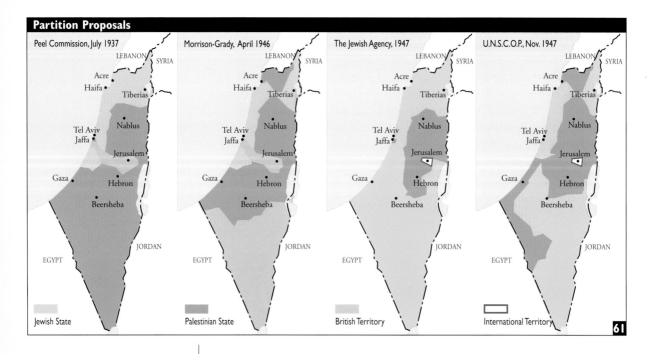

Partition Proposals

Peel Commission, July 1937
LEBANON SYRIA
Acre
Haifa
Tiberias
Tel Aviv
Jaffa
Nablus
Jerusalem
Gaza
Hebron
Beersheba
EGYPT
JORDAN

Morrison-Grady, April 1946
LEBANON SYRIA
Acre
Haifa
Tiberias
Tel Aviv
Jaffa
Nablus
Jerusalem
Gaza
Hebron
Beersheba
EGYPT
JORDAN

The Jewish Agency, 1947
LEBANON SYRIA
Acre
Haifa
Tiberias
Tel Aviv
Jaffa
Nablus
Jerusalem
Gaza
Hebron
Beersheba
EGYPT
JORDAN

U.N.S.C.O.P., Nov. 1947
LEBANON SYRIA
Acre
Haifa
Tiberias
Tel Aviv
Jaffa
Nablus
Jerusalem
Gaza
Hebron
Beersheba
EGYPT
JORDAN

Jewish State   Palestinian State   British Territory   International Territory

61

guerrilla warfare in the event of a German invasion. *Palmach* men fought for the British, for example providing the leading scouts for the attacks on the Vichy French in Lebanon and Syria. The IZL also opted to support the British but the *Lohamei Herut Israel* (LEHI) or 'Fighters for the Freedom of Israel' (also known as the Stern Gang) broke away and continued to oppose the British throughout the war; its first leader, Avraham Stern, was shot by the Palestine Police in 1942. The IZL, now led by Menachem Begin, renewed its terrorist campaign in 1944 as the end of the war was in sight. The Jewish Agency and the *Haganah* both condemned its activities while the war continued.

In 1945, following the British government's restriction on Jewish immigration to 1,500 people a month and its proposal for partition on very similar lines to that proposed in 1939, the *Haganah*, IZL and Stern formed an alliance known as the *Tenuat Humeri* or 'United Resistance Movement'. In October 1945 *Haganah* set off over 500 explosions mainly intended to disrupt the railway system; in November attacks were aimed at the police, the coastguard, and, on one occasion, a Royal Air Force camp. In January and February further attacks were made on RAF bases, resulting in the destruction of aircraft. Repression and counter-violence escalated and climaxed in July 1946, with an *Irgun* explosion at the King David Hotel which killed 91 and wounded 45 people. In February 1947 the British announced that they would refer the Palestine problem to the UN General Assembly; the UN sent a Special Commission to Palestine in July.

In addition to the *Palmach* which had three territorial battalions, the *Haganah* was organized into garrison (HIM) and field units (HISH). It also had a headquarters battalion which included naval, air, and reconnaissance forces; all told it numbered 2,100 with another 1,000 reserves ready for immediate recall. HIM had some 32,000 men and women whose main task was the defence of settlements and localities.

The King David Hotel, 1946.

HISH was made up of 9,500 young men between the ages of eighteen and twenty-five; organized into companies, they received more training than the members of HIM and had a more mobile role although they were still confined to their local areas. This policy was changed a few weeks before the UNGA Resolution when HISH was reorganized into six brigades, each allotted a regional responsibility; local tasks were allotted to HIM. Weaponry was in short supply and was limited to light weapons only because artillery and tanks could not be hidden from the British. However, procurement was under way in Europe. By the end of 1947 *Haganah* had some 8,300 rifles, 3,600 sub-, 700 light and 200 medium machine-guns, and 700 two- and three-inch mortars, but there was only sufficient ammunition for three days' fighting.

On the Arab side there were two Palestinian paramilitary groups, each about 1,000 men strong; known as the Army of Salvation, they were directed by the exiled Mufti of Jerusalem. Some 6,000 Palestinian Arabs had served in the British Army, where they had received only elementary training and their units had been disbanded. The most effective Arab army was the British-trained and -officered Jordanian Arab Legion, some 10,000 strong. The Egyptian Army, although by far the strongest, was only prepared to commit 5,000 men to the Arab League's plan to move into Palestine when the British withdrew. Other forces assigned to the operation were 8,000 Syrians, 2,000 Lebanese, and 10,000 Iraqis. As a result of Arab suspicions of the intentions of King Abdullah of Transjordan, the Arab Liberation Army under the Syrian Fauzi el-Kaukji, a former Turkish Army officer, was created to operate in Palestine before the British withdrawal.

Within two weeks of the UNGA's Resolution being adopted, 79 Jews had been killed with more than 30 Arabs being killed in these attacks and a further 60 in Jewish reprisal raids. Clashes continued for the next two months and from March to May the Arabs made great efforts to prevent the Jews reaching Jerusalem and the Kfar Etzion bloc. However, Kfar Etzion fell on 12 May 1948 after withstanding attack for a month; 100 Jews were killed, 15 of them after they had surrendered. Atarot and Newe Ya'aqov, the Jewish settlements north of Jerusalem, were evacuated after they had been attacked while the

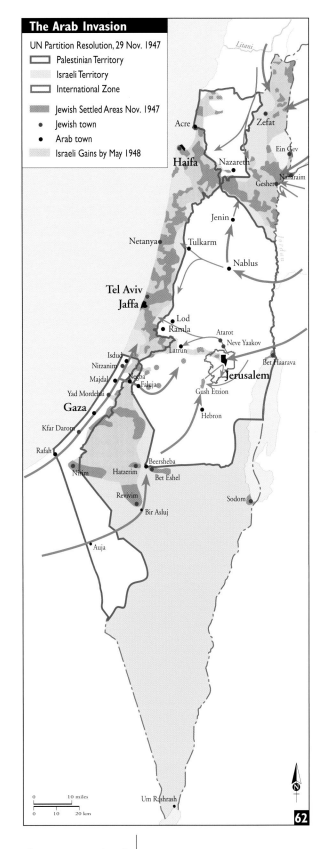

The Arab Invasion

UN Partition Resolution, 29 Nov. 1947
- Palestinian Territory
- Israeli Territory
- International Zone
- Jewish Settled Areas Nov. 1947
- Jewish town
- Arab town
- Israeli Gains by May 1948

62

population of Bet ha'Arava, east of Jerusalem, were evacuated by boat down the Dead Sea. There were also Arab attacks against isolated Jewish settlements in other parts of Palestine. Yehi'am, in Western Galilee, and Tirat Zevi, south of Bet Shean, both held out and mobile counter-attacks routed the besiegers. A serious battle which lasted nine days was fought at Mishmar Ha'emeq, north-west of Megiddo, and in the hills above it.

The Jews also made territorial gains, mainly consolidating their control of previously mixed areas. In Haifa on 21 April, after the British had concentrated in the docks, a surprise attack divided the Arab part of the city into three. At a meeting convened by the British the Jews demanded an Arab surrender but urged them to remain in their homes; however, the Mufti convinced the population that they should leave and return after the imminent Arab invasion had captured the whole city. Virtually the whole Palestinian population left, despite Jewish and British pleas, during a five-day truce. Also in April the Jews captured Bet Shean, Tiberias and Rosh Pinna, and, after ten days of heavy fighting, Safed (Zefat). Towards the end of April an operation was launched aimed at isolating, but not capturing, Jaffa, which was to have formed part of the Arab state, and opening the way to the airport at Lydda (Lod). On the 25th, without authority, the IZL attacked Jaffa from the north; the attack met with little success and the IZL had to agree to act in future only with *Haganah* authority. On the 27th the British deployed tanks and artillery and threatened Tel Aviv unless the attack on Jaffa was halted. On 13 May, when the British had withdrawn, Jaffa surrendered; only 3,000 of its 70,000 population remained in the city.

The first phase of the war, after the declaration of Independence, lasted until 11 June when the first truce was arranged. In the north the Iraqis failed to take the bridge over the Jordan at Gesher after a week-long battle against the settlers and elements of the 'Golani' Brigade, but the Jordanians captured the power station at Naharayim. The Syrians recaptured the Arab village of Zemah, taken earlier by the *Haganah*, on 18 May, and the settlements of Massada and Sha'ar HaGolan (both just south of the Sea of Galilee) had to be evacuated; they had held out for four days. On the 20th the two Degania settlements were attacked; at Degania A, defended by only seventy men, the Syrian infantry failed to keep up with the armour which had to withdraw with losses, having very nearly penetrated the Israeli defences. Fortunately for the Israelis, at Degania B the attack did not begin until the arrival of the first Israeli artillery unit whose two guns had only reached Israel a few days earlier and whose crews were untrained. Nevertheless, their fire, from the Crusader Castle Belvoir, caused the Syrians to break off the attack and withdraw, abandoning their earlier gains.

The Crusader castle at Kibbutz Yehi'am where Israelis held out against Arab attacks from January to March 1948. (Alain Roth Archive)

In the far north, as Lebanese forces prepared to attack the 'Finger of Galilee', a *Palmach* battalion captured both Malkiyya and Kadesh (Tel Kedesh) but the Lebanese counter-attacked immediately and the Israelis were forced to withdraw. On the night of 16/17 May the fort at Nebi Yusha (Mezudat Yesha) was finally captured; it had been occupied by the Lebanese Army when the British withdrew, and the *Palmach* had failed to capture it, losing twenty-eight men in a dawn attack some days earlier. The Lebanese took no further action on the Malkiyya front.

The Syrians meanwhile were preparing to attack Mishmar ha Yarden, north of the Sea of Galilee, and to forestall this the Israelis made a night raid on a Syrian base near the Customs House, just east of the Jordan above Bnot Ya'acov, on 18/19 May. The attack took the Syrians by surprise, and a number of armoured cars were destroyed and the ammunition stored there blown up. The Syrians postponed their attack until 6 June when two battalions were repulsed as their supporting tanks failed to cross the Jordan. On the 10th the Syrians attacked again, this time with two brigades. They captured the fords and, after tanks had penetrated beyond it, Mishmar ha Yarden was captured. As 11 June, the date of the first truce, approached, the Arabs redoubled their efforts but despite heavy attacks were unable to take Ein Gev on the eastern shore of Tiberias, nor could they expand their bridgehead at Mishmar ha Yarden.

On the Central Front the Iraqis concentrated three brigades at Nablus and on 25 May they attacked at Tulkarm in an attempt to cut Israel in two; by the 28th they had reached Kfar Yona and En Wered, where they were held but were now only 10 km from the sea. The Israeli response was to mount a counter-attack from the north to take Jenin; they also sent a force through Wadi Arah towards Tulkarm. The 'Golani' Brigade captured the village of Zarin on the 28th and next day were in control of Mount Gilboa and the hills north of the Valley of Dothan. On the night of 30 May the brigade surprised the garrison at Megiddo and captured it; the Iraqis counter-attacked throughout the day but were held off.

The attack on Jenin began with the capture of hills to the south-west and south-east by the 'Carmeli' Brigade supported by artillery and, for the first time, by two newly arrived Messerschmitt fighters. The objectives were captured by dawn but the Israelis found it impossible to dig in on the rocky ground. The attack in Wadi Arah was recognized as a diversion, and the Iraqis concentrated for a counter-attack on Jenin which Israeli patrols had found to be abandoned. The counter-attack began in the early

The End of the War

- ■ Israeli territory, summer 1948
- — Cease-fire lines
- Israeli gains by agreement
- Arab gains by agreement
- ⌁ The "Green Line" (armistice line)

Litani

Naqoura

Malkiyya

Sasa

Akko

Zefat

Haifa

Ein Gev

Nazareth

Jenin

Netanya

Tulkarm

Nablus

Tel Aviv

Jaffa

Ramla

Latrun

Isdud

Hartuv

Jerusalem

Majdal

Beit Hanun

Faluja

Hebron

Gaza

Rafah

Hatzerim

Beersheba

Nirim

Bet Eshel

Halutza

Sodom

Bir Asluj

Auja

Um RasRash

0   10 miles
0   10   20 km

63

afternoon, supported by heavy artillery fire and air attack, causing heavy casualties to the exposed Israelis. Although the Israelis moved their reserve into Jenin it was decided to withdraw that night because no further Israeli attack was going to be made on Tulkarm. No further offensives were made by the Iraqis during the war.

In the south the Egyptians advanced along the coast road and reached Gaza when a small seaborne force landed at Majdal; another smaller force crossed the border at Auja and entered Beersheba. There were twenty-seven widely separated settlements in the Negev, few of them having more than thirty defenders. The *Palmach* 'Negev' Brigade, only 800 men strong, defended the southern part of the country while the 2,700-strong 'Givati' Brigade, with its five battalions but no heavy weapons, was responsible for the area north of the Majdal–Beit Jibrin (Bet Guvrin) road.

The Egyptians attacked the isolated settlement of Kfar Doram, which had already been attacked by Moslem Brotherhood troops, with infantry, tanks and armoured cars. The infantry failed to keep up with the armour, which had several vehicles disabled, and the attack was broken off; after this the Egyptians only blockaded the settlement. At the same time Nirim, east of Rafah, was attacked on two successive days but both the Egyptian attacks were repulsed. After this the Egyptians decided to by-pass isolated settlements and push deeper into the country. The fight for Kibbutz Yad Mordechai, which the Egyptians had to attack as it controlled the main road, is described in detail later (see map 69).

The main Egyptian aim now was to cut off the Negev settlements completely and to occupy as much land as possible to prevent it from falling into King Abdullah's hands. They therefore established a line of strongholds along the Majdal–Beit Jibrin road but they were unable to capture Kibbutz Negba, whose defenders beat off an attack by 1,000 Egyptians on 2 June. Immediately before the first truce came into effect the Israelis captured a number of Arab villages but were unable to take the police fort at Iraq Suedan. The Egyptians gained control of the high ground which dominated the crossroads of the Majdal–Faluja and Kaukaba–Julis road and so when the truce came into effect the Negev was cut off.

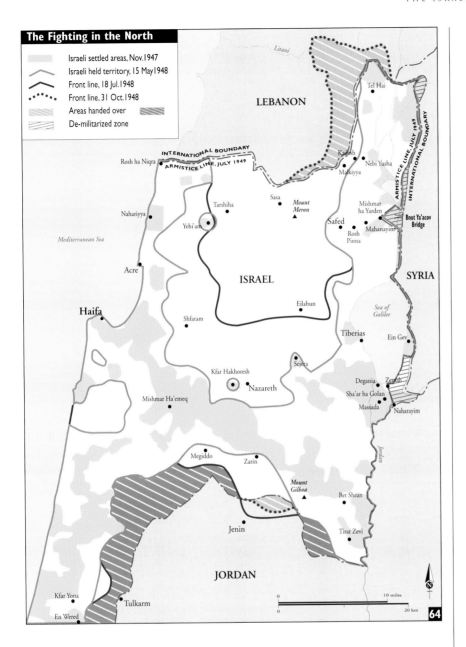

The Fighting in the North

	Israeli settled areas, Nov.1947
	Israeli held territory, 15 May1948
	Front line, 18 Jul. 1948
	Front line, 31 Oct. 1948
	Areas handed over
	De-militarized zone

Litani

LEBANON

Tel Hai

Kadesh

Rosh ha Niqra

INTERNATIONAL BOUNDARY

ARMISTICE LINE, JULY 1949

Nebi Yusha

Malkiyya

Sasa

Mount Meron

Mishmar ha Yarden

Tarshiha

Nahariyya

Safed

Bnot Ya'acov Bridge

Yehi'am

Mahanayim

Rosh Pinna

Mediterranean Sea

Acre

ISRAEL

SYRIA

Haifa

Eilabun

Sea of Galilee

Shfaram

Tiberias

Ein Gev

Kfar Hakhoresh

Sejera

Nazareth

Degania

Zemah

Sha'ar ha Golan

Mishmar Ha'emeq

Massada

Naharayim

Jordan

Megiddo

Zarin

Mount Gilboa

Bet Shean

Jenin

Tirat Zevi

JORDAN

Kfar Yona

Tulkarm

En Wered

0   10 miles

0   20 km

N

64

During the four-week truce both sides took the opportunity to reorganize and rearm, the Israelis receiving essential arms and equipment, mainly from Czechoslovakia, and carrying out intensive training. The freighter *Altalena* was organized by the IZL to bring weapons and recruits to Israel. The IZL were ordered by the government to hand over the arms and ammunition but refused to do so and fighting broke out between the IZL and *Haganah* in which fifteen died and the *Altalena* was sunk. From 28 June, after an oath of allegiance was taken, the IZL ceased to be an independent force.

The next phase in the war lasted until 15 October when the second truce came into force. In the north the Israelis concentrated on eliminating the strengthened Syrian bridgehead west of the Jordan by attempting to cut its lines of supply. On the night of 9 July the 'Carmeli' Brigade launched an attack aimed at capturing the Customs Post which overlooked the Bnot Ya'acov bridge but only one of the two battalions involved managed to cross the Jordan and so the attack was called off. Next morning the Syrians counter-attacked, threatening Rosh Pinna and Mahanayim; they also attacked Israeli forces still located east of the Jordan. In two days of hard fighting positions were lost and regained more than once.

To the south-west the 'Golani' Brigade attempted to drive the Arab Liberation Army away from the Coast–Tiberias road. The Arabs put all their effort into capturing the village of Sejera; many attacks had to be repulsed, the heaviest of which, on 14 July, was supported by Iraqi air strikes. The attack was only broken off because of the threat posed to Nazareth by the advance of the 7th Armoured Brigade from Acre. The 7th took Shfaram (Shefar'am), 16 km north-west of Nazareth, on the 14th; this surprised the Arabs who were expecting any Israeli attack to come from the south, and a blocking attempt by a company of armoured cars was quickly overcome by the 7th Brigade's only self-propelled gun. The Arab Army pulled out of Nazareth, which surrendered on the 16th; the Arabs then withdrew to the north-east, leaving the Israelis in possession of Lower Galilee when the second truce came into effect on the 18th.

On the Central Front Arab forces in Ramla and Lod still threatened Tel Aviv and denied the Israelis the use of Lod airport. Four complete brigades and elements of two more were assigned to an operation which in its first phase was to capture Lod and Ramla and in a second was to relieve Jerusalem by taking the police forts at Latrun and Ramallah, to the north of Jerusalem. The attack began on 9 July when the 'Yiftach' Brigade captured a number of villages to the south and east of Ramla and the 8th Armoured Brigade, which had twelve tanks, took the airport. A pincer movement was then supposed to converge at Ben Shemen before assaulting Lod from the east; the 'Yiftach' Brigade reached there but the 8th was held up, mainly by equipment problems. The 'Yiftach' had trouble entering Lod until a commando battalion (commanded by Moshe Dayan) drove into the town with all guns firing, causing panic before driving away. This daring raid allowed the brigade to complete the capture of the town when most of the population fled. The next day Ramla, attacked from the south, also surrendered. The British commander of the Jordanian forces, General Glubb, decided against attempting to recapture Lod and Ramla and concentrated his force at Latrun, which he guessed would be the Israelis' next objective. It was now clear that another UN cease-fire was about to be imposed and so the plan to take Ramallah was dropped and every effort was made to take Latrun, but it remained in Jordanian hands until 1967.

On the southern front the Egyptians, reinforced during the truce, were deployed with two brigades on the coast, one at Faluja, controlling the Majdal–Hebron road, and one (composed of Moslem Brotherhood units) on the Hebron–Jerusalem axis. Both sides were planning offensives to start when the cease-fire ended. The Israelis intended to open a road through to the Negev and to cut the Egyptians' east–west supply route; the Egyptians planned to widen their line blocking the way to the Negev. The Egyptians pre-empted the end of the truce by attacking on 8 July; they captured several positions but failed to take Beit Daras. The Israelis brought

Original Brigades of the Israel Defence Force

Haganah
North: 'Golani', 'Carmeli'
Jerusalem: 'Etzioni'
Central: 'Kiriati', 'Alexandroni'
South: 'Givati'

Palmach
North: 'Yiftach'
Central: 'Harel'
South: 'Negev'

forward their operation by 24 hours and attacked that night but failed to gain entry to the police fort of Iraq Suedan; they also captured the villages of Beit Affa, Ibdis and Iraq-Suedan but had to abandon the latter as the police fort had not been taken. An Egyptian counter-attack regained the village of Beit Affa but could not take Ibdis. The Egyptians next attacked Negba, considering this to be the key to the Israeli defence. The 150-man garrison managed to hold out, although attacked twice, causing over 200 Egyptian casualties. The fighting continued until the second cease-fire came into effect; the Israelis had secured a narrow route, subject to Egyptian fire, to the Negev and had blocked the coast–Hebron road. As the Egyptians had captured high ground south of Karatiya they managed to construct a by-pass round the village.

During the second truce the UN mediator, Count Bernadotte, produced a new partition proposal giving the Negev to the Arabs in return for western Galilee; it also gave Lod and Ramla back to the Arabs. These proposals were most unwelcome to the Israelis who realized they must pre-empt the UN by opening up the way to the Negev. Politically this became impossible after the murder of Count Bernadotte by, it was generally assumed, Israelis. Ben Gurion ordered the *Irgun* to disband its remaining force and some 200 members of LEHI were detained.

The Israelis now planned to take control of the whole of Galilee and destroy the Arab Liberation Army. Four Israeli brigades were available, now supported by four artillery batteries. Two brigades would carry out a pincer movement from Nahariyya and Safed, meeting at Sasa near the Lebanese border; a third brigade would protect the southern flank from the four Iraqi brigades deployed south of Jenin and carry out diversionary attacks, and the fourth would cover the Syrians who had three brigades east of the Jordan.

On 28 October the 7th Armoured Brigade advanced from Safed, forcing the Arabs to withdraw from Meron. They pushed on and captured Jish, where they surprised a recently arrived Syrian battalion, killing over 200 men. The brigade moved on to Sasa but found that the other arm of the pincer movement, the 'Oded' Brigade, had failed to take Tarshiha, 13 km west of Sasa. The plan was now changed accordingly. Sasa was taken by the 7th Brigade who found it only lightly held, and Tarshiha, after being heavily shelled, surrendered on the morning of the 30th.

The diversionary attacks in the south of the Arab-held enclave had misled the Arabs into believing that this was the main Israeli attack and so they had begun to withdraw to the north of the Acre–Safed road. The 'Golani' Brigade was therefore ordered to capture Eilabun, which it did on the night of the 29th. It then advanced northwards but was held up by a rearguard supported by artillery at Marar, which it occupied the next morning. The Arab Liberation Army withdrew into Lebanon but much of its equipment was captured. The 7th Brigade then moved northwards and surprised the garrison at Malkiyya which was less well prepared for an attack from the south. The 'Carmeli' Brigade crossed the Lebanese border and occupied a strip of land about 6 km wide from Malkiyya to the Litani; the return of this area was to be used later as a lever in negotiations with Lebanon. This operation ended the fighting in northern Israel.

Arab Commanders

Arab Liberation Army: Fawz el Din el Kaukji
Lebanon: Maj.-Gen. Fouad Shehab
Syria: Maj.-Gen. Abdullah Atfeh
Arab Legion (Transjordan): Maj.-Gen. John Glubb
Iraq: Maj.-Gen. Nur el-Din Mahmud
Egypt: Maj.-Gen. Ahmed Ali el Mawawi

Israeli Commanders

Chief of Staff: Maj.-Gen. Ya'acov Drori
Deputy: Brig.-Gen. Yigal Yadin
Northern Command: Brig.-Gen. Moshe Carmel
Central Command: Brig.-Gen. Dan Even
Jerusalem: Col. David Marcus
Southern Command: Brig.-Gen. Yigal Allon

In the south, with the encirclement of their force at Faluja, the Egyptians began to reinforce their positions close to Bir Asluj (Zomet Mash'abbim), were pushing eastwards, and once again threatened the isolated Negev settlements. The Israeli plan was to hold a defensive line from Nirim to Be'eri and then drive out all Egyptians east of this line. Operations 'Yoav' and 'Horev' which achieved this are described separately.

The Israelis carried out one more major operation to capture the southern tip of Palestine where it reaches the Red Sea; Operation 'Uvda' is described separately. After the end of the fighting a series of armistice negotiations were held. The first to be reached, at Rhodes on 24 February 1949, was with Egypt: the garrison of Faluja was allowed to return to Egypt, which retained the Gaza Strip. The Lebanese armistice was signed at Rosh ha Niqra on 23 March: Israel withdrew from Lebanese territory and the Lebanese from Rosh ha Niqra. The negotiations with Jordan, which also acted on behalf of Iraq, were the most complex. Eventually agreement was reached and signed on 3 April; by 22 May its military provisions had been implemented. Iraqi troops were withdrawn and Jordan gained control of what became known as the West Bank and of East Jerusalem. The Jordanians ceded a stretch of territory which widened the Israeli coastal strip and some land west of Bet Shean, while the Israelis withdrew from the area north of Jenin and in the south around Dhahiriya. The armistice line between Israel and the West Bank became known as the 'Green' line. Finally, agreement was reached with Syria, which pulled its troops out of the enclave it held at Mishmar ha Yarden. A compromise was reached over the former border between Palestine and Syria; the cease-fire line became the armistice line but the Syrians withdrew to the Mandatory Palestine/Syrian border and the areas between these two lines were declared Demilitarized Zones (DMZ). The Syrian armistice was signed on 20 July 1949 and the War of Independence was officially over. Independence had cost the Israelis 6,000 lives while some 15,000 had been wounded; Arab casualties are estimated to have been 15,000 dead and 25,000 wounded.

THE BATTLES FOR THE ROAD TO JERUSALEM

The battle for the road to Jerusalem opened on 30 November 1947, the day after the UN partition resolution was adopted, when a bus was fired on close to the airport and five Jews were killed. The route to Jerusalem from Tel Aviv first crossed the coastal plain but the most direct route was through the Arab town of Ramla and so the longer more southerly route via Kfar Bilu and Hulda was used for the resupply of Jerusalem. East of Hulda the road passed between the hills, at first some thousand metres away, but after Latrun the hills dominated the narrow winding road with Arab villages situated on the heights above it. It was 24 km from Latrun to Jerusalem.

At first the vehicles were fired on in the villages; later ambushes were laid and some road-blocks set up, although mines were not often laid as Arab and British vehicles also used the road. The Jews organized armed convoys, moved at night and on Saturdays when they were less expected,

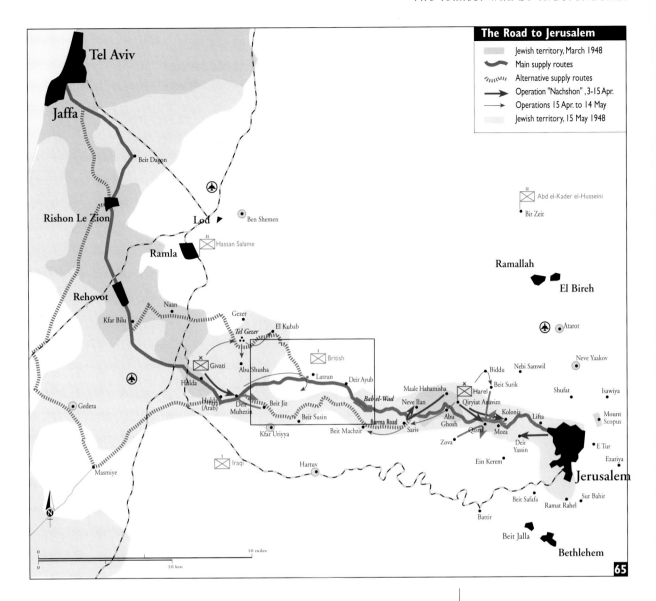

and constructed 'sandwiches' – vehicles protected by two sheets of steel with wood between them.

On 24 March 1948 a convoy was halted and attacked by hundreds of Arabs, encouraged by women and children. When the leading vehicle was knocked out the road was blocked and the convoy had to turn round and return to Tel Aviv, leaving behind fourteen burnt out 'sandwiches'. A convoy managed to reach Jerusalem the next day but a few days later another was attacked and was forced to turn back, suffering casualties. Jerusalem was then cut off from the coastal plain.

On 1 April the *Haganah* High Command met. Realizing that the loss of Jerusalem, now under siege, would be a fatal blow to Jewish morale, it decided to mount Operation 'Nacshon', which would create a safe corridor to Jerusalem by capturing and occupying the villages and strongpoints that dominated the road. A force of 1,500 men, the largest to take part in any operation so far, was assembled. Sufficient arms were only provided by the arrival of the first weapons consignments from Czechoslovakia.

'Sandwich' armoured trucks. (Alain Roth Archive)

Immediately before the operation the Headquarters of the Arab commander in Ramla was attacked and blown up, and at the eastern end of the road the village of Kastel, which commanded the road 8 km from Jerusalem, was captured and occupied. The operation began on the night of 5 April. At the western end a deserted British camp and the Arab villages Hulda and Deir Muhezin were occupied according to plan but the latter had to be abandoned when the British intervened. At the Jerusalem end the operation was less successful and the villages of Saris and Beit Machzir were not captured and the Jewish farm at Motza was taken by the Arabs. Nevertheless a convoy was despatched and reached Jerusalem with the first supplies for two weeks.

The Arabs concentrated on recapturing Kastel, which the Jews held on to for six days before withdrawing on 9 April. The Arab commander, Abdel Kader, had been killed as the Jews withdrew and when the *Haganah* mounted an attack the next day it was found that Kastel had been abandoned. On the same day forces of the IZL and LEHI captured the village of Deir Yassin, killing over 200 villagers; although the Jewish Agency expressed its disgust and regret over the affair, it is still used as propaganda by the Arabs. By 20 April five large convoys had reached Jerusalem, the men assembled for the operation had returned to their former units and the *Palmach* 'Harel' Brigade had taken over responsibility for the road corridor. The villages of Saris, Beit Surik and Bidu were captured and partially destroyed, but neither Beit Machzir nor Beit Jiz was captured as the *Palmach* had to be deployed to Jerusalem because of the build-up of Arab forces and the possibility of a British evacuation.

The 'Harel' Brigade was to move to Jerusalem with the next convoy which set out on the 20th. It was ambushed shortly after entering the defile; the ambushes were spread over a kilometre and a half of road and it was not until the evening that the trapped vehicles could be extricated, leaving ten behind. The 'Harel' Brigade suffered heavy casualties, including several commanders, in their efforts to rescue the convoy. Again Jerusalem was cut off.

Operation 'Maccabi' was the next attempt to open the road to Jerusalem with the 'Harel' Brigade operating in the east and the 'Givati' Brigade advancing from the west. The operation began on 8 May with the 'Givati' troops taking their objectives on the Hulda–Latrun road; the 'Harel' Brigade was unable to take Beth Machzir despite attempts on three successive days. The village finally fell on the 11th but by then the 'Harel' Brigade had suffered too many casualties to be able to continue to take Deir Ayub. On the 12th a force of 'Givati' tried to force its way past Latrun and Deir Ayub but came under fire from British armoured cars there and was halted with casualties.

Tel Gezer was captured by the 'Givati' Brigade during the night of 13/14 May, and the next day two more villages were taken. Despite the news that the Egyptian invasion had begun, it was decided to send one more convoy to Jerusalem before the 'Givati' were moved south. To the Israelis' surprise their objectives, Deir Ayub and the village of Latrun, had been virtually abandoned; their garrisons had been ordered to move to Syria as the Arab invasion was imminent. On the 16th the British evacuation from Jerusalem was completed. The road to Jerusalem was open but there was no convoy ready to go and it took forty-eight hours to send one through.

The Arab invasion was now well under way. The 'Givatis' moved south to face the Egyptians, while the 'Harel' Brigade moved up to Jerusalem; the Arab Legion occupied the fort at Latrun once the British had left. The road to Jerusalem was blocked again.

The 7th Armoured Brigade, a new formation based on Israel's first armoured battalion, was hastily formed, mainly from newly arrived immigrants. Having had minimal training, the force was tasked with opening the road to Jerusalem. On 24 May an attack was to be made by the new brigade; its armoured battalion was to protect the right flank, while a battalion of the 'Alexandroni' Brigade was to take the police fort and the village of Latrun. The infantry failed in their task; they did not reach the start line until dawn, while the artillery support only alerted the Jordanians, and the daylight attack was soon called off. The battalion suffered heavy casualties from fire from the villages of Bet Jiz and Bet Susin which were thought to have been unoccupied.

Two days later a second attack was launched; this time the 7th Brigade was to capture the fort and Latrun, and a battalion of the 'Givati' Brigade was to take the high ground overlooking the objective from the east. The infantry entered Deir Ayub unopposed but soon came under fire and withdrew without making any further effort to advance. The armour, unaware of this, mounted its attack and one company penetrated the fort compound but when a shell knocked out their engineers there was no way they could breach the walls of the fort and once more the force withdrew.

Then, by chance, a cross-country route south of the main road from Bet Susin, now held by the 7th Brigade, to the nearest positions of the 'Harel' Brigade was discovered. Most of the route was passable to vehicles, but there was a short but steep section just east of Bet Susin where the road

David Ben Gurion, Israel's first Prime Minister.

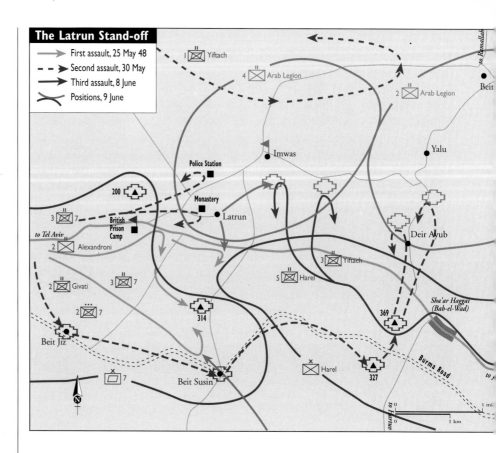

The Latrun Stand-off
→ First assault, 25 May 48
--→ Second assault, 30 May
→ Third assault, 8 June
Positions, 9 June

climbed 120 metres in 360 metres. Immediately, convoys of supplies were sent to Bet Susin, where the supplies were manhandled by porters from Jerusalem and transported by mule over the difficult section to the road running north from Hartuv where they were reloaded on vehicles. At the same time engineer equipment and workers were assembled to construct a road as soon as possible. The first convoy direct from Tel Aviv to Jerusalem crossed the 'Burma Road' (as it was called) on 10 June.

Just before the cease-fire and after a fourth attempt to take Latrun had failed, a Jordanian counter-attack took the settlement of Gezer and threatened the base at Hulda. The 'Yiftach' Brigade recaptured Gezer that night, only a few hours before the first truce came into effect.

At the end of the first truce the Israelis had planned to capture Lod and Ramla, to remove the threat to Tel Aviv, and then move on to take Latrun and finally Ramallah in order to raise the siege of Jerusalem. The first two objectives were achieved but it was clear that another cease-fire was about to be imposed so the capture of Ramallah was cancelled and every effort concentrated on taking Latrun. This was now defended by three Arab Legion battalions as General Glubb appreciated that it would be a key Israeli objective. On the night of 15/16 July four villages north of Latrun were captured by the 'Yiftach' Brigade supported by elements of two other brigades; this opened the way to by-pass Latrun; the Jordanians counter-attacked to prevent the fort being encircled. An attack by the 'Harel' Brigade on the Latrun ridge failed after another Transjordanian counter-attack. Israeli forces to the east and west of the fort were now only 3 km

The mosque at Nabi Samwil which the Haganah failed to capture in April 1947. (Photograph: Z. Radovan, Jerusalem)

apart and another unsuccessful attack was launched, this time from the north-east. On the night of the 17th, only hours before the second cease-fire came into effect, a further attack on the fort was made by tanks of the 7th Brigade and an infantry company of the 'Yiftach' Brigade. The attack had advanced half-way to the fort from its start line at El-Kubab when the gun of one tank jammed and it turned to take cover before clearing the barrel. Communications were not working and the other tank commanders, thinking this was a signal to withdraw turned back and the attack had to be called off. The Jordanians continued to occupy Latrun, blocking the main Jerusalem road, until 1967.

THE FIGHTING AT JERUSALEM

In general, before 1948 the Jews of Jerusalem lived in the western half of the city, as far as a boundary line drawn roughly northwards from the north-west corner of the Old City and south from there down the Gihon Valley to roughly the railway station, with Jews living south of the station being housed in isolated suburbs separated by about 1.5 km of Arab-occupied area. There were also two important Jewish institutions, the Hadassah Hospital and the Hebrew University on Mount Scopus, again separated by Arab areas. In the Old City the Jewish Quarter lay in the southern part, surrounded by Arab areas.

The outlying areas of Jerusalem and the settlements to the north and south could only be supplied by armed convoys. On 13 April 1948 a convoy heading for Mount Scopus was ambushed as it passed through the Arab district of Sheikh Jarrach and was trapped there. The British refused to intervene and after seven hours of fighting, numerous vehicles that had been taking some eighty people, mainly doctors and nurses, to the hospital, were captured and the occupants killed.

The *Haganah* High Command decided that an operation must be launched to create a permanent link with the outlying Jewish areas. The first phase of Operation 'Jebusi' was to create a corridor to Neve Ya'acov and Atarot by capturing the Arab villages of Nebi Samuel (Nabi Samwil), Beit Iksa and Shuafat. The attack, on 22 April, took two villages but the element of surprise was lost at Nebi Samuel on account of poor timing; the *Palmach* force was ambushed and its commander and thirty-two men were killed. Reinforcements were unable to reach the scene and the whole force withdrew, leaving Neve Ya'acov isolated.

The second phase, to capture Sheikh Jarrach and thus establish a corridor to Mount Scopus, took place on the 26th. Sheikh Jarrach fell after a night's fighting but the British demanded that the Jews withdraw as the main British evacuation route ran through that suburb. However, it was only after the British brought up a battalion with tanks and artillery which opened fire that the *Palmach* agreed to withdraw. The British ensured that the Arabs did not return and Sheikh Jarrach was occupied without opposition when the British finally withdrew.

On 29 April a Jewish attack was launched from Mount Scopus on the Augusta Victoria Hospital and the surrounding high ground in an attempt to cut Arab lines of communication between Jerusalem and Jericho and Jordan. Surprise was lost when a 'Davidka', a locally manufactured mortar, exploded, causing Jewish casualties; the attack was called off. On the same night the third phase of Operation 'Jebusi', the capture of the suburb of Katamon, to link up with the Jewish areas of Mekor Hayyim and Talpiyyot, was launched. Katamon was dominated by the hill on which the monastery of Saint Simon is sited, and which was held by Iraqi troops. Although the monastery was captured that night the Iraqis held on to a nearby house; the Jews decided to wait until the next night before taking it but the Arabs launched a fierce counter-attack which got close to entering the monastery before it was beaten off. The *Palmach* suffered heavy casualties and withdrawal was discussed. However, reinforcements from the 'Etzioni' (Jerusalem) Brigade were brought up and the area was cleared that night and Mekor Hayyim relieved the next morning. The nearby 'German Colony' area was also captured but further advance was stopped when the British enforced a cease-fire.

Both sides prepared to take over British-controlled areas as the date for their evacuation came closer. The Jews took the security zone known as 'Bevingrad' and the King David Hotel and so linked up with the Yemin Moshe area. The Arabs got into the Monastery of Notre Dame close to the north-west corner of the Old City first but were soon evicted by the Jews. A fierce battle was fought for the British 'Allenby' base and the Arabs were forced out. The *Haganah* proved unable to block the Jerusalem–Bethlehem road before units of the Jordanian Arab Legion entered the Old City.

The main force of the Arab Legion began crossing the Jordan on 13 May, shelled Jewish Jerusalem on the 15th, and had soon recaptured Sheikh Jarrach from its IZL defenders.

The Jordanians, despite strong efforts, failed to break into the Jewish part of the city at the Mandelbaum Gate and on the 23rd an armoured attack on the Notre Dame Monastery was beaten off. The Jordanians continued to shell and direct armoured car and sniper fire on the monastery but after the first disastrous attempt no further assault was attempted. The Jordanians were also unable to capture Kibbutz Ramat Rahel, just south of Talpiyyot, although it changed hands no fewer than three times.

The Jordanians now turned their attention to the Jewish Quarter of the Old City, ignoring the UN's declaration that it was an open, demilitarized, city. They first captured Mount Zion, which lies just outside the southern wall of the Old City, and then began to close in on the Jewish Quarter. Despite the appeals of the defenders, no relief attempt was made until the night of the 17/18th when the *Haganah* ordered an attack at the Jaffa Gate with a diversionary attack on Mount Zion. The attacking force was late and only arrived in daylight; the Arabs, forewarned, inflicted casualties on the Israelis as they dismounted from their transport. The attack on the Jaffa Gate that night was expected and was beaten back. The main attack now became the diversion and the *Palmach* company sent to Mount Zion surprised the Arabs by climbing the steepest approach and capturing it. Next night both attacks were renewed; the men at the Jaffa Gate failed again but at Mount Zion they blew open the Zion Gate and made contact with the Jewish Quarter. Reinforcements and more arms and ammunition were rushed in before Arab pressure at the Zion Gate forced the Israelis to abandon it and retire to Mount Zion, leaving the Jewish Quarter cut off again.

The Arab irregulars besieging the Jewish Quarter were now replaced by the Arab Legion and the attack was resumed. Slowly, street by street and house by house, the Quarter was captured. Another relief attempt was planned for the night of 28/29 May but on the morning of the 28th a delegation of Rabbis approached the Jordanians to negotiate terms of surrender; the Jordanians demanded unconditional surrender. Eventually the Old City surrendered, the defenders giving up their arms and being taken prisoner while the wounded and civilians were escorted to the Israeli lines.

Fighting continued, with neither side making any significant gains, until the First Truce came into effect on 11 June. There was little fighting in Jerusalem between the two truces. Israeli plans included the capture of Malhe and Ein Karim as a start towards opening the railway line to Tel Aviv, the capture of Sheikh Jarrach to block Jordanian approaches from the north and to link up with Mount Scopus, and the capture of the whole of the Old City. On the night of 9/10 July a company made up of sixteen- and seventeen-year-olds took the high ground now known as Mount Herzl, despite their commander being killed on the start-line for the attack. An attack by an LEHI unit failed to take the ridge controlling the track between Mahle and Ein Karim and had to retire after suffering heavy casualties. The 'Gadna' (Youth) Company took the LEHI objective the next night and the Arabs began to evacuate Ein Karim.

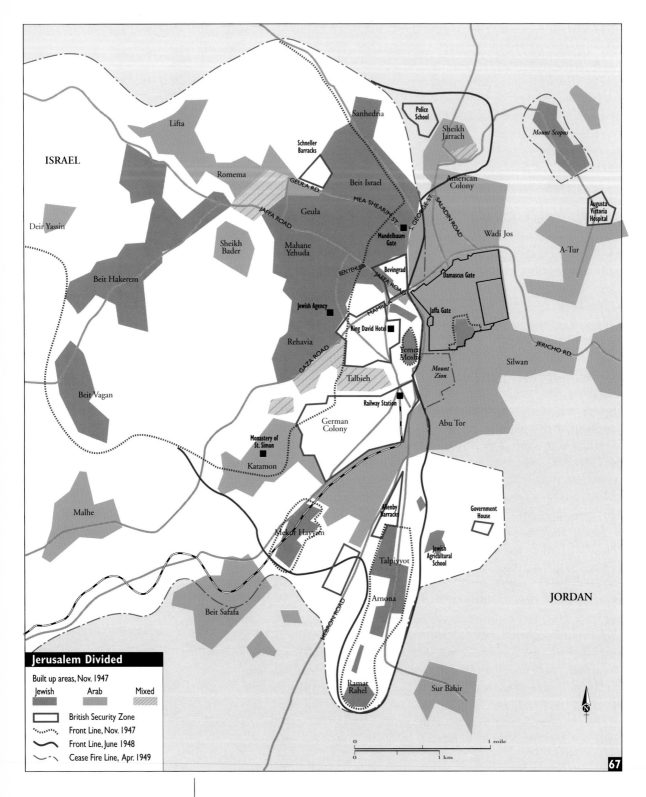

ISRAEL

Lifta

Sanhedria

Police School

Sheikh Jarrach

Mount Scopus

Schneller Barracks

Romema

GEULA RD.

Beit Israel

American Colony

Augusta Victoria Hospital

MEA SHEARIM ST.

Deir Yassin

JAFFA ROAD

Geula

S. GEORGE ST.

SALADIN ROAD

Wadi Jos

Sheikh Bader

Mahane Yehuda

Mandelbaum Gate

A-Tur

Beit Hakerem

BEN YEHUDA

JAFFA ROAD

Bevingrad

Damascus Gate

HAMIK

Jewish Agency

Jaffa Gate

King David Hotel

Rehavia

GAZA ROAD

Yemen Moshe

JERICHO RD.

Talbieh

Mount Zion

Silwan

Railway Station

Beit Vagan

German Colony

Abu Tor

Monastery of St. Simon

Katamon

Malhe

Allenby Barracks

Government House

Mekor Hayyim

Jewish Agricultural School

Talpiyyot

JORDAN

HEBRON ROAD

Beit Safafa

Arnona

Ramat Rahel

Sur Bahir

N

Jerusalem Divided

Built up areas, Nov. 1947

Jewish   Arab   Mixed

☐ British Security Zone

········ Front Line, Nov. 1947

⌇ Front Line, June 1948

⌇ Cease Fire Line, Apr. 1949

0   1 mile

0   1 km

67

    The other two attacks had to be postponed as one of the battalions earmarked for them had to be committed to recapturing the Mandelbaum Gate from the Arab Legion. It was apparent that a second truce would soon come into effect and any further attack must be launched that night. Although instructed to attack Sheikh Jarrach as a first priority, the

Jerusalem commander decided to make a frontal attack on the Old City. The *Irgun* managed to penetrate the New Gate but got no further, while at the Zion Gate a new 'device' failed to penetrate the wall and the attack was called off at dawn. The start of the second truce saw the Arab Legion still in control of the Old City.

Throughout the second truce Jerusalem witnessed exchanges of fire as sniper fire was returned by machine-guns, to be countered by mortars and then by artillery until the shooting was stopped by UN intervention. Supplies reached Jerusalem regularly along the 'Burma' road. After the Arabs had blown up the water pumping station at Latrun, a pipeline was built alongside the 'Burma' road. After the second truce no major operations were mounted on the Jerusalem front but a number of raids and artillery bombardments were launched by both sides. The last fighting to take place was a two-battalion attack by the Israelis on the night of 19/20 October which captured a number of Arab Legion outposts north of the railway line but failed to take the dominating features to its south.

THE BATTLE FOR YAD MORDECHAI

Kibbutz Yad Mordechai lies close to the Gaza–Tel Aviv road some 13 km north of Gaza City; although it was not the closest Jewish settlement to Egypt it was the first to seriously hinder the Egyptian advance as it controlled the main road. For some months before independence the Kibbutz had been preparing its defences: firing positions, communication trenches and outposts with overhead cover. A pill-box was constructed on a small rise nearly 300 metres south of the Kibbutz perimeter, a wire fence which was reinforced at various points with barbed wire entanglements. A *Palmach* platoon stationed at the Kibbutz laid minefields of 'shoe' mines. Shelters for the women and children were constructed and food and water stored and buried for protection.

For some time the transport taking Kibbutz produce to Tel Aviv had been subject to attack and the lorry cabs had been armoured. In return the Kibbutz mounted small ambushes to fire on Arab vehicles which passed by. They observed the withdrawal of the British Army and the flight of refugees from Jaffa. They also provided a machine-gun detachment to support the *Haganah* attack on the nearby Arab village of Breir, from which an ambush had been sprung in April on a small supply convoy for Yad Mordechai, after it had been cut off for a month.

To defend the Kibbutz there were some sixty men, over half of whom had either served in the British, Polish or Russian armies or had received training from the

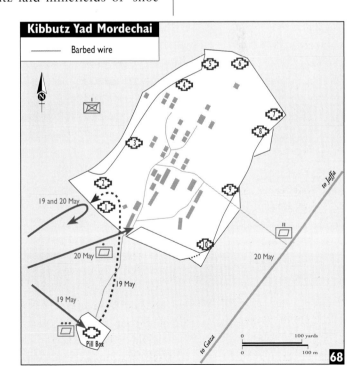

Kibbutz Yad Mordechai

Kibbutz Yad Mordechai was established on 1 December 1943 by a group of farmers and fishermen from Mitzpe Ha'yam near Netanya which was too small for its population. The Kibbutz was named after a hero of the Warsaw ghetto, Mordechai Anilevic.

The Kibbutz's Weaponry

(120 men and boys)
12 1911 Italian rifles
25 assorted rifles from Germany, Poland, Canada and Britain with 3,000 rounds
1 Tommy gun
2 Sten guns with 300 rounds
1 Schmeisser sub-machine-gun
1 Spandau light machine-gun
1 Browning machine-gun with 10,000 rounds
1 PIAT (Projectile Anti-tank) launcher with three rounds
2 Two-inch mortars with 50 bombs
400 hand-grenades

Collected from Egyptian dead:
12 .303 rifles and ammunition
2 Bren guns with 24 magazines
1 PIAT launcher with 12 rounds

Egyptian Army

(2 battalions with 2,000 men)
32 artillery guns
4 4.2 inch mortars
18 3 inch mortars
12 medium machine-guns
tanks
air support

Haganah. In addition, there was a group of twenty-five young male refugees from Europe who were there learning Hebrew. There was also the *Palmach* platoon but this was withdrawn at the beginning of May to strengthen its parent battalion for mobile operations; the Kibbutz objected, pointing out its strategic position on the main road, and was given a reinforcement of fourteen men. Weapons were also in short supply. They comprised some forty assorted rifles with 3,000 rounds of ammunition; five sub- and light machine-guns; a Browning machine-gun with 10,000 rounds of ammunition; one PIAT anti-tank projector with only three rounds; two 2-inch mortars with 50 bombs; and 400 hand grenades. The ambushed convoy brought a further seven Czech rifles.

After their failure to capture Kfar Darom and Nirim, the Egyptians reached Yad Mordechai on 16 May and then waited for reinforcements before attacking the settlement. Two Egyptian Spitfires strafed the Kibbutz on the evening of the 17th but caused no casualties as the people were in the shelters. After the air attack the Kibbutz decided to evacuate the children, although official policy was that women and children should remain in their settlements as evacuation was thought to lower morale. An armoured bus and three armoured cars were sent from the nearby *Palmach* base at Nir 'Am and they evacuated ninety-two children with their nurses and a number of young mothers that night. Just over fifty women remained at the Kibbutz.

The attack began on the 19th when the Egyptians had built up their forces to two infantry, one tank and one artillery battalions. After another air raid and three hours of artillery bombardment there was a pause in the firing and a plane dropped leaflets with an inappropriate message calling on the settlers to surrender within one hour or they would be attacked. After the hour was over the shelling was renewed and soon the Egyptian infantry advanced, surprisingly in a rather First World War manner but with their officers in the rear rather than in the lead. The seven defenders of the pill-box let the advancing infantry get to within 100 metres before opening fire; the Egyptians broke but were soon turned back by their officers. Again the Israelis held their fire and then concentrated on hitting the officers. This time the Egyptians' retreat could not be halted and the artillery redoubled its efforts to destroy the pill-box. Firing from the Kibbutz alerted the men at the pill-box that another attack was under way. This time they waited until the enemy were within grenade-throwing range, but after throwing their grenades they realized that they were about to be cut off and so withdrew to the settlement perimeter, covered by the smoke from burning wheat. The Egyptians then made three attacks on Post No. 1 which was on a hillock on the southern side of the Kibbutz and its strongest point. The first two were repulsed with rifle fire and the third, when the attackers started to cut their way through the wire, by grenades.

That night a patrol was sent out to collect arms and ammunition from the dead Egyptians. They managed to bring back 2 Bren guns with 24 loaded magazines, 12 rifles with ammunition, and a PIAT anti-tank launcher with 12 projectiles.

Next day an Egyptian tank and some armoured cars moved up to the pill-box and others took up fire positions on three sides of the Kibbutz so that all the posts were covered. At 10 am a spotter plane appeared overhead and a systematic bombardment of the defensive positions began. First, Post No. 9 received a direct hit, wounding its occupants and then Post No. 2, on the eastern side of the settlement, took another which killed its three defenders and destroyed the emplacement. The Egyptians then started to fire smoke and soon the defenders in Post No. 1 were blinded; fortunately, the wind suddenly shifted and the Egyptians were revealed to be already cutting the wire; they were soon dispersed. Another group was discovered cutting the wire at the main gate from where they could have got into the trench system; they too were forced to retreat but the Israeli defenders had had to expose themselves and suffered casualties. The second attack of the day, led by armoured cars, was again directed against Post No. 1, but the Egyptians were driven off by the fire of the 2-inch mortars. In all, the Egyptians made four assaults that day and all were beaten off, but 18 Israelis had been killed and 20 wounded. The Kibbutz called urgently for reinforcements and for more arms and ammunition and that night a platoon of *Palmach* joined the defenders.

A building at Yad Mordechai after the fighting.

For the next two days the Egyptians held off, contenting themselves with shelling the Kibbutz. On the 22nd the defenders reported that 'the settlement must be reinforced or abandoned. It is vital that the women and wounded be evacuated immediately.' On the 23rd the next Egyptian attack was made by two groups of tanks and armoured cars which penetrated the defences; although the defenders were virtually out of ammunition they managed to repulse the accompanying infantry. That night a unit of the 'Negev' Brigade with armoured cars broke through the encircling Egyptian lines and made contact with the settlement. The armoured cars were held up by an Egyptian strongpoint which was unsuccessfully attacked while the wounded were being evacuated. As the Kibbutz had received no reinforcements they had no alternative but to abandon it before dawn; the settlers moved north and the *Palmach* men east to join the defence of Gever Am, from where they had infiltrated into Yad Mordechai.

The loss of Yad Mordechai was a sad blow but its defence had provided the Israelis with five days in which to prepare a new defence line to the north and to bring into the country much needed heavy weapons and aircraft. Those five days were spent by the 'Givati' Brigade in preparing fortifications, digging tank traps, and blowing the bridges on the main road. It took the Egyptians four days to advance from Yad Mordechai to Isdud where they were halted by the lack of a bridge. Before a Bailey bridge could be constructed they were attacked by Israel's first Messerschmitts which had only just arrived and been assembled that morning. This was the furthest north the Egyptians penetrated.

OPERATIONS 'YOAV' & 'HOREV': TAKING THE NEGEV

During the second cease-fire the Egyptians continued to attack Israeli convoys resupplying isolated settlements in the Negev even though these were under UN escort. The attack on the convoy on 15 October was the signal for an Israeli operation to begin: four Israeli brigades, supported by

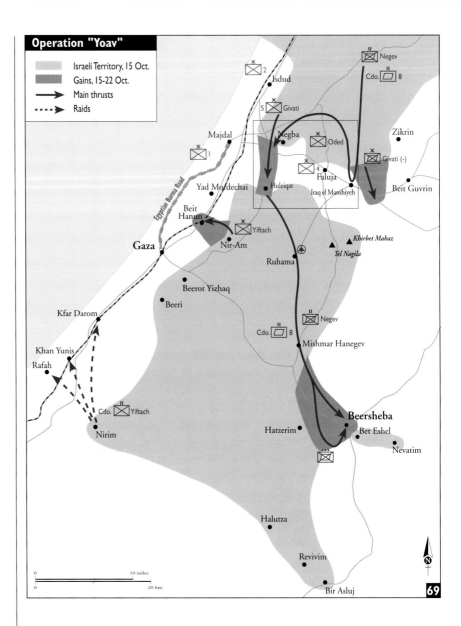

eight batteries of artillery, four of which were equipped with 75mm guns, were to break through to the Negev, cut the Egyptian lines of communications, separate and isolate the Egyptians and then defeat them in detail.

Before the operation started the *Palmach* 'Negev' Brigade which had been fighting in the Negev for nine months was relieved by the 'Yiftach' Brigade. To accomplish this, and to help build up Israeli strength in the Negev, an airstrip was constructed at Ruhama so that aircraft larger than Piper Cubs could be used to fly in the relieving troops. The first flight into Ruhama was made on the night of 22 August when equipment and ground staff were brought in. The plan was for the transport aircraft, Constellations and Commando 46s, to bring in 14 tonnes of supplies a night but by the third night some 75 tonnes a night was being achieved. All told 417 flights, averaging eight a night, were made into Ruhama, bringing in over 2,000 tonnes of stores and equipment and around 1,900 men.

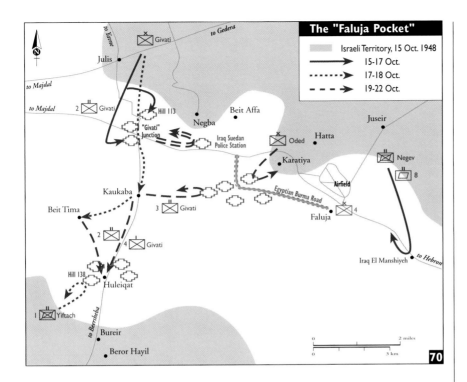

The 'Yiftach' Brigade was involved in fighting before Operation 'Yoav' was launched. Ruhama was in artillery range of Khirbet-Mahaz and Tel Nagila, hills close to the Faluja–Beersheba road, and it was decided that they must be occupied to protect the airstrip. The 'Yiftach' Brigade occupied the positions but before they could finish digging in they were attacked by the Egyptians and forced to withdraw. An Israeli counter-attack found the position unoccupied; the Egyptians had handed over to a local Arab unit which had run away. The next Egyptian attack, on 4 October, was made by armoured cars and infantry in Bren gun carriers which the Israelis had no way of stopping and the hill was lost again. The Israelis immediately mounted a pre-planned counter-attack and regained the position. All told the Egyptians mounted seven attacks but the Israelis hung on and the airlift into Ruhama was not interrupted.

After the attack on the convoy on 15 October Egyptian targets at Gaza, Majdal, Beit Hanun and El Arish were bombed, the railway and roads around Rafah were mined and camps attacked by commandos. The 'Givati' Brigade cut the road between Faluja and Bet Guvrin but an armoured and infantry attack on Iraq El Manshiyeh failed because of poor infantry/tank co-operation; the attacking armour was caught by artillery fire and sustained heavy casualties, including the loss of four Hotchkiss tanks and damage to all the other tanks taking part.

The Israelis now turned to taking the cross-roads (Zomet Givati), protected by fortified hills to the north and strongpoints to the west which were captured by dawn on the 18th after heavy fighting; four Egyptian counter-attacks were repulsed. On the night of the 18th Kaukaba was captured but Huleiqat remained in Egyptian hands. By now the coastal road had been cut at Beit Hanun and to avoid being cut off the Egyptians withdrew from Ashdod and Majdal towards Gaza. It was necessary to

Israeli Bren-gun carriers. (Alain Roth Archive)

capture Huleiqat if a corridor to the Negev were to be achieved, and this was the Israelis' next objective. The defences comprised six fortified and mutually supporting hills, manned by an Egyptian battalion, a Saudi-Arabian company and a heavy weapons company. On the night of 19/20 October the attack was launched and the first hill was taken by a bayonet charge; some thirty medium machine-guns were captured by the Israelis and immediately put into use. The whole position was taken only after hand-to-hand fighting. At the same time another attack on the police fort at Iraq Suedan was beaten off with heavy Israeli losses.

The last part of the plan could now be implemented and an attack on Beersheba, which surrendered shortly after it had been attacked early on the 21st, cut off the Moslem Brotherhood forces operating on the Hebron–Bethlehem road. The encirclement of Faluja and a 4,000-strong brigade was completed when forces from Jerusalem occupied Bet Guvrin. The fort at Iraq Suedan was finally captured on 9 November after the heaviest artillery bombardment the Israelis had yet fired. The garrison at Faluja refused Israeli offers of safe conduct to Egypt with military honours, and in December it repulsed a disastrous attack made by the 'Alexandroni' Brigade.

Operation 'Horev' began on the night of 22 December with the 'Golani' Brigade capturing Hill 86 which controlled the Gaza–Rafah road; the Egyptians counter-attacked strongly and the Israelis had to withdraw. However, the attack, together with the Israeli air attacks and naval bombardment, convinced the Egyptians that the main Israeli effort was to be made against the coastal strip, and so they concentrated their attention there. On 25 December, after a 24-hour postponement because of heavy rain, the 8th Armoured Brigade, avoiding the Egyptian defensive positions on the Beersheba–Auja (Nizzana) road, advanced down the old Roman road which led across the desert to the north and which engineers had been preparing for some days. When the brigade reached Wadi El-Abyad it swung west to the Rafah–Auja road, intending to block the road and then attack Auja from the north-west. Progress was slower than expected and the Egyptians were forewarned by an air attack made at 7 am, as originally planned. The tanks only reached the outpost at 4 pm, some nine hours behind schedule. The plan was hastily changed and Auja was attacked from the north-east where the Israelis, as they had expected, met well-prepared positions and were held up. By now Egyptian reinforcements from Rafah were engaging the road block from the north.

The 'Negev' Brigade, which on the night of the 25th had captured Bir E-Tamile and Mishrefe in wide outflanking movements, was ordered to speed up its advance along the main road in order to join the attack on Auja. On the 26th the Brigade's commando battalion approached a number of outposts from the rear, only to find they had been abandoned.

At dawn on 27 December the Egyptians renewed their attempts to get reinforcements past the Israeli road blocks, while the Israelis renewed their attack on Auja. The Egyptians were forced to withdraw and the Israelis, although heavily attacked from the air, silenced all resistance at Auja shortly after noon. Next day the 'Negev' Brigade crossed into Egypt and after an engagement at Um Katef entered Abu Ageila without opposition. On the 29th a battalion was sent west to El Arish, meeting some resistance at Bir Lahfan before reaching the airfield. At the same time another unit was sent from Auja south to Quseima and raids were made on Bir el Hama and Bir el Hassne, both over 80 km from the border. These incursions into Sinai caused the British to issue an ultimatum that unless the Israelis withdrew they would intervene under the terms of the Anglo-Egyptian Treaty of 1936. The Prime Minister ordered a withdrawal and the attempt to cut off the Egyptians in Gaza failed.

An Israeli machine-gun post on a Jerusalem rooftop, 1948. (IDF Archives)

The first Hotchkiss tanks handed over to 82 Battalion, 1948. (IDF Archives)

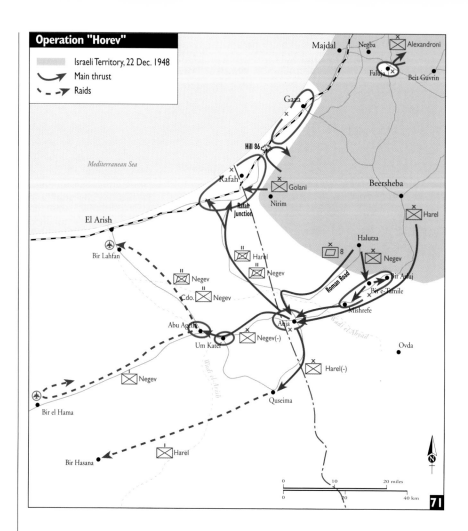

An Israeli Sherman tank at Kuntilla, 1948. (IDF Archives)

OPERATION 'UVDA': THE ADVANCE TO THE RED SEA

The final operation of the Israeli War of Independence was Operation 'Uvda'. It was launched in March 1949 with the aim of occupying the southern part of Palestine, which had been allotted to Israel by the UN partition plan, and gaining access to the Red Sea at Um Rashrash (Elat). During the armistice negotiations at Rhodes, Egypt had given up its claim to the region but Jordan did not as they had military control over it. Two brigades, the 'Negev' and 'Golani', were made available for the operation, but only one battalion from each was to take part so as to reduce the logistic load. The 'Golani' Battalion advanced down the Arava Valley where the bulk of Jordanian opposition was deployed, while the stronger 'Negev' Battalion took a cross-country route through the central Negev. Because of the talks at Rhodes the force was given strict instructions not to engage Jordanian forces.

Reconnaissance was carried out in late February and early March to map the cross-desert route and to make a logistic plan. It was decided to establish a forward airstrip at Iqfi (Sha'ar Zenifim) about 55 km north of Um Rashrash. The advance party of the 'Negev' Battalion set out from Beersheba on 5 March, passing by the ruins of the Nabataean city of Avdat, and crossing Makhtesh Ramon; from here on, the track became very difficult, and engineers had to blow up the large rocks blocking the way. The first transport planes landed at Ifqi at about 6 pm on the 6th.

The 'Golani' column left its assembly area at Kurnub (another ruined Nabataean city), taking with it seven days' supplies as there would be no air resupply. On 7 March it established an advance base at Ein Hussub at the junction of the Beersheba– Sodom and Sodom–Um Rashrash roads. The next advance was to Ein Webe (En Yahav) which had been occupied by the Jordanian Arab Legion but it was found to be deserted on arrival. On the 8th a complaint was raised by the Jordanian delegation at Rhodes that 'Jewish forces in jeeps and armoured cars crossed our lines on the morning of 7 March, 1.5 km west of Bir-ibn-Auda. The situation will be most delicate unless Israel ceases all military activity during the course of negotiations.'

Also on the 8th the 'Golani' column was held up by the Arab Legion at Ein Amer, 11 km south of Ein Webbe; obeying their orders, they did not return the Jordanian fire but forced them to withdraw by outflanking them from the east. The column pressed on to Bir Meliha and the entrance to Wadi Hayon (Nahal Ya'alon). The 'Negev' Brigade sent a company to establish a base about 20 km south of the airstrip, from where they carried out further route reconnaissance. Air reconnaissance reported Arab Legion

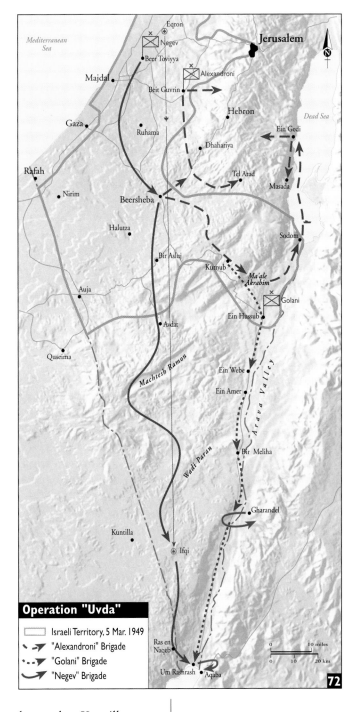

forces in Um Rashrash and to the north-west on the road to Kuntilla.

On the 9th the 'Golanis' continued southwards and found that the expected outposts on the road had been withdrawn. The Arab Legion had prepared an ambush in the foothills of Har Qetura but they opened fire too early and the Israelis avoided the trap. Once again an outflanking movement that night caused the Jordanians to withdraw. On the 10th the Israelis learnt that Ras en Naqeb and Um Rashrash had been vacated and once air reconnaissance had confirmed that the outposts above the town had been abandoned the 'Negev' Brigade set out on foot. By midday they had reached the heights from where they could see the Red Sea. By 3 pm

*Armoured cars en route for Um
Rashrash. (IDF Archives)*

*Hoisting the Israeli flag at Elat,
10 March 1949. (IDF Archives)*

they had reached the sea; two hours later the advance guard of the
'Golanis' met up with them.

At the same time as Operation 'Uvda', the Israelis mounted a separate
operation to clear the area of the north-eastern Negev and to establish a
line from Ein Gedi on the Dead Sea westwards to Um el-Burge, 16 km
north of Beersheba. The operation was carried out by the 'Givati' Brigade
and included, on 6 March, an amphibious landing at Ein Gedi by an
infantry company. The Israelis also occupied Masada, the site of Herod's
fortress and of the last Jewish stand against the Romans in AD 73.

Although the last of the armistice agreements, that with Syria, was not
signed until July 1949, the War of Independence was now in effect over.

THE ARAB–ISRAELI WARS

THE FIGHTING BETWEEN THE MAJOR WARS

At the end of the War of Independence Israel signed armistice agreements with its Arab neighbours; since then there have been two major Arab–Israeli wars, in 1967 and 1973, and the Israeli–Egyptian war in 1956. These are described separately. This section covers the period of 'no war–no peace' between these wars from 1949 to the present day.

From the date of Independence until the Sinai campaign in 1956, Israel suffered an increasing number of terrorist attacks carried out by Palestinians known as Fedayeen. The majority of the attacks came from territory controlled by Jordan and Egypt but some also came across the borders with Syria and Lebanon. Initially, the raids were carried out for the most part by refugees seeking anything that would improve their lives, either food or goods, even telephone wire, that could be sold for food. Next the raids escalated into attacks by gangs who, as well as stealing anything of value, also committed acts of sabotage and murder. Israeli reprisal raids began in 1951 but on the whole these were poorly executed; out of eighty-five mounted up to the end of 1953 only thirty-eight were considered successful and the majority of the remainder were classed as unqualified failures.

In an effort to neutralize a persistent saboteur living at Nabi Samwil, the Jerusalem District Commander persuaded a former paratroop officer, Arik Sharon, then a university student, to lead a reprisal raid. This led to the establishment, under Sharon's command, of a commando unit specializing in reprisal raids. Known as Unit 101, Sharon's group carried out a number of increasingly ambitious raids into the West Bank and Gaza Strip. In October 1953 a much larger-scale raid was planned against the village of Kibya after the murder, by hand grenades, of an Israeli woman and her two children. A larger force than Unit 101 was needed but the paratroop commander chosen was reluctant to take charge of an operation he did not think his men were up to. Sharon therefore took overall command. All the inhabitants of Kibya were thought to have fled, and during the raid forty-six houses were blown up, killing sixty-nine men, women and children who, unknown to the Israelis, were still hiding there.

In August 1955 the Fedayeen campaign of raids into southern Israel intensified and the Israeli Cabinet was divided over what response should be made. Initially only small-scale raids were authorized but even these were

*Abdul Nasser
Battalion Commander, Faluja
Pocket, 1948; President and Prime
Minister of Egypt 1954–70.*

halted by the Prime Minister, Moshe Sharett. After a successful Fedayeen attack on the night of the 29th, Dayan, the Chief of Staff, tendered his resignation with the result that the Government authorized the large-scale retaliatory raid that Dayan had been demanding. On the night of 31 August/ 1 September three companies of Israeli paratroops, again led by Arik Sharon, attacked Egyptian and Fedayeen positions at Khan Yunis, killing 72 and wounding 58. The raid halted the Egyptian Fedayeen campaign for fear of further escalation and casualties. Instead Nasser turned his attention to tightening the blockade of the Straits of Tiran, and closed the Gulf of Aqaba airspace to Israeli civil aircraft. At the same time Fedayeen in Jordan, Syria and Lebanon were instructed to step up their raids. The slide towards war had begun.

In the last months of 1955 Egyptian–Israeli confrontation centred on the Demilitarized Zone (DMZ) established by the armistice agreement; this lay around the Auja oasis some 45 km south-east of Rafah, on the eastern side of the former Egyptian/Palestine border. Neither side could deploy troops there and while Israel considered it was under its sovereignty Egypt treated it more as a no-man's-land. On the other side of the border there was a similar-sized triangular-shaped area in which the Egyptians were barred from establishing defensive positions.

Clashes in the DMZ involving Egyptian check-posts and Israeli border markers led, eventually, to an Egyptian raid on 26 October 1955 on the Israeli police post at Be'erotayim, 200 metres inside the DMZ. In retaliation the Israelis mounted a raid on Kuntilla where they killed 12 Egyptian soldiers and took 29 prisoner. The Egyptians remained in the DMZ and so the Israelis launched a brigade-scale operation against Egyptian positions on both sides of the border at El Sabha and Wadi Siram. The Egyptian positions were destroyed, 81 soldiers were killed and 55 taken prisoner.

Following the 1956 war and the deployment of UNEF in Sinai and Gaza, Arab incursions switched from Israel's southern border to the north and east. Syria shelled Israeli settlements in the Hula valley from the Golan Heights and laid mines across the border in Israel. Fishing boats on the Sea of Galilee were attacked and farmers attempting to cultivate the DMZs were fired on. An Israeli reprisal raid on Khirbet Tawfiq in 1960 did nothing to abate the attacks. There were, of course, instances where the Israelis provoked attack so that they could be justified in retaliating strongly. In 1964, with support from an Arab summit meeting and in retaliation for the construction of the Israeli National Water Carrier to pipe water down to the Negev, the Syrians began to divert the waters of the Banias in Syria and the Hasbani in Lebanon from the Jordan, Israel's main supply of water. The Lebanese were dissuaded from continuing the project but the Syrians did not abandon it until the Israelis reacted with artillery and long-range tank fire on the work sites; in November they carried out air strikes on areas out of artillery range.

Also at the Arab Summit the Palestinians were recognized and the Palestinian Liberation Organisation (PLO) was established with a $1,100 million grant from Arab states. The PLO was formally created at a conference in Jerusalem in 1965 when the Palestinian Covenant, which called for the destruction of the state of Israel, was adopted. One

Palestinian group, known as Fatah and led by Yasser Arafat, realizing they were not going to get military support from Arab countries, embarked on their own campaign of sabotage and terrorist attacks, in part hoping to provoke an Arab–Israeli war.

Syrian shelling of Israeli settlements and infiltration attacks across the Lebanese and Jordanian borders from bases located in Syria continued. The level of attacks from Jordanian territory became so high that in November 1966 the Israelis mounted their first daytime counter-raid employing both armour and air attack. Syrian shelling intensified in April 1967, and on 7 April, after a particularly heavy attack, the Israeli Air Force was sent in to attack the artillery positions; in the ensuing air battle the Syrians lost six MiG fighters. The precursors of the 1967 war were under way.

The victory in 1967 added to Israel's security problems in that they were now responsible for maintaining law and order in the West Bank and Gaza Strip. However, the threat from the Syrian front was much reduced; apart from the Druse in a number of villages in the north of the Golan the Syrian population had fled, and Syrian artillery was now out of range of Israeli settlements in the Hula Valley.

On the Egyptian front the confrontation along the line of the Suez Canal became known as the War of Attrition. It began within three weeks of the end of the war, on 1 July 1967, with the ambush of an Israeli patrol on the narrow dike east of the Canal, connecting El Qantara with Port Fouad. A number of artillery exchanges took place between July and October. On the 21st, the Israeli naval flagship, the destroyer *Elat*, was sunk by Egyptian missile boats when close to Port Said; the Israelis retaliated by shelling the oil refinery near Suez. On 8 September 1968 the Egyptians initiated a massive artillery bombardment, firing over 10,000 shells at Israeli positions along the whole length of the Canal; again the Israelis retaliated by firing at the Suez refinery. The Egyptians repeated their bombardment on 26 October; this time the Israeli response was a number of commando raids against two Nile bridges, a power transformer between Aswan and Cairo, and the Naj Hammadi Dam.

The Israelis now constructed the Bar-Lev line of fortifications to protect their troops manning positions along the line of the Canal. The war escalated with both sides launching commando raids; in July 1969 the Egyptians surprised an Israeli armoured unit at Port Tawfiq after which the Israelis began to employ their air force in a further escalation. The Israelis carried out large-scale seaborne raids in July and September against the radar sites on Green Island in the Gulf of Suez and Ras Za'afrana 50 km south of Suez; two Egyptian torpedo boats were sunk by frogmen at Ras Sadat. On the night of 25/26 December a helicopter-borne raid captured and flew back to Israel a new low level/long range radar from Ras Gharib, 175 km south of Suez. From January 1970 the Israeli Air Force embarked on a series of raids deep into Egyptian territory.

All this time the Egyptians, with Russian help, were installing a massive air-defence system and initially a proportion of this was manned by as many as 16,000 Russians. The Israelis were also aware that some fighter aircraft were being flown by Russian pilots and deep raids were suspended in order to avoid direct confrontation with Russia. The effectiveness of the SAM belt increased and in July, twenty Israeli aircraft were shot down. On

Moshe Dayan
Palmach, *1941; Commander,
Jerusalem, 1948; Chief of Staff,
1954–8; Minister of Defence,
1967–74; Foreign Minister, 1977–9.*

Ariel Sharon
Platoon Commander, 1948; CO
101 Battalion, 1953; Airborne
Brigade Commander, 1956;
Divisional Commander, 1967 and
1973; Minister of Defence, 1981–3;
Minister for Trade and Industry,
and Housing and Construction,
1984–92; Minister for National
Infrastructure, 1996.

30 July a squadron of Israeli Phantoms attacked a radar site; this provoked a force of MiG-21s to intercept them, but these in turn were attacked by waiting Israeli Mirage fighters which shot down four. The War of Attrition continued until a cease-fire was agreed in August 1970. By then over 300 Israelis had been killed in engagements across the Canal while Egyptians casualties are believed to have been at least 2,000 dead.

Palestinian attacks which had previously been mounted in the West Bank now had to come from Jordan. This, of course, led to Israeli reprisal raids into Jordan. The most serious incident was the Israeli raid on the village of Kerama in March 1968. The Jordanians observed the Israeli preparations, which included the assembly of an airborne brigade and a brigade-sized force of armour in the Jiflik/Jericho area, and to counter the threat they deployed the 1st Infantry Division with a brigade covering each of the three Jordan bridges. The Israelis crossed the Jordan at 5.30 am on the 21st and engaged the Jordanians; an airborne battalion was lifted by helicopter beyond Kerama where they linked up with armoured troops before systematically destroying the village and PLO camp. The Israelis withdrew early that night and both Israelis and Jordanians claimed a victory. As a result the PLO moved their camps further to the east and carried out a large-scale recruiting campaign.

Clashes between the growing Palestinian forces and the Jordanian Army were inevitable and there were frequent incidents between November 1968 and July 1970 when more serious fighting broke out. In September 1970 King Hussein dismissed the civil government and replaced it with a military command bitterly opposed to the Palestinians. In eleven days' fighting the army cleared the PLO from Amman and most other main towns and destroyed a number of their guerrilla camps. The Syrians now took a hand, invading northern Jordan; but their air force, fearful of provoking Israeli intervention, gave their ground forces no air cover and within a week they were driven out by the Jordanians. In October Hafez al Assad seized power in Syria; he continued to actively support the PLO but ensured that they did not mount raids across the armistice line on the Golan Heights. The bulk of the PLO now moved to Lebanon, swelling the number of Palestinian refugees already there; PLO terrorists operated from Lebanon against northern Israel from October 1968 until June 1982. After the murder of members of the Israeli team at the Munich Olympics in 1972 Israel attacked PLO bases in Lebanon by land, sea and air.

Gaza was a hotbed of Palestinian terrorist activity but much of it was aimed as much at keeping control of the local population as against Israelis. General Sharon was now in charge of Southern Command; this included responsibility for Gaza where the Israeli presence was kept to a minimum. He was authorized by Dayan to eliminate the PLO. This was done primarily by intelligence collection leading to the discovery of hidden bunkers, both in the city and in the dense agricultural areas, where the terrorists lived. Undercover squads were deployed, houses in the refugee camps were demolished to create wide roads to make patrolling easier, and the fathers of boys caught throwing stones at soldiers were deported. Between July 1971 and February 1972 Sharon's troops killed 104 terrorists and arrested 742 others.

PLO 'Katyusha' rocket launcher.
(Alain Roth Archive)

Following the 1973 war, United Nations peacekeeping forces were deployed on the Golan Heights and along the Suez Canal in Sinai. Israeli control of the borders with Jordan and Lebanon was tightened so that illegal crossing and the smuggling of arms and explosives into Israel and the West Bank became extremely difficult. The pattern of terrorist attacks on Israel changed: infiltration still took place but the infiltrators were often caught by the army before they could reach their target. This tactic was superseded by the firing of 'Katyushas' at Israeli border settlements. These were short-range rockets with little accuracy normally fired singly from simple and easily hidden launchers. Israel retaliated with air raids and coastal shelling.

The Lebanese civil war from April 1975 to October 1976 was primarily a struggle between the Christian and Muslim communities but it also involved the Palestinians whose armed groups were seen as a counterweight to the predominantly Christian-led Lebanese Army. The war weakened the authority of the government and enhanced the position of the Palestinians; at the same time Syria much increased its influence by first intervening unilaterally and later as part of the Arab peacekeeping force. Syrian troops remained in some strength in Lebanon after the other Arab contingents withdrew.

In March 1978, following a seaborne PLO raid into Israel which resulted in the deaths of thirty-seven Israelis, the Israelis mounted an invasion of south Lebanon, codenamed Operation 'Litani', which occupied the country as far north as the Litani River. The Israelis finally

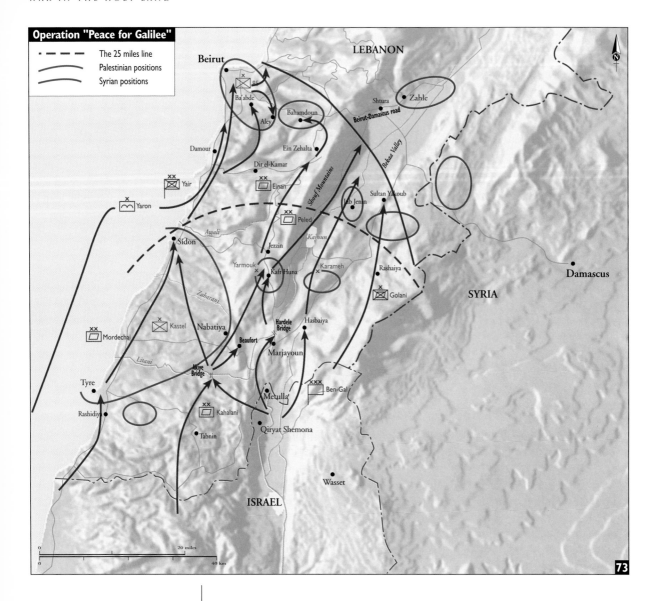

Operation "Peace for Galilee"

- – – – – The 25 miles line
- ───── Palestinian positions
- ───── Syrian positions

LEBANON

Beirut

Ba'abde

Aley

Bahamdoun

Shtura • Zahle

Damour

Ein Zehalta

Beirut-Damascus road

Dir el-Kamar

Einan

Bekaa Valley

Yair

Yaron

Shouf Mountains

Peled

Ifb Jenin

Sultan Yakoub

Awali

Sidon

Jezzin

Karoun

Yarmouk

Kaft Huna

Karameh

Rashaiya

Damascus

SYRIA

Zaharani

Golani

Kastel   Nabatiya

Hardele Bridge   Hasbaiya

Mordechai

Beaufort

Marjayoun

Litani

Akiye Bridge

Tyre

Ben-Gal

Metulla

Rashidiy

Kahalani

Tabnin

Qiryat Shemona

Wasset

ISRAEL

20 miles

40 km

73

withdrew by 13 June after a UN peacekeeping force (UNIFIL) had been deployed. However, the UN were not allowed right up to the Israeli border and a security zone between 5 and 15 km wide was established and policed by the paramilitary force of Major Saad Haddad with Israeli support. This force is now known as the South Lebanese Army.

In 1978 the Egyptian President, Anwar Sadat, made his historic visit to Jerusalem which initiated the peace process and led to the Egyptian–Israeli Peace Treaty, described in the next section.

Palestinian attacks on Israel, despite the much-increased military activity along the border with Lebanon, continued until a cease-fire was arranged in July 1981. The Israelis were determined to destroy the PLO as a force in Lebanon and the Defence Minister, Arik Sharon, actively prepared for an invasion while waiting for an excuse to launch it. The opportunity came with the attempted assassination of the Israeli ambassador in London. The Israelis mounted a series of air raids against PLO targets in Lebanon, and as expected the Palestinians retaliated with artillery and rocket fire. The Israeli invasion, which began on 6 June 1982, was then authorized by the cabinet.

Operation 'Peace for Galilee' has been described as Israel's only non-defensive war; its official aim was to clear an area so that Israeli settlements were no longer within range of PLO artillery. This was taken, though not explicitly stated, to mean a strip of land 40 km wide north of the border. Sharon, whose other aim was to force the Syrians out of Lebanon, kept changing the Israeli plan, and has been accused of misleading the government and even the General Staff as to his intentions. (In November 1997 Sharon lost a libel suit when the Supreme Court ruled it was true that he had deceived the Prime Minister over the war's aims.) The 40 km line was swiftly reached along the coast and in the centre but to the east the Syrians in the Bekaa Valley refused Israel's demands to order the PLO behind their lines to pull back and to withdraw Syrian reinforcements which included SAM batteries. Clashes with the Syrians were inevitable, and eventually some 70 Syrian aircraft were shot down and 19 SAM batteries were destroyed. The Israelis reached Beirut and laid siege to the western part of the city, where the PLO was concentrated, while being welcomed by the Christians in the north and east. Palestinian bases and offices were destroyed and a vast amount of military hardware captured. A cease-fire was agreed with the Syrians on 11 June after heavy tank fighting in the Bekaa, but the PLO went on fighting. Finally, on 12 August a cease-fire was arranged and the Palestinians agreed to leave Lebanon; their withdrawal began on the 21st and by the 30th over 7,000 Palestinian fighters had left for other Arab countries. As the PLO left two new enemies of the Israelis emerged in Lebanon: first, the mainly Shiite population in the south backed by the Amal faction, and a new force, the *Hizbullah* ('Party of God'), formed round a core of Iranians whom the Syrians allowed to establish themselves in Baalbek.

The Israeli Army remained in Lebanon for over two years, until May 1985, despite reaching an agreement with the Lebanese government in May 1983; the invasion had cost the Israeli Defence Force over 500 lives. During this time it was engaged in a guerrilla war with Lebanese factions who saw the Israelis as an occupying rather than a liberation force. The experience further reduced the IDF's image as a confident offensive force as its morale and tactical ability were both shaken by the operational situation for which it was not prepared. The massacre carried out by Christian Lebanese Phalangists at the Sabra and Shatilla Palestinian refugee camps led to an Israeli Committee of Inquiry which strongly criticized Arik Sharon, General Eitan, the Chief of Staff, and other Israeli generals. Eventually Sharon moved from the defence post to another in the cabinet. In retrospect he has been blamed for the conduct of the war which he managed to direct personally by ensuring there was no contact between the political and military elements of the government other than through himself. While the war achieved the removal of the PLO from Lebanon and lifted the threat to northern Israel, it did nothing to help solve the Palestinian issue nor did it reduce Syria's influence in Lebanon; on the contrary, it had been strengthened.

December 1987 saw the start of the *Intifada* or uprising, a home-grown Palestinian movement in the West Bank and Gaza, which had its origins in the Palestinian belief that they had been abandoned by the Arab world, as illustrated by the dropping of the Palestinian problem from the agenda for the Arab Summit at Amman; there was also an increasing disenchantment with the PLO and the Palestinian Diaspora. During 1987 there had been a growing pattern of civil disturbance: the numbers of demonstrations and riots, and incidents of stone-throwing and tyre-burning all increased by over 100 per cent compared with the previous year. At roughly the same time a new clandestine organization, the Islamic Jihad, was formed; this was dedicated both to Islamic revival and to the destruction of Israel. The Palestinians were encouraged by the action of a Palestinian fighter who crossed the Israeli/Lebanese border by hang-glider in November 1987; landing near an army camp whose guards he surprised, he killed six Israeli soldiers before himself being killed. The first riot was sparked off by a traffic accident in the Gaza Strip when an Israeli lorry killed four Palestinians. The Israeli army was caught unprepared; they were untrained, ill-equipped, and to some extent unwilling to cope with the mass of demonstrations and the constant harassment they had to withstand. Mistakes were made and the army was pilloried by the international press and media. The Palestinians confined themselves to civil disturbance including stone-throwing and burning tyres in the street; in the first year of the *Intifada* only twenty attacks on Israelis involving the use of firearms were recorded. On the other hand in the same period over 300 Palestinians were killed and about 8,000 wounded. The generals soon realized that there was no military solution to the *Intifada* and that a political solution must be found. Shortly after the start of the *Intifada* a new Palestinian Islamic extremist organization, Harakat al-Muqawana al Islamiyya (*Hamas*), based mainly in Gaza, emerged and increasingly rivalled the PLO for control of the Palestinians of the West Bank and Gaza. In addition to its military wing, *Hamas* was active in many fields such as health and education and so gained considerable local support. Israeli extremists did not remain inactive during the *Intifada* and a number of reprisal attacks, normally involving the smashing of car windscreens, and some shootings took place. The *Intifada* opened Israeli eyes to the fact that the occupation of Gaza and the West Bank could not continue forever.

Israel did not form part of the coalition formed to liberate Kuwait after its invasion by Iraq in 1990. During the war Iraq, in an attempt to provoke Israel into attacking it (and thus splitting the coalition), launched thirty-nine Scud missiles at targets in Israel. No one was killed in these attacks but over a hundred people were injured and three died of heart attacks. No chemical warfare (CW) warheads were fired although it is now known that Iraq had such warheads; had they been employed Israel would undoubtedly have reacted extremely strongly, and it seems likely that Iraq was deterred from their use by Israel's nuclear capability. Whether this augurs well for the possible future use of CW missile warheads against Israel remains to be seen.

Palestinian Terrorist Organisations

PLO Radicals:
Popular Front for the Liberation of Palestine (George Habash) based in Syria.
Democratic Front for the Liberation of Palestine (Naif Hawatmeh) Syria.
Arab Liberation Front (Abdul Rahim Ahmed) Iraq.
Palestine Liberation Front (Mohammed Abbas) Iraq.

Opposed to the PLO
Fatah Revolutionary Council (Abu Nidal) based in Libya.
Popular Front for the Liberation of Palestine General Command (Ahmed Jebril) Syria.
Popular Struggle Front (Samir Gosheh) Syria.
Saiqa (al-Khadi) Syria.
Fatah Dissidents (Abu Musa) Syria/Lebanon

Violent clashes continued (and still do) on Israel's northern border where a security zone north of the border in Lebanon was established, controlled by the South Lebanese Army backed by a permanent Israeli military presence. On two occasions when the level of attacks on Israel became unacceptable, and in an effort not to repeat the trauma of the 1982 invasion, Israel carried out massive air and artillery attacks intended to neutralize the area from which most of the attacks were mounted. In July 1993 over 250,000 Lebanese were forced from their homes by the ferocity of the Israeli artillery, aircraft and naval gunfire attacks. In April 1996, only weeks before the Israeli elections, and after the sixth and heaviest rocket attack on northern Israel by *Hizbullah*, the Israelis launched massive reprisal raids. This time some 200,000 villagers fled from their homes in south-western Lebanon, north of the security zone. *Hizbullah* targets across the country were attacked, including helicopter gunship raids on offices in Beirut. After a week of bombardment an agreement was brokered by the US between Israel and the *Hizbullah*; in return for Israeli guarantees not to attack civilian targets, *Hizbullah* would not fire into Israel; attacks on Israeli troops in Lebanon, however, were permitted.

By 1993 the Palestinian peace process was well under way but it was opposed by extremists on both sides. On 25 February 1994 a Jewish extremist settler from Qyriat Arba shot dead thirty Arabs who were praying in the mosque at Abraham's tomb in Hebron. The Israeli government outlawed two fanatical groups, Kach and Kahane Chai. *Hamas* promised there would be five reprisal attacks: by November they had killed thirty-eight Israelis in four bomb attacks, including three by suicide bombers. On 4 November 1995 the Israeli Prime Minister, Yitzhak Rabin, was assassinated by an ultra right-wing Israeli; his successor, Shimon Peres, saw a massive swing to his Labour Party and so advanced the date of the election from late October to May 1996. *Hamas* reacted violently to the murder of their leading bomb-maker, Yehiya Ayash, known as the 'engineer', who was killed by a bomb planted in his mobile telephone. Suicide bombers killed fifty-eight Israelis in four suicide bomb attacks in February and March, which in turn caused the Israeli electorate to vote for the Likud leader, Benjamin Netanyahu.

Israel now has peace treaties with Jordan, one with Syria will follow eventually, and the Palestinian issue must be settled. Whether this will bring peace to the Holy Land is not certain. Iran and Iraq still remain implacably opposed to the state of Israel and both are known to have ambitions of acquiring nuclear, chemical and biological weapons and the long-range missiles with which to deliver them. Whatever arrangements are reached over a Palestinian state there will always be a hard-line group that will not accept less than the full recovery of Palestine for the Palestinians; terrorism will continue to be a threat. In Israel the differences between the religious and the secular communities widen each year and, as they disagree on the way forward for peace with their Arab neighbours, there may not be peace even within Israel.

THE 1956 SINAI CAMPAIGN

In mid-1955 Fedayeen attacks on southern Israel intensified. By then Israel had realized that these were not spontaneous incidents but part of the

Arab campaign against Israel which included economic sanctions and the closing of the Suez Canal to Israeli shipping. After the successful Israeli retaliation raid on Khan Yunis on 31 August Nasser called off Fedayeen attacks from Gaza while instructing that they should be increased from Jordan, Lebanon and Syria. He also tightened the blockade of the Straits of Tiran and closed Gulf of Aqaba airspace to Israeli civil aircraft.

In September 1955 the Israelis learnt that the Egyptians were to be supplied with arms by Czechoslovakia; these would include over 100 MiG-15 fighters, about 50 Ilyushin-28 bombers and over 200 tanks. The Israelis believed it would take the Egyptians up to six months to absorb these new weapons, and there was a growing body of opinion, led by Dayan, that the Egyptian Army must be destroyed before it became too powerful. In October Syria and Egypt signed a mutual defence pact, with Egypt leading the joint command.

Towards the end of 1955 Israel had managed to persuade France to sell it a substantial quantity of arms after the US had refused to do so. In April 1956 the first Mystère IV fighters were delivered, followed by large numbers of tanks (380 by October), APCs and anti-tank weapons. By the spring of 1956 the French had decided that the only way they could defeat the Algerians was for President Nasser to be overthrown, and they began to consider the possibility of an attack on Egypt involving the Israelis; this possibility led to French willingness to supply even more arms to Israel.

In December the Egyptians in the Gaza Strip began sniping at Israeli patrols across the border and this continued until 2 April 1956 when an Israeli patrol was ambushed on their own side of the border. On the 4th another patrol was fired at from several Egyptian positions, killing three Israelis. Next day, after an exchange of small-arms fire, the Israelis mortared and then shelled Egyptian positions; the Egyptians responded by mortaring four Israeli kibbutzim. Very soon afterwards the Israelis shelled the centre of Gaza, killing 58 civilians and wounding 100.

Israel expected to see an increase in Fedayeen attacks from other Arab countries as retaliation for the shelling of Gaza, but Nasser had decided to attack from Gaza. Some 200 Fedayeen, organized into squads of between four and seven men, were given targets in southern Israel stretching from Qiryat Gat to Beersheba to Kibbutz Gevulot, and were told that Nasser expected 60 Israelis and 100 to be wounded. The raids began on 7 April and were over by the 12th after the Fedayeen had lost 16 dead and 5 captured. The Fedayeen made no distinction between military and civilians: the worst atrocity was the attack on children in the school at Moshav Shafir. In all, 11 Israelis had been killed and 49 wounded.

In July the US had decided not to finance the construction of the Aswan High Dam and the British had also pulled out of the project. Within a week, Nasser had nationalized the Suez Canal and was on a collision course with France and the UK. France and Britain agreed a plan in which an Israeli attack on Egypt would act as a trigger for them to land at Port Said, ostensibly to protect the Canal for international shipping. The plans were finally agreed at a conference held at Sèvres on 21 October and attended by the French and Israeli Prime Ministers and the British Foreign Secretary. The plan was for the Israeli invasion to start as if it were purely a retaliatory attack and could be halted if the French and British landing

---

Egyptian Order of Battle

C-in-C: Gen. Abd el Hakim Amer
Sinai Command: Maj.-Gen. Ali Amer
3rd Infantry Division
4th, 5th, 6th Brigades
8th Palestinian Division
86th, 87th Frontier Brigades
26th National Guard Brigade
4th Armoured Division
1st, 2nd Armoured Groups
2nd Infantry Brigade

50,000 men committed
500 tanks and assault guns
200 APCs
500 artillery pieces
255 combat aircraft

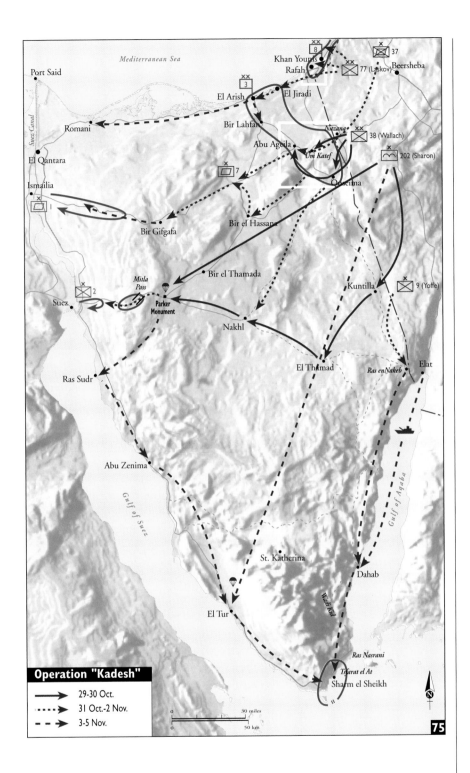

Operation "Kadesh"

→ 29-30 Oct.
┄┄▸ 31 Oct.-2 Nov.
╌╌▸ 3-5 Nov.

0   30 miles
0   50 km

75

failed to materialize. The timing was thought to be right as the US was then in the middle of a Presidential election and the Soviet Union was concerned with the popular liberation movements in Hungary and Poland.

The Israelis mounted an attack on the Jordanian police fort at Qalqilya on 10 October following the murder of two Israeli farmers; this raid and the subsequent tension between Israel and Jordan served as a cover for the Israeli mobilization for the Sinai campaign. Israel's aims for the campaign were threefold: to remove the Egyptian threat by destroying its army in Sinai; to destroy the Fedayeen organization; and to open the Straits of Tiran.

Egyptian forces in Sinai consisted of two infantry divisions: the 8th Palestinian Division, manned by Palestinians but officered by Egyptians, was deployed in the Gaza Strip, and the 3rd Division, with brigades located at El Arish, Abu Ageila and Quseima. In addition, there was a brigade east of Suez, to the west of the Mitla Pass, two infantry battalions garrisoned Sharm el Sheikh, and an armoured brigade was based at Bir Gifgafa. The Israelis had mobilized six infantry, one parachute, two mechanized and one armoured brigade for the attack.

The campaign began on 29 October, with a parachute drop of one battalion at the eastern end of the Mitla Pass in central Sinai; a second airlift dropped anti-tank guns, mortars and jeeps to the battalion. The remainder of the 202nd Airborne Brigade, commanded by Colonel Sharon, had to cover 100 km from its assembly area at Ein Khussub, where it could be seen as threatening Jordan, to link up with the battalion at the Mitla. It crossed the border at Kuntilla where the Egyptian garrison immediately withdrew; at Bir el Thamada Sharon attacked at dawn on the 30th and took the position after a 40-minute battle. The last position to be taken before linking up was at Nakhl, which fell at 5 pm after an artillery bombardment; the paratroops linked up at 10.30 pm. The Egyptians sent forward one of the Suez Brigade's battalions into the Mitla where, after losing many vehicles to Israeli air attack, it established itself in caves on either side of the pass. Sharon's task was to block Egyptian movement through the Mitla Pass; he was refused permission to move through the pass as all air support was needed for the main battle but he was allowed by Dayan to send a patrol through. The 'patrol' comprised two companies plus tanks, heavy mortars and artillery. It soon came under fire from the Egyptians in the caves and was held up, suffering casualties, and its mortars and artillery came under air attack. They were pinned down under fire for seven hours. Eventually the Egyptians in the caves either withdrew or were eliminated by a second battalion which had to fight its way along the high ground on either side of the pass.

The main Israeli attack was launched by the 38th Ugda (Divisional Group), comprising the 7th Armoured and 4th and 10th Infantry Brigades, with the aim of clearing the Egyptian defences at Abu Ageila and Quseima so as to open up the central axis into Sinai. On the evening of 29 October the 4th Brigade crossed the frontier to advance on Quseima. The heavy going meant that the assault could only be made early next morning; as Quseima fell the 7th Brigade, which was being held back for the attack on Um-Katef, arrived to ensure the first phase was swiftly completed. The plans were now changed and a battle group of the 7th was sent to test the southern approach to Um Katef which was found to be strongly held. Another battle group manoeuvred to the west seeking a better and less defended approach and found the Daika Pass; this narrow defile required engineer work before it could be crossed and then only by tracked vehicles. The armour advanced and found itself on the Egyptians' main supply route; they were ordered to attack Abu Ageila while a third armoured battle group was sent to block the Bir Hasana road to the

---

Israeli Order of Battle

Chief of Staff: Maj.-Gen. Moshe Dayan
Southern Command: Brig.-Gen. Assaf Simhoni
  77th Ugda (Divisional Group)
1st, 11th Infantry Brigades
27th Mechanised Brigade
  38th Ugda
4th, 10th Infantry Brigades
7th Armoured Brigade

202 Parachute Brigade
9th Infantry Brigade
12th Infantry Brigade
45,000 men committed
400 tanks
450 half-tracks
150 artillery pieces
155 combat aircraft.

south-west. An attack on Um Katef was now essential as this was the only way for resupply to reach the armour which had crossed the Daika Pass.

The 10th Brigade attacked on the evening of the 30th, first taking the outposts at Auja Masri and Tarat Um-Basis before advancing on Um-Katef. An armoured attack was made on the heavily defended Egyptian base of Abu Ageila at first light on the 31st, but it had lost surprise and came under heavy fire when still 3 km away. The infantry, in half-tracks, pressed on covered by tank fire and the position fell within the hour. A number of Egyptian counter-attacks were repulsed with the help of air support. The first battle group, still dug in south of Um Katef, was now ordered to block the approach of a strong Egyptian armoured force advancing from Bir Gifgafa but this had already been attacked by the Israeli Air Force and had turned back. The armoured force pursued them until they had crossed the Canal and halted 16 km beyond it.

The Israeli armour now at Abu Ageila was ordered to attack the Ruefa Dam, a strongly held position to the south-east, and it came under heavy anti-tank fire. The Israelis pressed on even though many had no ammunition except hand-grenades, and overran the Egyptian position in the dark, crushing many of the posts with their tracks. Next morning, 1 November, the 10th Brigade made two attempts to take the Um-Katef-Um-Shihan position and an attack by the 37th Mechanized Brigade, which had been held in reserve, was also repulsed. That night the Egyptians slipped away before they could be cut off, and their positions were found abandoned next morning.

To the north Ugda 77, commanded by Brigadier-General Laskov, had the task of taking Rafah and clearing the Gaza Strip. It started its advance on the night of 30/31 October with a battalion of the 'Golani' Brigade crossing, on foot, the minefields south of Rafah; another battalion crossing in vehicles struck mines, blocked the route, and also had to cross on foot. By 5.30 am the battalion had captured the southernmost position on the road to Nizzana and then joined the leading battalion to assault three positions protecting the Rafah road junction; after taking these the Israelis dug in and waited for the tank force to move forward. To the north the other two Golani battalions had attacked and taken positions south of the El Arish–Gaza road and further north the motorized battalion of the 27th Armoured Brigade had taken the most northerly positions astride the main road.

The remainder of the 27th Brigade now crossed the minefield breached by the Golanis at 10 am before turning south towards El Arish. They met resistance at El Jiradi which they attacked from the south after outflanking it. The brigade spent the night concentrating 5 km north of El Arish and in the morning found that the Egyptians had evacuated the town following the Anglo-French air raids on Egyptian air-bases. Held up only by the large numbers of vehicles destroyed in air attacks or abandoned by the roadside, the 27th Brigade reached Romani and halted 16 km from the Canal. Patrols from the 27th and 7th Armoured Brigades and the 202nd Airborne Brigade established contact across the Sinai front.

Dayan now ordered the final phases of the Israeli operation, the clearing of the Gaza Strip and the advance to Sharm el Sheikh, to begin. The Gaza task was allotted to the 11th Infantry Brigade, supported by a

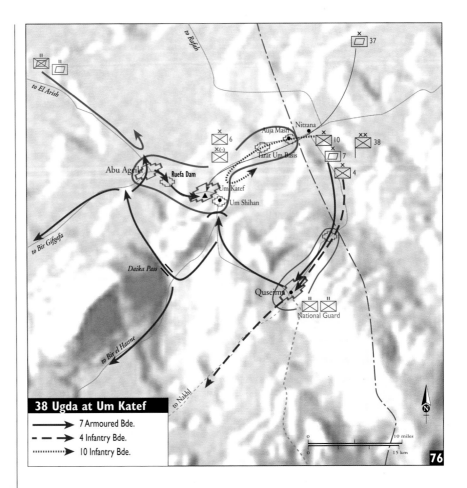

38 Ugda at Um Katef

→ 7 Armoured Bde.
--→ 4 Infantry Bde.
·····→ 10 Infantry Bde.

combat team from the 37th Brigade, which broke through the defences on the Ali Montar Ridge at 6 am on 2 November. An infantry battalion entered the city to mop up resistance and the city surrendered at midday. The brigade then moved south to Khan Yunis where the 86th Palestinian Brigade now found itself sandwiched between the 11th and the 'Golanis'; the Palestinians continued to fight and it was not until 1.30 pm on the 3rd that Khan Yunis was cleared.

In the far south operations had begun on the evening of 29 October when the reconnaissance company of the 9th Infantry Brigade, commanded by Colonel Yoffe, captured the police fort and the important road junction at Ras en Naqb. The remainder of the brigade then set out from Elat, taking a wide northerly route so as not to reveal Israeli intentions, to join the recce company at Ras en Naqb. The brigade began its 240 km cross-country advance to Sharm el Sheikh on 2 November, reaching the coastal oasis of Dahab on the 3rd where they fought a section of the camel-mounted Frontier Force before being resupplied and refuelled from a landing ship sent from Elat.

Advancing down the narrow Wadi Kid, where they met some slight opposition, the brigade reached Ras Nasrani by midday on the 3rd to find the heavily fortified position there had been abandoned. Elements of Sharon's 202nd Brigade were close by, having advanced down the Gulf of Suez coast after being parachuted in at El-Tur; they had halted 25 km north of Sharm el Sheikh. The outer defences of Sharm at Tsfarat el At fell to the 9th's reconnaissance company during the afternoon of the 4th after an Israeli air attack, but the first attack on Sharm itself, made from the west in the dark, was repulsed with losses. At 5.30 am another attack was launched from both west and east of the town and by 9.30 the fighting was over and the coastal guns which had dominated the Straits were destroyed. The war had cost Israel 189 lives and 900 men wounded; Egyptian losses from Israeli action were about 1,000 killed, 4,000 wounded and 6,000 taken prisoner.

The British and French operations had been postponed and they did not land at Port Said until 6 November, preceded by parachute drops the day before, a week after the first air strikes had taken place. The British had not penetrated more than 37 km down the Canal, to just south of El Cap, when the force of political pressure from Russia, the US and the UN caused the British to agree to a cease-fire from midnight on the 6th, which the French had no option but to join. United Nations observers arrived to monitor the front line on 12 November and the first Danish peacekeeping troops deployed, taking over the forward positions, on the 30th; French and British troops completed their withdrawal from the Canal Zone on 22 December.

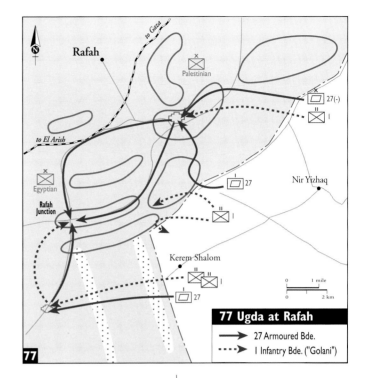

77 Ugda at Rafah

→ 27 Armoured Bde.
┈┈▶ I Infantry Bde. ("Golani")

The armistice between Israel and Egypt required the withdrawal of all Israeli troops from Sinai, as the United Nations deployed a peacekeeping force (United Nations Expeditionary Force (UNEF)). UNEF was to occupy both Gaza and Sharm el Sheikh but in the event they were unable to control Gaza and so withdrew, contenting themselves with patrolling its border. The Israelis withdrew from Sinai in stages. The first stage, completed by 8 January 1957, was to a line from Abu Ageila–Quseima–Ras Mohammed (the tip of the peninsula). El Arish was evacuated a week later and, with the exception of the west coast of the Gulf of Aqaba and Gaza, the withdrawal was complete by 22 January. Israel withdrew from Sharm el Sheikh and Gaza, after UNEF had deployed there, on 8 March 1957.

JUNE 1967: INTRODUCTION TO THE SIX DAY WAR

While the immediate causes of the 'Six Day War' were actions taken by Egypt (then known as the United Arab Republic), in particular the demand for the withdrawal of the United Nations Emergency Force (UNEF) and the blockade of the Straits of Tiran at the southern end of the Gulf of Aqaba to both Israeli and Israeli-bound shipping, tension between Israel and its Arab neighbours had been mounting for some time. The presence of UNEF on the Sinai border and the Gaza Strip ensured there was no direct confrontation between Israeli and Egyptian forces but Palestinian attacks were mounted from both the Waest Bank and Lebanon and there were a number of incidents involving Syria. Attempts by Syria to divert the sources of the Jordan led to Israeli artillery and tanks shelling the construction sites and in November 1964 there was an air attack. In November 1966 the level of raids from Jordanian-held territory was such as to provoke the Israelis into launching their first daytime reprisal raid employing both armour and air support against the village of al Samu in the Hebron Hills. In April 1967 Syrian artillery shelling of border settlements increased until on the 7th the Israeli Air Force engaged the artillery positions; in the ensuing dogfight six Syrian aircraft were shot down.

On 16 May the Egyptians demanded that UNEF leave its border posts and concentrate in its camps, and on the 17th the Egyptian Army began its build-up in Sinai and had concentrated seven divisions with a thousand tanks there by the 20th. Israel and the other Arab armies mobilized. The UN Secretary General agreed to withdraw UNEF troops on the 19th but insisted on a complete withdrawal. On the 22nd the closing of the Gulf of Aqaba was announced by President Nasser. Israel initially waited for the international community to assemble a naval task force to ensure Israeli access to the Gulf of Aqaba but it soon became clear that this would not materialize. Israel also lost the support of France, its main arms supplier. On 30 May King Hussein returned from a reconciliatory visit to Egypt where he signed a defence agreement and agreed to the appointment of an Egyptian general to command Arab forces in Jordan. Two Egyptian commando battalions were flown to Jordan and took up positions in the West Bank.

Israel formed a government of National Unity which appointed Moshe Dayan as Defence Minister and included Menachem Begin in the cabinet. The Israelis launched a series of pre-emptive air strikes on the morning of 5 June. The first wave took off at 7 am to strike four targets in Sinai, three more close to the Suez Canal, and Cairo West airport. Further Egyptian targets were attacked during the day, as were Syrian and Jordanian air bases and the Iraqi airfield at H-3, after raids had been carried out over Israel by these three air forces. The Egyptian Air Force lost 309 out of a total of 340 combat aircraft plus transports and helicopters. By evening the Jordanian Air Force had been eliminated, while Syria had lost over sixty aircraft (or two-thirds of its force) and the Iraqis had lost their planes at H-3. In all the Israelis lost twenty-six aircraft in these raids. Israeli armoured forces crossed the border into Sinai at about 8 am.

The battles to capture Jerusalem, the Golan Heights and the Sinai peninsula are described in the following pages; fighting also took place in the Gaza Strip and in the West Bank, opposite Israel's narrow waist and in the north. The task of guarding the 15 km between Tulkarm and Netanya was the responsibility of Central Command's 'Givati' Brigade. They were facing the Jordanian 1st Infantry Brigade which occupied the hills east of Tulkarm and Qalqilya; the 25th Jordanian Infantry Brigade was deployed around Jenin. On 5 June the Jordanians kept moving their few tanks so

Remains of an Egyptian coastal gun at Ras Nassrani, guarding the Straits of Tiran.

that there appeared to be many more; the Israelis remained on the defensive despite the heavy artillery fire which fell on their positions. The 'Givati' Brigade was finally authorized to attack at midday on the 6th and its first task was to take the strong position at Suppin; from there it was only allowed as far east as Azun so as to not to clash with the forces moving on Nablus.

North of Jenin Israel's Northern Command had positioned an armoured division. When the expected Jordanian and Syrian tank attacks did not materialize, this division was ordered, during the afternoon of the 5th, to attack with the aim of neutralizing the artillery in the Dotan Valley (Emeq Dotan) which was shelling the Ramat David airfield. The attack successfully overran the artillery positions and moved on to Qabatiya Junction, cutting off Jenin from Nablus. Jordanian armour counter-attacked and was routed after a night tank battle. An infantry brigade with tank support entered Jenin from the south. Another Jordanian

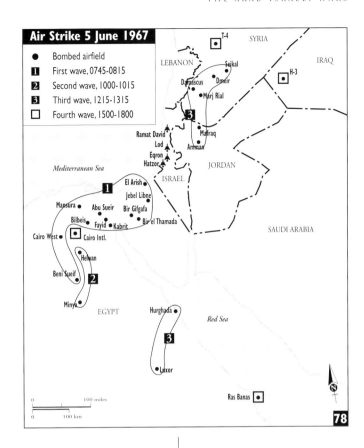

tank force was reported advancing from Tubas; leaving the infantry to complete the capture of Jenin the Israeli armour returned to Qabatiya to engage this force in fighting that lasted twelve hours. The Israelis sent another armoured brigade east of Mount Gilboa which broke through at Tilfit but was then held up by Jordanian tanks at Zababida until nightfall when they took first Aqaba and then Tubas. Leaving the main part of the brigade to cover the road to the Damiya Bridge, the brigade commander pushed forward to Nablus where they were at first mistaken for Iraqis; the 'Golani' Brigade managed to take the city by the evening of the 6th while the armour was engaging the Jordanian tanks which had been deployed to the west of the city.

The Gaza Strip, the Egyptian-occupied region of Palestine, is 40 km long and 13 km wide and was defended by three Palestinian infantry brigades armed by the Egyptians. A parachute brigade supported by armour following up the initial Israeli breakthrough took Khan Yunis and turned north up the coast towards Gaza; by that evening they had reached the Ali Montar Ridge. At the same time Israeli infantry attacked Gaza from the west, which was taken on the 6th, and the whole Strip was under Israeli control by early on the 7th.

A major factor in the Israeli victory was the information policy followed by both sides. The Egyptians kept news of their defeats, particularly the loss of their air force, secret and broadcast false claims of success which led to their allies making unwise decisions. The Israelis also deliberately kept quiet about their speedy success which probably led to the failure of the Soviet Union to influence the outcome of the war.

The Israelis had won an outstanding victory, due in the main to good leadership, the speed of decision making and action, good intelligence and courage, which ensured the momentum of the attack was maintained despite heavy casualties. Of course the achievement of total air domination played a major part. With hindsight a number of observers have suggested that the ease of the Israeli victory resulted in over-confidence and serious mistakes resulting in Israeli setbacks in the early days of the 1973 Yom Kippur War.

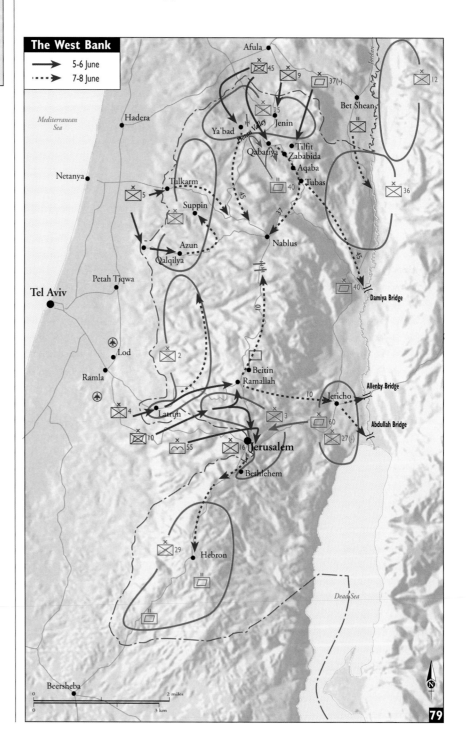

THE CAPTURE OF THE OLD CITY

The capture of Jerusalem had no strategic value. Indeed, before the 1967 war began the regional commander was instructed to remain on the defensive and not initiate any attacks; it had, of course, immense political significance. Jerusalem was the responsibility of Israel's Central Command led by Major-General Uzi Narkiss. The forces available to him at the start of the war were the Jerusalem Brigade, which was deployed mainly along the dividing line but with two battalions and a tank company held in reserve; Colonel Yotvat's Brigade, which was deployed west of Latrun; and the 10th 'Harel' Armoured Brigade with fifty 1940-vintage Sherman tanks, which was the Command Reserve and was concentrated in the Ben-Shemen woods, close to Lod. Jerusalem was surrounded on three sides by Jordanian-held territory and on the fourth, the western, side the main road ran perilously close to positions on high ground just over the 'green' line. At the entrance to the Jerusalem corridor the Jordanians held a strong position at Latrun. There were four Jordanian infantry brigades which could operate against Jerusalem: one just north of Latrun poised to cut the Tel Aviv road, one in East Jerusalem, one to the south around Hebron, and one in reserve west of Jericho. There was also an armoured brigade in the Jordan Valley near Jericho.

The war began on 5 June with Israeli air raids on the Egyptian Air Force starting at 7.45 am; the first shots were fired in Jerusalem by the Jordanians at about 10.45 am, close to the Italian Hospital and later at the Israeli position on Mount Zion. The first Israeli action was to seek a cease-fire through the Military Armistice Commission and by 10.30 am King Hussein had received a message transmitted by the UN Chief Observer, General Od Bull, from the Israeli Foreign Minister saying: 'We are in thick of a defensive war in the Egyptian sector. We shall take no action against Jordan unless Jordan attacks us first. Should Jordan attack Israel, we shall direct all our might against her.' The king rejected the warning, as fighting had already begun and Jordanian bombers had taken off. Since then he has said he knew he would lose but had no alternative but to join the Arab assault.

Jordanian attacks were expected against the Mount Scopus enclave, which lay less than 2 km from the dividing line, and Mevaseret Yerushalayim, a small settlement about 6 km west of Jerusalem close to the Tel Aviv road but dominated by the Jordanian position at Sheikh Abdul Aziz. In fact the first Jordanian attack was made on the demilitarized zone at Ra's Maqabir, the 'Hill of Evil Counsel' where the United Nations had set up their headquarters in Government House, which they occupied at about 1 pm. The Jerusalem Brigade prepared to take the hill but there was uncertainty over whether offensive action was authorized or not; it had not been, but by the time this point had been confirmed the Jerusalem Brigade had captured the compound and evacuated the UN staff there.

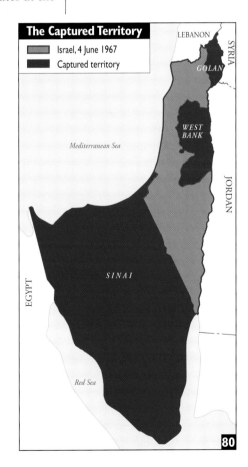

The Captured Territory

Israel, 4 June 1967

Captured territory

LEBANON
SYRIA
GOLAN
WEST BANK
Mediterranean Sea
JORDAN
EGYPT
SINAI
Red Sea

80

Relative Strengths

Tanks:

Egypt 1,300
Jordan 290
Syria 750
Arab Total: 2,340
Israel: 1,000

APC/Half-tracks:

Egypt 1,050
Jordan 210
Syria 580
Arab Total: 1,840
Israel: 1,500

Artillery

Egypt 575
Jordan 260
Syria 315
Arab Total: 1,150
Israel: 200

Combat Aircraft:

Egypt 430
Jordan 20
Syria 125
Iraq 105
Arab Total: 680
Israel: 285

To forestall an attack on Mount Scopus it was planned to block the Jordanians by occupying the high ground at Tel el Ful, 6 km north of the Old City, and the 10th Brigade was ordered forward to the Ma'ale ha Hamisha Forest while authority from general headquarters was obtained. The plan was now modified to include using part of the Jerusalem Brigade to attack a Jordanian strongpoint in Sheikh Jarrach on the northern edge of the city. At this stage GHQ allocated one battalion of the 55th Parachute Brigade, later allotting the whole brigade commanded by Colonel Motta Gur, to Central Command and authorized the attack on Sheikh Jarrach. The commander of the 10th Brigade was briefed on his task, which now included taking Abdul Aziz and 'Radar', a hill where three radar sets were sited, surrounded by defensive positions, and which lay just north of the 'green' line between Ma'ale ha Hamisha and Bidu, en route to Tel el Ful. The attack on Sheikh Jarrach now fell to the 55th Parachute Brigade who would then reinforce Mount Scopus, and they were warned also to be ready to storm the Old City even though this had never been included in any contingency plan.

Shortly after 3 pm on the 5th, the attack on Government House went in and drove the Jordanians out. Beyond the compound was a feature known as the 'sausage', through which the only road to Bethlehem and Hebron ran; taking this would cut the West Bank in two and permission to take the feature was given. It fell after a short, hard fight leaving thirty Jordanians dead. At 4.15 pm came the order to take the village of Sur Baher and the 'bell' strongpoint, south of the UN compound. This was the first operation over the 'green line' to be authorized and a battalion set out on foot from its reserve position at Mount Hertzl, 6 km away. However, 'bell' was taken by armoured troops moving on from 'sausage' but who moved back to the UN Compound once the infantry had arrived and consolidated to block the road to the south.

The move forward of the 10th Brigade had not gone smoothly: no one had remembered to close the road to civilian traffic and this caused delays as did Jordanian artillery fire which resulted in both vehicle and personnel casualties. Nevertheless, four hours after leaving the assembly area, the brigade crossed the 'green' line at 5.30 pm. It advanced on three axes. The western axis led to the radars and two of the positions had been taken by 7.30 pm, but mines caused both casualties and delay and the third radar post was only taken with the help of the infantry, which had been defending Ma'ale ha Hamisha, at 1.30 am on the 6th. On the centre axis the Israelis were heavily shelled and the two strongholds on it could only be taken by dismounting and fighting on foot, then the minefield had to be cleared before the half-tracks could come forward. Hirbet el Lauuza fell at 10.30 pm but the advance could not be resumed until 4 am. On the third axis from Motza through Beit Kika to Tel el Ful the tanks encountered extremely rocky ground and only six reached Hirbet Zahara, the hill opposite the objective. The Jordanian tank brigade had moved up from Jericho during the evening and it was only at Narkiss's insistence that the Air Force could be persuaded to attack it that night.

Authority to capture Latrun was given at about midnight on the 5th of June and, although the move forward of Yotvat's Brigade and the assimilation of various other units which were placed under its command was incomplete, he decided to attack straight away. Blocks were established on the road running north-east from Latrun, and a feint attack was made on the village, while the main assault came down the road from Mishmar Ayalon after an hour's artillery fire on the fortified police station. A stream of refugees with soldiers among them could be seen moving towards Beit Nuba (Mehov Khoron); a company with tank support burst into the fort to find it only recently vacated and its successful capture was reported at 5 am. Once the villages of Beit Nuba, Beit Sira and Beit Liqya had been cleared the brigade was ordered to move as fast as possible past the last-named and on to Beit Horon and the Beitaniya junction west of Ramallah.

Before the 55th Parachute Brigade could reach Mount Scopus it had to take the Jordanian positions sited on the northern edge of Jerusalem which blocked its route. At 2 am on 6 June the artillery fire plan began and at 2.20 am two battalions began their assault, one on the heavily fortified Police Training School and to its north Ammunition Hill, while the other went for Sheikh Jarrach. The fighting lasted over four hours and at dawn the third parachute battalion entered Sheikh Jarrach and occupied the Rockefeller Museum at the north-east corner of the Old City. By mid-morning the brigade was well established in the valley between the northern city wall and Mount Scopus but it had suffered heavy casualties.

By 6.30 am on the 6th, when the first Jordanian tanks, which had survived the overnight air attack, were seen, no Israeli attack on Tel-el Ful had been made as only 6 tanks and 14 half-tracks with infantry and reconnaissance men and some mortars had reached Hirbet Zahara and they needed refuelling. Slowly other elements of the brigade began to assemble. The brigade commander arrived by helicopter and quickly issued orders, and one battalion set out to outflank the objective from the north with covering fire from the other which was then to take out the artillery at Hizma. Before long it had dispersed the Jordanians and reached the summit; the tank threat to Mount Scopus had effectively been destroyed. The battalion was then ordered south to link up with the 55th Brigade and to take Givat Hamivtar. The first attack was unsuccessful and had to withdraw but it was enough for the Jordanians who pulled out before a second attack could reach them; by 11 am both Givat Hamivtar and French Hill had been captured. Also by 6.30 am Yotvat's Brigade had reached lower Beit Horon and it captured upper Beit Horon at 8 am on the 6th.

The next task for the 55th Brigade, which had been reinforced by an airborne reconnaissance unit, was to take control of the ridge which overlooks the city from the east – the Victoria Augusta Hill and the Mount of Olives – and these were attacked by one battalion, the reconnaissance unit and a tank company supported by tank and artillery fire. However, the advance did not begin until 10 pm and in the dark the leading tanks missed the turning which would take them to the ridge and continued on to Gethsemane where they came under heavy fire from both the Mount of Olives and the Old City. Eventually the tanks were extricated but only after heavy casualties had been inflicted on the platoon sent to find them and guide them back. Before they could continue towards the ridge the attack was called off as Jordanian tanks were reported to be approaching from the east.

Jordanian Order of Battle

C-in-C: Field-Marshal Habis el Majali
25th Inf Bde Janin
1st Inf Bde Tulkarm
2nd Inf Bde Latrun
3rd Inf Bde Jerusalem
29th Inf Bde Hebron
27th Inf Bde Jericho
36th Inf Bde Jordan Valley
12th Inf Bde Irbid
40th Armd Bde Damiya
60th Armd Bde Jericho

Israeli Order of Battle

Central Command: Brig.-Gen. Uzi Narkiss
5th Inf Bde Netanya
4th Inf Bde Latrun
10th Mech Bde
16th Inf Bde Jerusalem
55th Para Bde Jerusalem

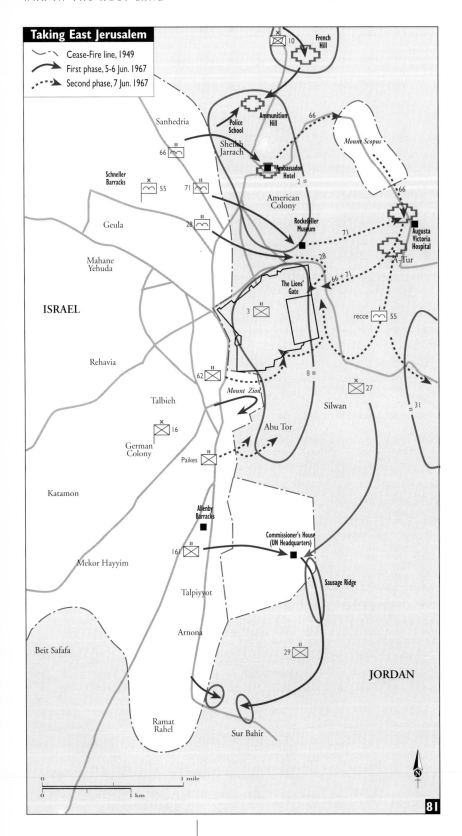

Taking East Jerusalem

- ⌒⌒ Cease-Fire line, 1949
- → First phase, 5-6 Jun. 1967
- ⋯► Second phase, 7 Jun. 1967

Sanhedria

Police School

Sheikh Jarrach

Ammunition Hill

Mount Scopus

66

Schneller Barracks

Ambassador Hotel

American Colony

2 =

66

Geula

Rockefeller Museum

71

Augusta Victoria Hospital

Mahane Yehuda

28

A-Tur

ISREAL

The Lions' Gate

66 ÷ 71

28

66 + 71

recce 55

Rehavia

3

8 =

62

Talbieh

Mount Zion

Silwan

31

German Colony

16

Abu Tor

27

Paikes

Katamon

Allenby Barracks

Commissioner's House (UN Headquarters)

161

Mekor Hayyim

Sausage Ridge

Talpiyyot

Arnona

JORDAN

Beit Safafa

29

Ramat Rahel

Sur Bahir

0   1 mile

0   1 km

N

81

That evening the Ministerial Committee on Matters of Defence had met in Tel Aviv; it had not altered the policy that the Old City was not to be entered. The Defence Minister, Moshe Dayan, after hearing of the Jordanian withdrawal, said 'we must finish taking Jerusalem tonight and tomorrow'; however, no orders to do so were issued even though the Jordanians were now in full retreat. Early on the 7th the BBC announced that the UN Security Council had declared a cease-fire to start at noon and the Israelis, fearing that the cease-fire would come into effect before the Old City surrendered, at last gave Narkiss permission to enter the City.

At 8.30 am on the 7th the Air Force attacked the Jordanian positions on Augusta Victoria and the artillery bombardment started immediately afterwards. One battalion that had reached Mount Scopus attacked from the north and a second took an exposed route through Gethsemane; fortunately there was little resistance and no Jordanian artillery fire and Augusta Victoria was captured by 9 am. The supporting tanks were sent on to A Tur. Gur's third battalion, following the line of the city wall to St Stephen's (or Lion) Gate, was overtaken by the brigade commander whose half-track was the first to enter the Old City and move on to the Temple Mount. Here the Governor surrendered the City. After mopping up to the south of the Old City through Mount Zion and Silwan, elements of the Jerusalem Brigade entered through the Dung Gate.

The Jerusalem Brigade was sent south and took Bethlehem, Etzion (the Jewish settlement area lost in 1948) and Hebron. To the north Ramallah was taken by the 10th and Yotvat's Brigades, and the 10th then went on to capture Jericho while Yotvat was given the task of mopping up north of Jerusalem. At 8 pm on the 7th both Israel and Jordan accepted the UN's call for a cease-fire, leaving Israel in control of Jerusalem and the West Bank.

THE CAPTURE OF SINAI, 1967

When the 1967 war began the Egyptians had seven divisions, five infantry and two armoured, with 100,000 men and 1,000 tanks in Sinai. They were deployed in three lines, the first close to the border with heavily fortified areas at Rafah, Um-Katef and Quseima. The second ran from El Arish through Jebel Libni and Bir Hasana to Nakhl; the third comprised the armoured reserve and was positioned between Bir Gifgafa and Bir el Thamada. The initial Israeli strategy was to have been to restrict their attack to Gaza and around El Arish but the scale of the Egyptian build-up meant that the Straits of Tiran could only be opened by defeating the Egyptian Army in Sinai. The Israeli plan was to attack with three Ugda (divisional task forces), one on the coast route and one from Nizzana towards Um-Katef and Abu Ageila. Once the first Egyptian line had been broken a third Ugda would be introduced with the task of making a deep south-

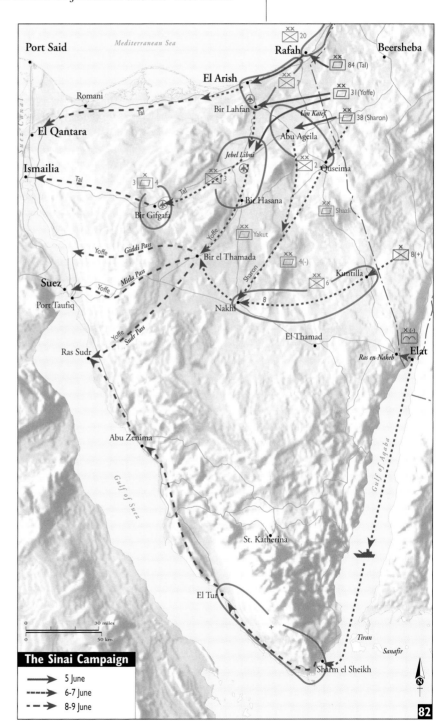

The Sinai Campaign
→ 5 June
--→ 6-7 June
- -→ 8-9 June

Israeli Patton M-48AZ tanks advance near Rafah, 5 June 1967. (IDF Archives)

westerly penetration and blocking the Mitla Pass. Infantry units were to remain on the defensive at Gaza, Kuntilla and Elat.

On the northern axis Major-General Tal probably faced the hardest task as the Egyptian defences were much stronger than the Israelis expected and their location on the coast did not allow the Israelis to exploit their superior manoeuvrability. Tal set out at 8 am on 5 June with the 7th Armoured Brigade which, avoiding the minefields and fortified positions, broke into and took Khan Yunis but was ambushed as it reached Rafah junction. A two-pronged attack which encountered an Egyptian tank counter-attack was successful and the brigade pressed on, taking the position at Sheikh Zuweid, and elements passed through El Jiradi where the Egyptians were asleep. At the same time the weak 202nd Brigade, consisting of only one paratroop battalion mounted in half-tracks and one tank battalion, had by-passed Rafah to the south but got into trouble when it turned north as the tanks became separated from the infantry who were counter-attacked by a tank battalion. Tal recalled the 7th Brigade but the Air Force had dealt with the Egyptian tanks and the paratroops went on to destroy the artillery south of Rafah. The 7th Brigade now tried to clear the El Jiradi defile but its attack failed. Tal's third brigade, the 60th, however, had made slow progress through soft sand as it advanced parallel with the coast and was now short of fuel. Tal therefore decided to commit his only reserve of two tank companies; these secured the entrance to the defile and then gave covering fire as the mechanized battalion of the 7th Brigade drove straight through with only artillery illumination to light the route.

A Centurion tank of 200th Armoured Brigade firing in Sinai, 1967. (Alain Roth Archive. Photo Nahum Gutman)

On the central axis Major-General Sharon's Ugda first captured the eastern edge of the Egyptian defensive position at Tarat Um Basis and then outflanked the main position, taking up blocking positions north and west of the Abu Ageila crossroads; in a separate southern movement they also blocked the Um-Katef–Quseima road. Sharon's artillery then moved forward and at dusk a parachute battalion was helicoptered behind the Egyptians to attack their artillery. The Egyptians were then attacked from both east and west and by 6 am on the 6th the road from Um-Katef to Abu Ageila was in Israeli hands, but mopping up was to take a further twenty-four hours.

With the road now open it was possible for the third Ugda under Major-General Yoffe to pass through Sharon's Ugda and head for the passes it was to block. Yoffe's force had already crossed soft sand dunes considered to be impassable and was blocking the roads from El Arish to Jebel Libni and Abu Ageila at Bir Lahfan. On the evening of 5 June an Egyptian force was ambushed there by one of Yoffe's brigades which routed it. Yoffe then moved south-west to Jebel Libni where, aided by one of Tal's brigades from the north, he attacked and by dusk on the 6th had captured the fortified Egyptian base area and airfield. Yoffe moved straight on to Bir el-Hasana.

On 7 June Tal's forces advanced on two axes. In the north they met opposition 16 km east of El Qantara: here the tanks provided a firebase for the paratroopers who outflanked the enemy to the south. This force reached the Suez Canal early on the 8th. The remainder of Tal's Ugda was directed against Bir Gifgafa and in a coordinated movement Yoffe

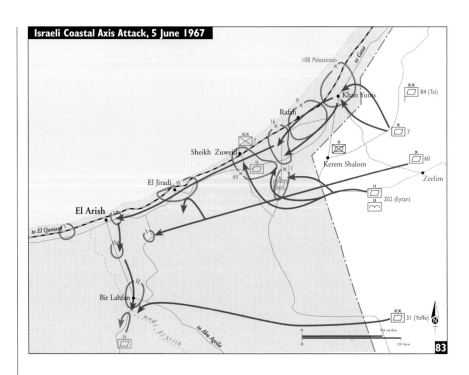

Israeli Coastal Axis Attack, 5 June 1967

Egyptian Order of Battle

Front Commander: Gen. Abd el Mohsen
Mortagui
2nd Infantry Division
3rd Infantry Division
4th Armoured Division
Armoured Task Force
6th Mechanized Division
7th Infantry Division
20th Palestinian Division

Israeli Order of Battle

Southern Command: Brig.-Gen.
Yeshayahu Gavish
31st Armoured Division
38th Armoured Division
84th Armoured Division
8th Infantry Brigade

advanced on Bir el Thamada and then to the Mitla Pass. Sharon moved south towards Nakhl, threatening to cut off the Egyptian armoured force which was to have attacked the southern Negev from Quseima; this force, along with all the remaining Egyptian units in Sinai, now headed for the Mitla Pass. All day the Israeli Air Force had been attacking the retreating Egyptian columns and had destroyed hundreds of vehicles. Yoffe's leading tanks managed to reach the Mitla entrance although four tanks which had run out of fuel had to be towed. Other Israeli tanks got tangled up in the fleeing Egyptian columns in the dark. Sharon caught up with two Egyptian brigades at Nakhl and in the ensuing battle the Israelis destroyed 60 tanks, 100 guns and 300 other vehicles; Sharon then moved on to Bir el Thamada to link up with Yoffe.

Finally, on the 8th both Tal and Yoffe reached the Canal. Tal linked up with his northern detachment opposite Ismailia, while Yoffe crossed both the Mitla and Gidi Passes and sent a detachment down the Red Sea coast to meet the paratroopers who had been landed by torpedo boat at Sharm El-Sheikh, which they found deserted. The Egyptian Army had lost 800 tanks, several hundred guns and over 10,000 vehicles; they suffered between 10,000 and 15,000 casualties, and over 5,000 were taken prisoner. Israeli losses were some 300 dead and over a thousand wounded.

THE CAPTURE OF THE GOLAN HEIGHTS, 1967

When the 1967 war broke out the Syrians, who had encouraged the Egyptian provocation of Israel, and despite the near destruction of its air force on the afternoon of 5 June, did not initially attack Israel. It was only after the Egyptians had been defeated that the Syrians began to shell settlements in northern Israel and attempted to capture two. The Golan

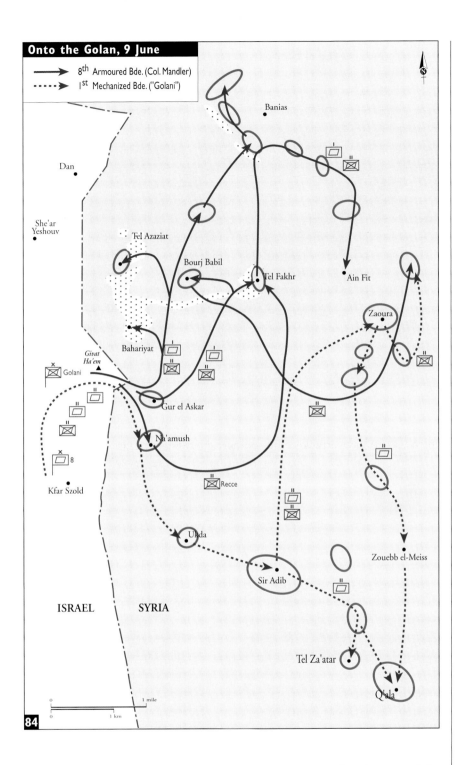

Onto the Golan, 9 June

→ 8th Armoured Bde. (Col. Mandler)
┅▶ 1st Mechanized Bde. ("Golani")

Banias

Dan

She'ar
Yeshouv

Tel Azaziat

Bourj Babil

Tel Fakhr

Ain Fit

Zaoura

Bahariyat

Givat
Ha'em

Golani

Gur el Askar

Na'amush

8

Recce

Kfar Szold

Ukda

Sir Adib

Zouebb el-Meiss

ISRAEL   SYRIA

Tel Za'atar

Q'ala

0   1 mile
0   1 km

84

Heights is a plateau rising to some 900 metres immediately east of the
Jordan River and Sea of Galilee; at the northern end lies Mount Hermon,
2,200 metres high, and 72 km to the south the plateau ends at the
Yarmouk River and the Jordanian border. The western edge, which
overlooked Israel, was heavily defended with bunkers, minefields and gun
emplacements, as were the routes leading to Damascus, only 80 km from
the border. The normal Syrian garrison on the Golan had been reinforced
and consisted of six infantry brigades each with a battalion of tanks, four

holding the front line with two in depth; there were also two armoured and one mechanized brigades ready to counter-attack any Israeli incursion. Israel's Northern Command was led by Major-General Elazar whose forces comprised three armoured brigades, two of which took part in the capture of the northern West Bank, and five infantry brigades.

Dayan held back Northern Command until the Egyptians had been defeated in Sinai and the Jordanians had been thrown out of the West Bank, despite the appeals of the settlers in the Hula Valley who had experienced years of Syrian harassment. The Israeli attack on Syria began only on 9 June. The Israeli breakthrough was concentrated at Gur el Asker where the 'Golani' Infantry Brigade and Colonel Mendler's 8th Armoured Brigade advanced following concentrated air, artillery and direct tank fire on the forward Syrian positions. The 'Golanis' first had to take the position at Tel Fakhr (Mizpe Golani) so that they could attack the dominating stronghold of Tel Azaziat (Givat Azaz) from the rear before clearing the area bounded by Kfar Szold, Zaoura and Banias. The 'Golanis' had a hard fight, suffering many casualties, particularly officers and NCOs, before they took Tel Fakhr at 6 pm; with reinforcements they then captured Tel Azaziat by dusk.

The 8th Armoured Brigade had only two battalions, one of tanks and one mechanized; it was therefore organized into three infantry/tank battle groups. It first cleared Na'amush, about halfway up the heights, where it split. One battle group fought its way up the steep slope, led by bulldozers, through Ukda to Sir Adib where it met strong resistance, losing

The Golan Heights viewed across Lake Tiberias. (Photograph: Z. Radovan, Jerusalem)

Looking down on the Bnot Ya'acov bridge. (Photograph: Z. Radovan, Jerusalem)

several tanks and the battalion commander before taking the position after an air strike. The second battle group turned north-east to take positions at Ain Fit and Zaoura. The third battle group and brigade headquarters was to have followed the second but lost its way until reaching Sir Abid where it turned north, reaching Zaoura where the second group was in some trouble. After an air strike Zaoura was overrun. The first battle group, as it approached Q'ala, found the road blocked by 'dragon's teeth' covered by two positions; it managed to clear the northern position after another air strike and to break through the block, only to come under heavy fire from tanks in the village. Only two tanks reached the edge of the village, which was taken by one of the battle groups from Zaoura.

To the south of the main attack, two infantry brigades crossed the Jordan at Mishmar ha-Yarden taking the three villages along the road running north from the Bnot Ya'akov bridge, and they also took the Upper Customs House. This allowed an armoured brigade to advance up the slope and take the position at Rawiya.

By the 10th there were three Israeli armoured brigades on the Golan. One joined the 'Golani' Brigade to take the southern slopes of Mount Hermon, while the other two advanced on Quneitra from Q'ala and from Kfar Naffakh. Quneitra was captured without opposition by 2 pm. A unit of 'Golanis', lifted by helicopter, occupied the lower peak of Mount Hermon. In the middle of the morning the Syrians broke and began to flee in panic, leaving behind much of their equipment undamaged. The Israelis were now less than 50 km from Damascus.

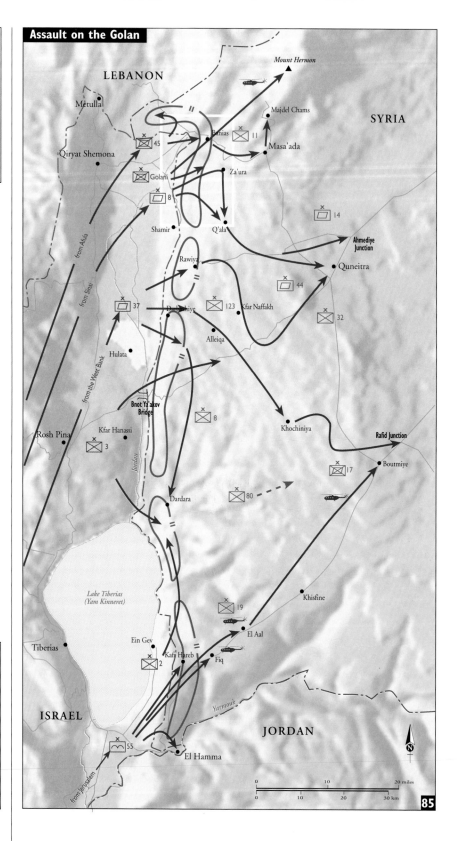

Assault on the Golan

Syrian Order of Battle

Maj.-Gen. Ahmed Souedani
11th Infantry Brigade
123rd Infantry Brigade
80th Infantry Brigade
19th Infantry Brigade
32nd Infantry Brigade
17th Mechanized Brigade
14th Armoured Brigade
44th Armoured Brigade

Israeli Order of Battle

Northern Command: Brig.-Gen. David Elazar
1st 'Golani' Brigade
3rd Infantry Brigade
2nd Infantry Brigade
Reinforcements
8th Armoured Brigade
37th Armoured Brigade
45th Mechanized Brigade
55th Parachute Brigade

LEBANON

SYRIA

Mount Hermon

Métulla

Majdel Chams

Qiryat Shemona

Banias

Masa'ada

Za'ura

Golani

Shamir

Q'ala

Ahmediye Junction

Rawiya

Quneitra

Darbashiye

Kfar Naffakh

Alleiqa

Hulata

Bnot Ya'akov Bridge

Kfar Hanassi

Rosh Pina

Khochiniya

Rafid Junction

Boutmiye

Dardara

Lake Tiberias (Yam Kinneret)

Khisfine

Ein Gev

El Aal

Tiberias

Kafr Hareb

Fiq

ISRAEL

JORDAN

Yarmouk

El Hamma

85

*The southern Golan Heights
photographed from the road to
Hammat Gadder.*

Another force, including the 55th Parachute Brigade which had come north after capturing the Old City of Jerusalem, began an attack south of the Sea of Galilee which employed helicopters to lift paratroops ahead of the main column to take Fiq (Afik), El Aal (Eli Al) and finally Boutmiye (Hanot Oreha) and Rafid Junction. When the Israelis accepted the UN cease-fire, which came into effect at 6.30 pm, they held a line running from Mount Hermon, east of Masaada, Quneitra and Rafid and down the Yarmouk River to the Jordan.

The capture of the Golan had been achieved in under two days. It had cost Israel 141 lives; Syrian losses totalled an admitted 170 killed (the Israeli estimate is 500), 2,000 wounded, 61 aircraft shot down, and 85 tanks and over 100 guns captured.

THE OCTOBER WAR: YOM KIPPUR, 1973.
BACKGROUND AND OVERVIEW

In this section the course of the war on the Golan Heights is described separately, as are the Egyptian crossing of the Suez Canal and the Israeli crossing and encirclement of the 3rd Egyptian Army. This introduction covers general points and outlines other events in the war.

The main cause of the 1973 war was the increasing frustration of the Arabs, particularly the Egyptians, in their inability to open negotiations with Israel over the return of territory lost in 1967. They did not

Relative Strengths	
Tanks	
Egypt	2,200
Syria	1,820
Jordan	150*
Iraq	300*
Others 370*	
Arab Total:	4,840
Israel:	2,000
APC/Half-tracks	
Egypt	2,400
Syria	1,300
Jordan	200*
Iraq	300*
Others	120*
Arab Total:	4,320
Israel:	4,000
Artillery/MRL	
Egypt	1,280
Syria	670
Jordan	40*
Iraq	50*
Others	100*
Arab Total:	2,140
Israel:	570
Combat Aircraft	
Egypt	690†
Syria	390†
Iraq	70*
Others	90*
Arab Total:	1,240
Israel:	400**

* numbers committed only
† includes aircraft delivered during the war

necessarily expect to recover all the territories lost in the war but hoped to gain some and to be able to convince the United States in post-war talks that a long-term settlement was needed. A new war had been anticipated by the Israelis for some time but it was judged that the Egyptians would not go to war until they were able to take out Israeli airfields and this would not be possible until they had acquired sufficient suitable aircraft. An Israeli mobilization had been ordered in May 1973 by the Chief of Staff, General Elazar, when he rejected the intelligence assessment that war was not imminent and that Egyptian military movements were purely an exercise in brinkmanship. The Egyptians fostered the Israeli belief that they were unready for war with a successful misinformation campaign and although all Egyptian preparations were noted by Israeli intelligence their assessment remained that the Egyptians could not go to war until various pre-conditions were attained.

The Egyptians had prepared well. Their new Chief of Staff, General Saad el-Shazly, began to plan the war shortly after his appointment in May 1971. The Syrians had agreed to a coordinated simultaneous attack, and other Arab assistance was promised. A major lesson for the Arabs in the 1967 war had been the effectiveness of the Israeli Air Force. To counter this both Egypt and Syria invested heavily in Soviet surface-to-air missiles (SAMs). The Egyptians had 150 batteries, most with SAM-2 and SAM-3 but over half with the highly mobile SAM-6; over one-third of the batteries were deployed along the line of the Suez Canal. The Syrians had some thirty batteries of SAM-6. Even with this defence the Arabs realized that their chance of successfully bombing Israeli targets was low and to compensate for this both countries obtained Soviet Frog surface-to-surface missiles (SSMs) with a range of 88 km, and in April 1973 a number of 300-km range Scud SSMs were delivered to Egypt. President Sadat has said that he decided to go to war when these SSMs arrived. Israeli armour would be halted by an unusually high deployment of anti-tank missile launchers in the attacking infantry; the Egyptians concentrated virtually all their hand-held launchers in the assaulting units. The Egyptian aim was not to retake the whole of Sinai but to establish a strong bridgehead over the Canal with the expectation that this would lead to peace talks; however, plans for deeper penetration were prepared and the Syrians believed this was the Egyptian objective.

In September the Egyptians began manoeuvres in the Canal Zone. These were regarded by the Israelis as a major exercise; this was the Egyptian intention, as it was the eighteenth such exercise since Shazly had assumed command. The Israeli armoured division in Sinai was put on alert but was instructed not to make any moves which might escalate the situation. By 3 October the divisional commander, General Mendler, was convinced that war was imminent, as was a junior intelligence officer at Southern Command HQ, but their warnings were not heeded, and nor were the indications noted by 5 October that the Egyptians were in a position of readiness for an attack on a scale not seen before. Soviet naval ships had left Egyptian ports on the 4th, and it was learnt that Soviet families had been evacuated. At the same time reports of an unprecedented Syrian build-up of forces were being received but still Israeli military intelligence maintained that the likelihood of war was small, and this assessment was accepted by the inner cabinet on 3 October. On the morning of the 5th the standing army was placed on the highest state of alert; meetings held by the Defence Minister and the Prime Minister confirmed the alert status but ordered no further action other than putting the reserve mobilization centres also on alert.

The Chief of Israeli Military Intelligence was woken at 4 am on the 6th to be told that the war would start before the end of the day; somehow this assessment got translated into the expectation that the attack would be made at 6 pm. Before 6 am the Chief of Staff was recommending general mobilization and a pre-emptive air strike against the Syrians. Dayan, the Defence Minister, would not agree to either of these actions and the decision was left to the Prime Minister. Golda Meir eventually authorized the mobilization of 100,000 men; the Chief of Staff actually ordered the mobilization of more and orders were also given for the reserves to deploy piecemeal as sub-units were ready and not as planned as full brigades or divisions. The cabinet was meeting and was in the process of asking why 6 pm was certain to be H-Hour when at 2 pm the news arrived that the war had begun.

The Egyptians had chosen 6 October as the date for their attack as it was the Jewish holy day, Yom Kippur, or 'Day of Atonement', when it was thought that readiness would be lower than normal; however, a better choice would have been Jewish New Year when most Israelis would have gone to the beaches rather than remaining at home as they all do on Yom Kippur. As a result mobilization was achieved much more quickly than had been anticipated.

From the start of the war the Israelis gave priority to the northern front, as the distance before Israel itself was reached was so much less than in Sinai.

The Israelis had some 350 combat aircraft, US A-4 Skyhawks and F-4 Phantoms and French Mirages, while the Arabs had some 900 planes, virtually all Soviet-made MiG-17s, MiG-19s and MiG-21s. The Arab air forces did not attempt to penetrate deeply into Israeli-held territory. The Egyptians kept west of the line Refidim–Mitla Pass; the deepest they penetrated was to El Arish in a raid from the sea in which three of six Mirages were shot down, and a failed attempt to reach Elat. The Egyptians had Kelt air-to-surface missiles (ASMs) which they fired at targets in Israel but the Israelis managed to shoot down most of these. The Syrians concentrated their air attacks on Israeli fighting units; they also attempted to raid Haifa and the radar site on Mount Meron, losing planes in both attempts.

The Syrians fired Frog SSMs at the Ramat David airbase in northern Israel; the Israelis responded by destroying the Barouk early warning radar in Lebanon and then made a series of raids against the Syrian oil and electric-generating installations. The Egyptians fired only one of their Scud SSMs, on the 22nd; it caused no damage, landing in Sinai. All told the Arab air forces lost 514 aircraft, of which 172 Egyptian and 162 Syrian planes were shot down in aerial combat. The Israelis lost 102 aircraft, 50 of these being lost in the first three days of the war; only 5 Israeli aircraft were shot down by Arab fighters, the rest falling to SAMs. One lesson learnt by the Israelis was not to under-estimate the effectiveness of

Golda Meir
Foreign Minister, 1956–66;
Prime Minister, 1969–74.

SAMs; since then electronic warfare and the use of anti-radar measures have had the highest priority in the Israeli Air Force.

Naval forces had little influence on the war. Egypt's navy had 3 destroyers, 2 frigates, 10 submarines, 12 missile boats and some 26 torpedo boats; Syria had 9 missile boats and 11 torpedo boats; Israel had only 14 missile boats. The Israeli Navy pre-empted an Egyptian plan to ferry troops across the Gulf of Suez, destroying a number of boats assembled in the Bay of Mersa Talamat on the first night of the war. The Israelis mounted naval operations along both the Egyptian and Syrian coasts which tied down ground forces there. On the night of 6/7 October a force of five Israeli missile boats encountered and sank a Syrian torpedo boat as it retreated towards Latakia; next a Syrian minesweeper was sunk and then the Israelis found themselves engaged by a waiting force of Syrian missile craft. In the ensuing fight three Syrian vessels were sunk with no Israeli loss. On the night of the 8th/9th six Israeli missile boats were sailing to engage coastal targets between Damietta and Balatin when they were engaged by four Egyptian boats with missiles of longer range than those of the Israelis. However, the Israelis continued to approach until they came within range and then sank three of the Egyptian boats.

The Arabs confined their attacks to Sinai and the Golan; there were no attacks launched from Jordanian territory against either Israeli territory or the West Bank, the Jordanians contenting themselves with tying down Israeli forces without incurring air attack from them. Egypt received ground force reinforcements from Algeria, Kuwait, Libya, Morocco, Sudan and Tunisia; Syria was supported by two divisions of Iraqis, two Jordanian tank brigades and an infantry brigade from Morocco. Saudi Arabia sent an infantry brigade to Jordan. Algeria, Libya and Iraq sent squadrons of aircraft to Egypt, and Iraq sent four squadrons to Syria. Jordan entered the war only on the 13th when its 40th tank brigade crossed the border at Dera'a.

Both the Arabs and the Israelis depended on resupply from their super-power backers. The Soviet Union had prepared supplies ready to ship before the war started; at its peak the Soviet airlift to Egypt landed an aircraft every ten minutes, and large numbers of freighters landed weapons and ammunition at Syrian and Egyptian ports. The US airlift did not begin until 14 October; all told there were 565 US resupply sorties while 250 Israeli cargo flights crossed the Atlantic.

The war ended with a UN-negotiated cease-fire. At first, the UN Security Council Resolution 338 of 22 October 1973 was accepted by Egypt and Israel but not Syria; in any event it was quickly broken and so fighting continued. A second UNSC Resolution 339 was accepted by Syria on the 24th when it came into effect although some fighting continued on the 25th around Suez. Military talks were held at Kilo 101 on the Cairo–Suez Road from 28 October when supplies were allowed through to the 3rd Army. A UN peacekeeping force, UNEF 2, began to deploy in Egypt in November and was completely deployed by February 1974. A Separation of Forces Agreement was reached between Israel and Egypt and signed at Kilo 101 in January 1974 and the separation was completed by 4 March. In Geneva an agreement between Israel and Syria was signed on 31 May 1974, and disengagement and Israeli withdrawal began on

---

United Nation Security Council Resolution 338 (1973)

Calling for a cease-fire and for the implementation of Resolution 242 in all its parts.

United Nations Security Council Resolution 339 (1973)

Confirming Resolution 338 and requesting the dispatch of UN observers to supervise the cease-fire.

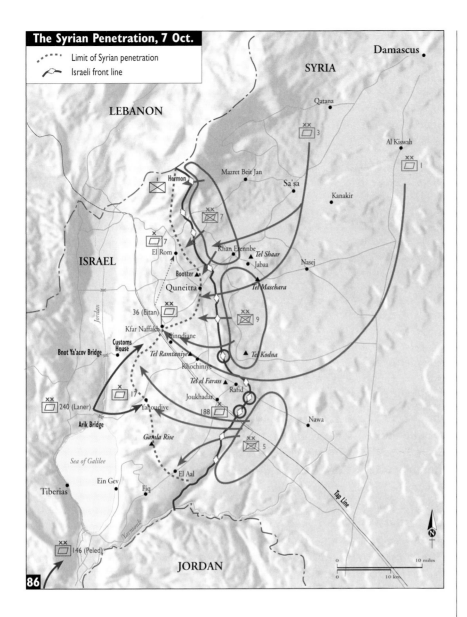

The Syrian Penetration, 7 Oct.

- Limit of Syrian penetration
- Israeli front line

Damascus

SYRIA

LEBANON

Qatana

Al Kiswah

XX 3

XX 1

Hermon

Mazret Beit Jan

Sa'sa

Kanakir

XX 7

El Rom

X 7

Khan Erennbe

Tel Shaar

Jabaa

Nasej

ISRAEL

Booster

Quneitra

Tel Maschara

36 (Eitan)

XX

Kfar Naffakh

Sinndiane

Customs House

Jordan

Bnot Ya'acov Bridge

Tel Ramtaniye

Khochinniye

Tel el Farass

Rafid

Joukhadar

Yahoudiye

188

X 17

XX 240 (Laner)

Arik Bridge

Gamla Rise

Sea of Galilee

Ein Gev

Fiq

El Aal

Nawa

XX 9

Tel Kodna

XX 5

Tap Line

Tiberias

N

XX 146 (Peled)

Yarmouk

0   10 miles

0   10 km

JORDAN

86

1 June from the 840 square km it had captured beyond the 1967 armistice line. Another United Nations Peacekeeping Force, UNDOF, was established in a Demilitarized Zone on the Golan Heights and zones of limited armaments monitored by the UN were agreed to.

Israeli losses amounted to 2,521 men killed of whom 24 per cent were officers: a very high proportion. No Arab figures have ever been published but estimates give a figure of 12,000 dead for Egypt and 4,000 for Syria. A number of serious lessons were learnt by the Israelis, a key one being that tanks need to be closely supported by infantry if they are to survive against short-range anti-tank weapons. The effectiveness of the Arab SAM defences pointed up Israel's shortage of artillery. The army was considerably expanded and reorganized after the war, a process which took a good many years as new equipment was acquired mainly from the US and so could only be supplied in limited numbers each year. The Soviet Union resupplied Egypt and Syria much more quickly; for example, it provided Syria with replacements for the thousand or so tanks it had lost in the war in a matter of months, and supplied the other Arab armies with a further thousand tanks within a year.

The war led to a super-power crisis. The Soviet Union claimed that Israel had violated the first cease-fire and continued to encircle the Egyptian 3rd Army, threatened to intervene and as evidence of their determination placed their airborne divisions on high alert. The US responded by changing its nuclear alert status, a measure which also involved conventional forces, including those in Europe. Tension was high for several days until it became clear there would be no direct Soviet intervention and while the US insisted that the Israelis should not destroy the 3rd Army.

THE SYRIAN ATTACK ON THE GOLAN HEIGHTS

In October 1973 Israeli forces on the Golan consisted of a string of infantry-manned fortified outposts overlooking the obstacle belt of a tank-ditch with barbed wire entanglements and minefields on either side of it along the length of the 1967 cease-fire line (the Purple Line). These were backed by two armoured brigades: the 7th, which had only been sent to the Golan a few days earlier, deployed to the north of the Bnot Ya'acov Bridge–Quneitra road, and the 188th, situated to the south of it. All told the Israelis numbered some 4,500 men and 177 tanks. The Syrian plan was to make its main attack in a north-westerly direction along the disused Tapline with the 5th Mechanized Division followed by the 1st Tank Division ready to break through once the Israeli defences had been penetrated. Two other mechanized divisions, the 7th and 9th, were to advance from east to west, take Quneitra and make a holding attack in the north aimed at Wasset. The 3rd Tank Division was held in reserve. Syrian forces numbered about 45,000 men with 1,400 tanks.

The attack was launched at 3 pm and was preceded by an hour's intense artillery barrage from some 700 guns and an air strike. In the north the leading Syrian tanks, which were fitted with mine-ploughs or rollers, and their bridge-laying tanks were all knocked out before they reached the obstacle but on the Tapline approach a number managed to cross the ditch. The Syrians also captured the Israeli radar station on Mount Hermon in a helicopter-borne attack. The situation was so serious that the Israeli Air Force was committed to close air support rather than gaining air superiority; in the first two days they lost fifty aircraft to Syrian SAM fire. By the evening of the 6th the 188th Brigade, commanded by Colonel Ben-Shohar, had only 15 tanks left to face the Syrians' 450; by dawn the Syrians were closing on El Aal and were only 10 km from the Arik Bridge, just north of the Sea of Galilee. Further north the Syrians were approaching Kfar Naffakh where General Eytan had his 36th Division's headquarters.

The first Israeli reinforcements of the 240th Armoured Division began to arrive at the Arik Bridge that evening. From here, the commander, General Laner, who had been given responsibility for the southern Golan, sent them piecemeal either up the road to Naffakh or to Yahoudiye to join his two brigade commanders who had gone on ahead. During the night the two Syrian mechanized divisions in the north broke through the

Syrian Order of Battle

Chief of Staff: Maj.-Gen. Youssef Chakkour
1st Armoured Division
3rd Armoured Division
5th Mechanized Division
7th Mechanized Division
9th Mechanized Division
3rd Iraqi Armoured Division
40th Jordan Armoured Brigade
Moroccan Brigade

Israeli Order of Battle

Northern Command
Maj.-Gen. Yitzhak Hoffi
36th Mechanized Division
146th Armoured Division
240th Armoured Division

minefields and anti-tank ditch and engaged the Israeli 7th Brigade, led by Colonel Ben-Gal. At dawn the Syrian 1st Tank Division under Colonel Tewfiq Jehani took the lead and forced the remnants of the 188th Brigade back to Naffakh from which General Eytan withdrew northwards to El Rom, as the Syrians entered the camp. Other Syrian tanks almost reached the Customs House above the Bnot Ya'acov Bridge. The Syrians then called a halt as their tanks were in danger of getting ahead of Syrian SAM cover, and a conference was held. Then, instead of reinforcing the success of their 1st Division, the Syrians split their other tank division, sending one half to reinforce the battle against the Israeli 7th Brigade and the other to outflank Rafid and support the 1st Division.

During the night of the 7th General Peled's 146th Armoured Division arrived, having been diverted from its war role of reinforcement in Sinai. Peled was ordered to mount the Golan Heights from south of the Sea of Galilee, attack the Syrians on the Gamla Rise and at El Aal, then advance north-eastwards to an objective just beyond Rafid. Laner's two brigades were to attack up the Naffakh and Yahoudiye roads and then to swing south-east to encircle the Syrian 1st Division. The Syrians had established strong defensive positions at Sinndiane, Tel Ramtaniye, Tel el Farass and Joukhadar; that at Joukhadar withdrew in front of Peled's attack during the night of the 8/9th and this exposed the tank division's supply line. The Syrian tank brigade sent to counter-attack was repulsed with the help of close air support. Syrian infantry failed to infiltrate into and take the Israeli positions the next night. On the morning of the 10th the two Israeli divisions met up near Khochniye and virtually wiped out two of the 1st Division's brigades and repulsed a mechanized brigade's attack from Tel Kodna; by midday they had reached the Purple Line and recovered all lost territory in the southern Golan, but an attack by the 146th on Tel Kodna was broken off when they met heavy opposition.

In the north the 7th Brigade, encouraged by General Eytan, had fought the Syrians for over forty-eight hours in what became known as the Valley

Mount Hermon, viewed from beyond Lake Tiberias. (Photograph: Z. Radovan, Jerusalem)

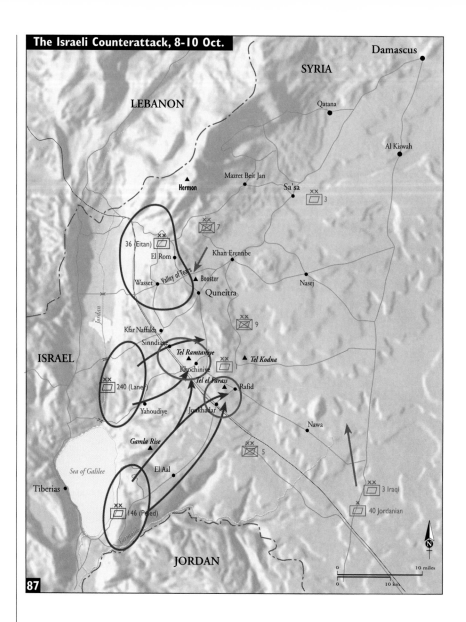

The Israeli Counterattack, 8-10 Oct.

87

of Tears and, by the morning of the 9th, had only thirty-four tanks left when a helicopter force inserted infantry behind them. These were eliminated by the brigade reconnaissance unit just as a major Syrian attack, supported by twenty-three artillery and MRL batteries, was mounted, forcing the 7th off the 'Booster' Ridge. Eytan ordered in a reconstituted force from the 188th Brigade with only eleven tanks, which caught the Syrians in the flank and drove them back. By then the Syrians had decided to break off and pull back from the Golan. The 7th Armoured Brigade had fought continuously for seventy-two hours, losing all but nine of their original tanks, but they had destroyed 260 Syrian tanks and over 500 other vehicles.

The Israelis now decided that they should push forward to within artillery range of Damascus. Eytan's two brigades, which had been reinforced with reservist battalions, attacked in the north. The 7th, in the foothills of Mount Hermon, took its objective, Mazret Beit Jan, from a

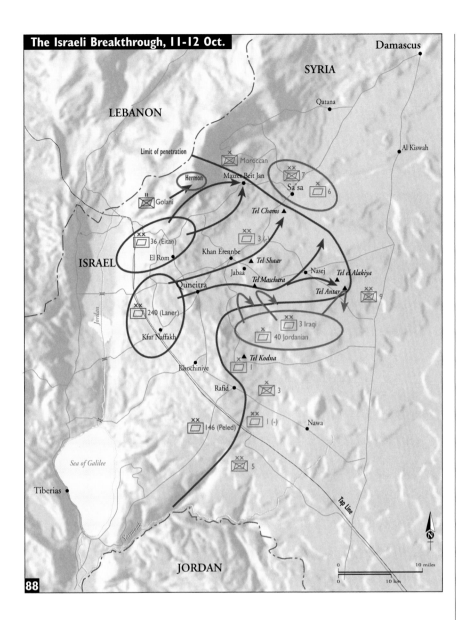

The Israeli Breakthrough, 11-12 Oct.

88

Moroccan brigade on the afternoon of the 12th. The 188th, now with only four of its original officers unharmed, was not so successful, being held up by Syrian tanks and anti-tank guns; a paratroop battalion was brought in to capture its objective, Tel Chams, on the night of the 13th.

The 240th Division attacked a strong Syrian defence on the Damascus road and the 17th Brigade was reduced to five tanks before two fresh armoured brigades could take the Khan Erennbe cross-roads. On the 12th two of Laner's brigades made a wide outflanking movement through Nasej with the aim of taking Sa'sa from the south.

During the afternoon Laner spotted a large tank force about 10 km to the south of Tel Shaar (Jabaa) moving towards him; it was two brigades of an Iraqi division. Laner prepared an ambush, deploying four brigades facing inwards in a horseshoe formation from Nasej to Tel Shaar to Tel Maschara (Oumm Batne). Although the Iraqis had virtually reached the Israeli positions in the late afternoon, they halted just short of the trap as they were waiting for their third brigade before moving forward just before first light. Their attack was launched at 3 am and they had reached within 180 metres of Tel Shaar before the Israelis opened fire, knocking out eighty tanks and most of the division's mechanized brigade; the Iraqis withdrew in disorder.

The Jordanians and Iraqis launched a number of unsuccessful attacks over the next few days and the Israelis went over to the defensive as they saw they could make little further ground. On the night of 21/22 October, the last night of the war, Israeli airborne troops lifted by helicopter retook the radar site on Mount Hermon, while a battalion of 'Golani' infantry fought their way up the mountain track to link up with them just before the cease-fire came into effect.

The fighting on the Golan had cost Israel 772 men killed, 2,450 wounded and 55 taken prisoner; of the 250 tanks knocked out 150 were able to be repaired. Estimates of Arab losses were some 3,500 men killed and up to 1,300 tanks lost.

THE EGYPTIAN ATTACK ACROSS THE CANAL

The Israeli defences in Sinai began with a string of fortifications along the Suez Canal known as the Bar-Lev line. Behind this lay a large number of prepared tank-firing positions and a system of roads, headquarters and logistic facilities. There were three roads running parallel to the canal: the nearest, linking the forts of the Bar-Lev line, was known as Lexicon; 8 km to the east was the 'artillery' road; and 16 km further east (but still west of the passes) was the 'lateral' road. In 1970, during the August cease-fire, the Israelis further strengthened their defences by building a second line of forts some 8 to 10 km behind the Canal and by building up the sand-bank along the eastern side of the Canal. Caused by dredging, this bank was as high as 25 metres in some places, making egress from the Canal even more difficult (the banks had been concreted to prevent erosion and, at high water, the water level was 1 metre below the concrete lip – an impossible climb for amphibious vehicles). There was insufficient time to raise this bank so that the Egyptians, who had built a bank on their side of the Canal up to 40 metres high, could no longer see Israeli deployments across the Canal. There was opposition to this emphasis on securing the line of the Canal from those generals who believed a mobile tank defence was a better use of resources; a compromise was adopted which meant the Bar-Lev line was only weakly held, with a number of forts usually being unmanned. The Israelis normally deployed the 252nd Armoured Division of three armoured brigades, then commanded by General Albert Mendler, in Sinai, with a fourth reserve brigade added in times of tension; the Bar-Lev line was manned by reservist units on their annual duty.

The attack across the Canal, which had been rehearsed countless times, began just before 2 pm on 6 October and was preceded by a short but massive artillery barrage employing some 2,000 guns and mortars, a Frog SSM brigade, and an air strike by 240 aircraft directed at the Sinai airfields, radars, SAM sites and suspected command posts. Then some 10,000 infantry crossed the Canal in rubber dinghies to establish

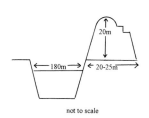

Israeli Suez Canal bank defences.

Destroyed Israeli Centurion tanks of the 7th Armoured Brigade in the 'Valley of Tears' on the Golan, 1973. (IDF Archives/Bamahane)

bridgeheads and to attack the Bar-Lev forts which were manned only by some 400 reservists from the 16th Jerusalem Brigade with only three of the forward deployed tanks being on the Canal line. The Egyptian attack was successful and by dark 80,000 men, the best part of five infantry divisions, were across the Canal, having suffered very light casualties. The garrisons of the forts put up a brave fight but were unable to stop the Canal crossings. One fort, manned by only forty-two soldiers, at the southern end of the line held out for a week while the most northerly one, 'Bucharest', was the only fort not taken by the Egyptians despite being cut off for long periods and repeated attacks by tanks, infantry, commandos and aircraft. An Israeli relief force was ambushed and destroyed and seven Israeli aircraft were shot down while attempting to attack the Egyptian commando force.

The Israeli armoured brigades deployed in Sinai had been ready to move forward to meet the forecast H hour of 6 pm but had not moved by the time of the Egyptian attack. In the early stages there was no apparent Egyptian area of main effort for the Israelis to concentrate their counter-attacks against and so the three brigades moved forward separately. In the north Colonel Amir's 460th Brigade soon became involved in fighting to link up with the Bar-Lev forts which reduced his tank strength to only twenty. In the centre Colonel Reshef's 14th Brigade found that their planned positions had already been occupied by Egyptian infantry with anti-tank weapons and they also came under fire from longer range ATGW and tanks still on the ramp on the west of the Canal. To the south Colonel Shomron's 401st Brigade advanced through the Giddi and Mitla Passes and managed to support the forts from the junction of the two Bitter Lakes to Suez, with the exception of the fort at Port Tawfiq, but by evening Shomron had lost 77 of his 100 tanks. He withdrew and concentrated his remaining tanks to engage the Egyptians at long range, halting any attempts to attack his force. On the 9th two Egyptian mechanized brigades attacked towards the Mitla Pass. Shomron surprised

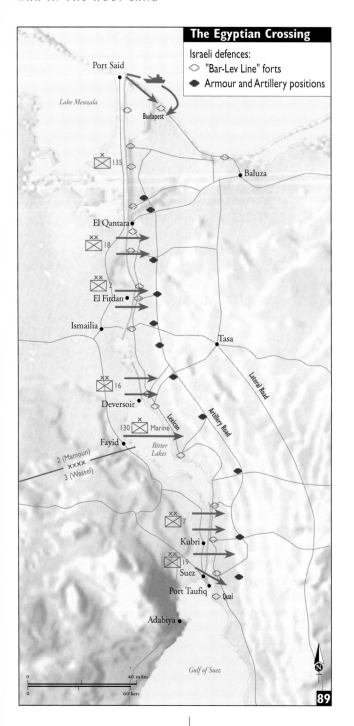

The Egyptian Crossing

Israeli defences:
- ⬡ "Bar-Lev Line" forts
- ⬢ Armour and Artillery positions

Port Said

Lake Menzala

Budapest

135

Baluza

El Qantara

18

2

El Firdan

Ismailia

Tasa

Lateral Road

16

Deversoir

Luxton

Artillery Road

130 Marine

Fayid

Bitter Lakes

2 (Mamoun)
3 (Wassel)

7

Kubri

19

Suez

Port Taufiq   Quai

Adabiya

Gulf of Suez

N

0   40 miles
0   60 km

89

them with a counter-attack which knocked out twenty tanks and many other armoured vehicles and the attacking brigades withdrew.

The Israelis shot down a large number, though not all, of the helicopters lifting commandos to block the Khatmia, Giddi and Mitla Passes and the 130th Marine Brigade, which had crossed the Great Bitter Lake in amphibious armoured vehicles, met and was destroyed by tanks of the 401st Brigade. By evening the Israelis had three armoured brigades in the front line, but by first light only 90 of their 280 tanks were serviceable. That night ten bridges were thrown across the Canal to get the Egyptian armour across and the sand ramparts were blown away by high-powered hoses; all Israeli attempts to attack the bridging sites were beaten off by the thick anti-tank missile belt while the Israeli Air Force was held off by the SAM belt.

During the afternoon of the 7th two Israeli reserve armoured divisions began to arrive and took over the sectors of the brigades, and command of them, in the centre and north of the line, with General Adan's 162nd in the north and the 143rd commanded by General Sharon in the centre. That evening counter-attack plans were discussed with the Chief of Staff; he decided there would be no attempt to cross the canal but ordered a north–south operation in which, first, Adan's division would move down the line of the Canal, but about 1 km away from it so as to be out of ATGW range. Once Adan had reached the Great Bitter Lake then Sharon's division was to carry out a similar operation towards Suez. The aim was to eliminate any Egyptians deployed ahead of their bridgeheads; no attempt was to be made to relieve any Bar-Lev fortifications still holding out.

Unfortunately General Gonen, the southern front commander, then changed the plan and issued new orders which further confused things. The 162nd Division, which was to clear the Egyptians east of the Canal between El Firdan and Deversoir, and, it was hoped, capture some bridges intact, suffered heavy casualties in its attacks on the Egyptian bridgehead which was well protected by ATGW. At 2.30 pm Gonen ordered Sharon's division, which had been sent to surprise an Egyptian bridge near Suez and

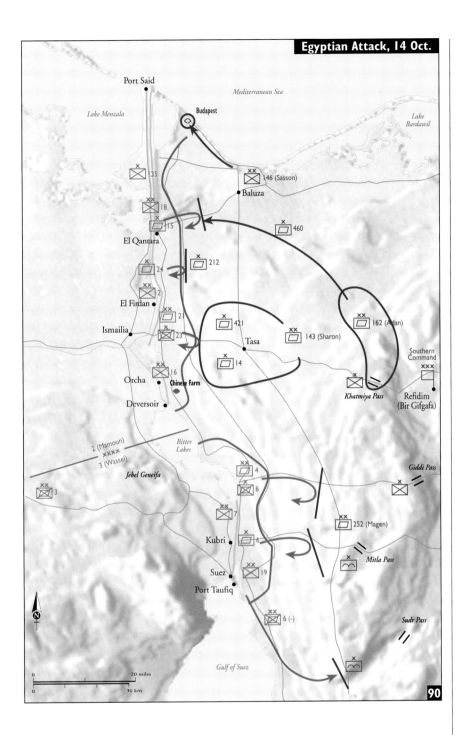

Egyptian Attack, 14 Oct.

Port Said

Budapest

Mediterranean Sea

Lake Menzala

Lake Bardawil

135

146 (Sasson)

Baluza

18

460

15

El Qantara

212

24

El Firdan

421

162 (Adan)

143 (Sharon)

Tasa

Ismailia

21

23

14

Southern Command

16

Orcha

Chinese Farm

Khatmiya Pass

Refidim (Bir Gifgafa)

Deversoir

2 (Mamoun)

3 (Wassel)

Bitter Lakes

Giddi Pass

Jebel Geneifa

3

4

6

252 (Magen)

7

Kubri

6

Mitla Pass

Suez

19

Port Taufiq

6 (-)

Sudr Pass

N

0   20 miles

0   30 km

Gulf of Suez

90

so was stretched out on the road as far south as the Mitla Pass, to return and support Adan. At the same time the Egyptians launched a counter-attack against Adan's southern flank, which threatened to cut the road to Tasa which was now unprotected after Sharon's move. One of Sharon's brigades managed to restore the situation at Tasa but the Egyptians beat off two counter-attacks which Sharon made without orders (and despite being ordered to stop his attack); Gonen asked for Sharon to be replaced. Adan withdrew his division in the dark to regroup and repair its tanks; he had lost 70 out of 170. The Israeli attacks had failed because of the lack of infantry to winkle out the Egyptian ATGW crews and because of insufficient artillery support. At this stage General Bar-Lev, a former Chief of Staff and then Minister of Trade and Industry, was sent to take over the southern front, leaving Gonen as his Chief of Staff. Bar-Lev also asked for Sharon to be removed but this was refused on political grounds.

The Israelis remained on the defensive while the Egyptians expanded their bridgeheads so that the divisions in each army linked up with each other but there was no physical contact between the two armies east of the Canal. Any eastward movement forward of the bridgeheads, once it had got beyond SAM protection, was halted by the Israeli Air Force. On the 9th a divisional attack was made on Adan's centre brigade and he was able to smash it by attacking with his other two brigades on either flank. Attacks on Adan continued throughout the 10th and Sharon's division was attacked by elements of the Egyptian 21st Armoured Division; he defeated the attack in a mobile battle in which the Egyptians lost fifty tanks.

The Israelis were already making plans to cross the Canal but were unready to do so while the main Egyptian tank force of some 900 tanks remained west of the Canal. The Syrians were pressing the Egyptians to step up their operations so as to relieve Israeli pressure on them; the Egyptian generals first resisted President Sadat's instructions to mount a major attack into Sinai but had to do so after receiving a direct order. The Egyptians therefore deployed their two remaining armoured divisions, two mechanized divisions and two independent tank brigades east of the Canal; the move was noted by the Israelis with satisfaction. Instead of concentrating their attack on the 14th along one axis the Egyptians dissipated their forces by attacking along the whole front including attacks on the edge of the marshes in the north towards Romani and down the Red Sea coast towards Ras Sudr in the south.

Early on the morning of the 14th, after a heavy artillery bombardment, the 2nd Army in the north attacked astride the road through Tasa to Refidim (Bir Gifgafa), which was defended by Sharon's division. The 14th Brigade, sited on high ground, allowed the Egyptians to advance towards its positions before opening fire, knocking out 93 tanks for the loss of only 3 of its own. To the south a similar battle was fought by Colonel Erez's 421st Brigade which also held off the Egyptians. To the north one of the brigades of Adan's division, which had been withdrawn into reserve to reorganize, had to be sent to counter the thrust towards Romani which it achieved, knocking out some fifty Egyptian tanks.

The 3rd Army attack was directed against both the Giddi and Mitla Passes where the 252nd Division (Mendler had been killed two days before and his division taken over by General Magen) had been reinforced by a brigade of airborne troops. The division gave some ground and then counter-attacked, accounting for some forty tanks. Further south an Egyptian armoured brigade making a wide outflanking movement met another Israeli airborne brigade, backed by some of Magen's tanks, holding the Sidr Pass and was virtually destroyed. Once halted the 3rd Army's armour turned south and when they had left the cover of their SAMs suffered heavily from Israeli air attack.

The Egyptians now proposed moving the remnants of their armoured divisions to the west of the Canal but this was vetoed on the grounds that

---

Egyptian Order of Battle

Chief of Staff: Lt-Gen. Saad el Shazli

2nd Army

18th Infantry Division
2nd Infantry Division
16th Infantry Division
23rd Mechanized Division
21st Armoured Division
135th Infantry Brigade
160th Marine Brigade

3rd Army

7th Infantry Division
19th Infantry Division
6th Mechanized Division
4th Armoured Division

Israeli Order of Battle

Southern Command: Maj.-Gen. Shmuel Gonen
Maj.-Gen. Haim Bar-Lev
16th Infantry Brigade
252nd Armoured Division
143rd Armoured Division
162nd Armoured Division

*Syrian tanks destroyed as they
crossed the Israeli anti-tank ditch
on the Golan, 1973.
(IDF Archives/Bamahane)*

the army's morale would be shattered. The Israelis were now ready for
their counter-attack.

THE ISRAELI CROSSING OF THE CANAL AND THE ENCIRCLEMENT OF THE EGYPTIAN 3RD ARMY

The Israelis had started planning to cross the Canal as early as 10 October,
but General Bar-Lev, commander of the southern front, was opposed to a
crossing as long as the bulk of the Egyptian tank strength remained on the
west bank; in any event Israel was still giving top priority to operations on
the Golan and thus priority for air support. The Egyptians had moved
their tank force across the Canal and launched unsuccessful attacks
against the Israelis in Sinai on the 14th. On the 13th the Israelis had
broken the back of the Syrian attack on the Golan and had recovered most
of the territory lost earlier; equally encouraging was the start of the US
resupply airlift on the same day.

There were three choices for the crossing site, all of which had been
prepared before the war with bridging material pre-positioned and the
canal ramp discreetly thinned. The sites were opposite El Qantara,
Deversoir and Kubri, 16 km north of Suez. Bar-Lev chose Deversoir as it
was close to the Egyptian inter-army boundary and the 20 km gap
between them; also the Israeli left flank would be protected by the Great

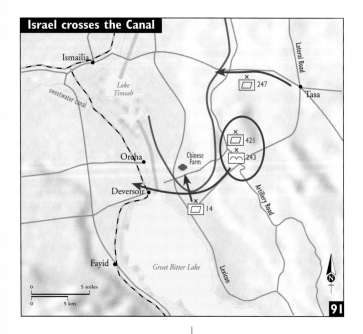

Israel crosses the Canal

Bitter Lake. Sharon's division was not only to make the assault crossing and protect a bridgehead over the Canal to allow Adan's division to cross and swing south towards Suez, but also to clear two metalled roads leading to the canal on the eastern side to assist the move forward of bridging and follow-up forces.

Sharon's plan was to make a diversionary attack with the 247th Armoured Brigade down the Tasa–Ismailia road to pin down the Egyptian 16th Infantry Division; this was to be followed, an hour later, by Reshef's reinforced brigade which was to approach from the south across the sand dunes to the northern end of the Great Bitter Lake and then to clear a 5 km length of canal bank where the crossing would be made. Rehsef was also to capture the area of Chinese Farm and to clear from the west the two roads leading back to Artillery Road. An attached airborne brigade, the 243rd, would make the first crossing to secure bridging and rafting sites, and would also secure crossing sites over the Sweetwater Canal and prevent Egyptian observation of the Suez Canal crossing sites. Finally Sharon's third armoured brigade, the 421st, would cross and create a gap in the Egyptian SAM belt so that the air force could give cover to the operation.

The attack was due to start as soon as it got dark in order to give the maximum time for bridge-building and crossing during darkness but it was soon clear to Sharon that there was insufficient time to meet the timetable. If Sharon had consulted Bar-Lev the attack would have been postponed for twenty-four hours but he decided to press on, ignoring the timetable and hoping to muddle through. At 5 pm on the 15th the diversionary attack began and two hours later Reshef's brigade began its approach march. The area of the Canal crossing sites was secured without opposition but the attempt to capture an Egyptian bridge some 5 km further north failed with many casualties. Nor was the attack on Chinese Farm and the features north-east of it any more successful as there was strong opposition from the Egyptian infantry and elements of the 21st Armoured Division who were in the area.

The airborne brigade began to cross the Canal at 1.30 am and by 8 am had secured a bridgehead 5 km long by 1.5 km deep with one crossing site over the Sweetwater Canal. The first armoured battalion was rafted across by 10.30 am and, leaving

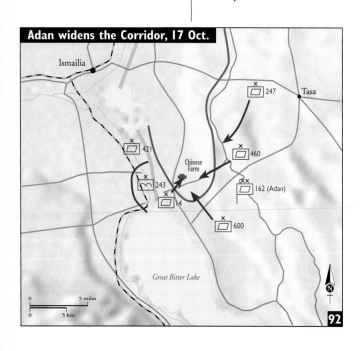

Adan widens the Corridor, 17 Oct.

some tanks to support the paratroops, it pushed some 24 km westwards and destroyed four SAM batteries. Without a bridge there could be no fast build-up across the Canal and the pontoon bridge units could not reach the Canal without a road; Reshef's brigade was unable to clear a road. By now the units across the Canal were running short of ammunition and it was agreed that unless a bridge could be built that night, they would be withdrawn. That night a fresh paratroop battalion was brought in and it managed, in bright moonlight, to clear the southern of the two roads for long enough for one pontoon bridge to get through; it was built by 4 pm on the 17th but the paratroops had suffered 50 per cent casualties.

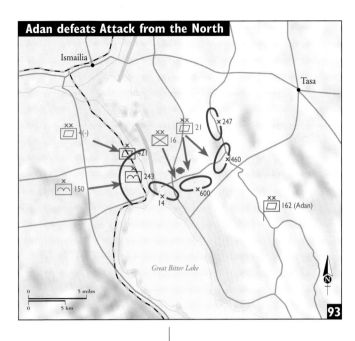

Adan defeats Attack from the North

Bar-Lev now reinforced Adan's division with the 247th Brigade which had carried out the diversionary attack and ordered him to clear the Chinese Farm position. Keeping the 212th Brigade in reserve, Adan sent the 247th Brigade from the north to take the high ground north-east of the farm, the 460th from the east down the two approach roads and the 600th from the south to cut across the roads opposite the farm. The Egyptians now mounted two uncoordinated counter-attacks: from the north two tank brigades drove southwards only to find themselves in a horseshoe-shaped killing zone in which they were crippled by the four Israeli brigades forming the horseshoe. Rather later, a 3rd Army tank brigade approached from the south, giving Adan sufficient time to regroup to meet it; he turned about the 460th Brigade on the line of the approach roads, moved the 600th south to the Edra Hills and sent his reserve 212th Brigade further south still to cut off any retreat. The plan worked perfectly and the Egyptians lost all but 10 of their 96 tanks. The battle was over by 5 pm.

By 11 pm Adan's division was on the move again, this time crossing the Canal. Next morning his men began to expand the bridgehead to the west against strong opposition. They also destroyed two more SAM batteries. The 252nd Armoured Division now crossed the Canal and took up position on Adan's right, and a two-divisional advance was made southwards. During the day a prefabricated bridge some 190 metres long and weighing 500 tonnes arrived, having been towed right across Sinai by fourteen tanks; it and another pontoon bridge were positioned across the Canal. On the 19th the Israelis had reached Jebel Geneifa where they met

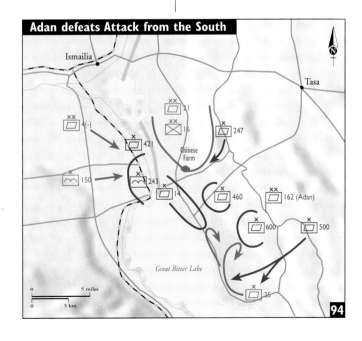

Adan defeats Attack from the South

An Egyptian pontoon bridge over the Suez Canal with Commander-in-Chief General Ahmed Ismail Ali crossing to Sinai.

heavy opposition, including units from the 4th Armoured Division sent back across the Canal, which they managed to overcome on the 20th but with heavy casualties.

Sharon, responsible for securing the bridgehead and keeping open the corridor to it, was authorized to move north on Ismailia but movement was slow owing to the agricultural nature of the area. The 243rd Airborne Brigade reached the outskirts of Ismailia and Reshef's 14th Brigade attacked the strongpoint at Orcha which they captured after heavy

The Israelis cross the Suez Canal, 17 October 1973. (IDF Archives/Bamahane)

An Israeli truck approaches knocked-out tanks near Chinese Farm. (IDF Archives)

fighting in which the Egyptians lost over 300 killed. At one time they saw a large number of Egyptians crossing the Canal, only to be fired on by Egyptian positions on the west bank. Sharon proposed that he should by-pass Ismailia and attempt to cut off the 2nd Egyptian Army but this suggestion was vetoed and he had to be ordered more than once to take the high ground north of Chinese Farm from where Egyptian artillery was able to shell the resupply corridor. The cease-fire came into effect before Sharon could mount an attack on Ismailia.

Egyptian MiG-17 attacks Headquarters 162nd Armoured Division. (Alain Roth Archives. Photo Nahum Gutman)

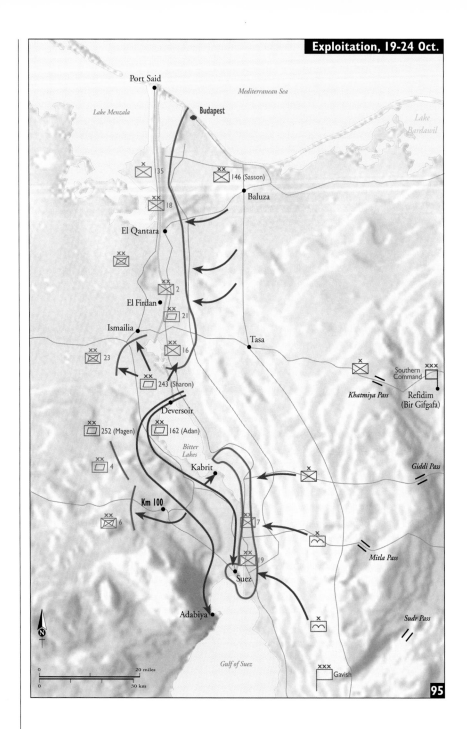

On the 22nd Adan's tanks reached the western shore of the Little Bitter Lake; that evening the first cease-fire came into effect. The cease-fire was soon broken, mainly by Egyptian units attempting to escape the Israeli encirclement, and the Israelis took full advantage of the violations to press further south. Adan attacked but was unable to take Suez, while the 252nd Division crossed the Suez–Cairo road and reached the shore of the Red Sea at the small port of Adabiya. The second cease-fire came into effect on the 24th but by then the 3rd Egyptian Army, with some 45,000 men and 200 tanks, east of the Canal, had been cut off.

PEACE AT LAST?

The process that began with President Sadat's visit to Jerusalem in 1977 has led so far to peace treaties being signed by Israel with Egypt and Jordan, and to its recognition by and improved trade relations with a number of Arab states. Negotiations, now stalled, have been held with the Syrians, and secret talks with the Palestinians led to the Oslo Process as the basis for a solution to the Palestinian issue. Other Arab states, particularly Iraq and Iran, still remain implacably opposed to peace with or for Israel. Both Iraq and Iran have ambitions to produce nuclear, chemical and biological weapons and the long-range missiles to deliver them that threaten Israel with massive casualties and destruction. These weapons would also threaten their neighbours in the Persian Gulf and Arabian Peninsula, and their Western Allies and the international community headed by the US is determined to ensure that their weapons programmes do not come to fruition. States cannot be forced to make peace with Israel and, as has been seen elsewhere in the world, even when peace is reached there is always a hard-line element that refuses to accept any compromise.

PEACE WITH EGYPT

Following secret meetings between Egyptian and Israeli government ministers, President Sadat surprised the world by visiting Israel in November 1977; detailed peace negotiations quickly followed. However, it took US President Carter to finalize an agreement when he invited Prime Minister Begin and President Sadat and their advisers to meet at Camp David until they had agreed on the terms of the Treaty. The Treaty was signed in Washington in March 1979; the basis of the agreement was the exchange of land for peace, and so far the peace has held.

Both Israel and Egypt had to accept conditions that they would have preferred not to, and for Israel a number of precedents were set that could have implications for future treaties with other Arab states. The first of these was a full withdrawal by Israel from Egyptian territory, including the Taba enclave just south of Elat that both sides claimed. The border here had been marked by the British Royal Navy in 1900, and eventually Israel accepted Egypt's claim. Other precedents more favourable to Israel were that the withdrawal was conducted in stages, an international observer force was established in Sinai, and Egypt accepted limitations on the level of forces it could deploy in Sinai.

After the Israeli withdrawal Sinai was divided into three zones. Zone C was a strip, varying from 25 to 40 kilometres wide running along the

Menachim Begin, Israeli Prime Minister.

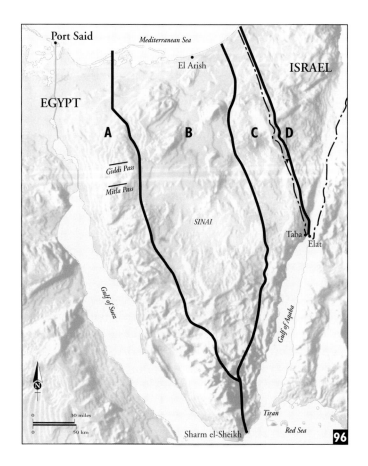

The Sinai Agreement

`– - —` International border

Armament limitations	A	B	C	D
men	22,000	4,000	Police	4,000
tanks	230	-	-	-
artillery	126	-	-	-

western side of the Israeli/Egyptian border and down the eastern coastline of the Gulf of Aqaba; in this zone the Multi-national Force and Observers established checkpoints and observation posts and carried out patrols. The Egyptians are not allowed to deploy any military forces in this zone but can keep armed civil police there. Zone A was another strip, this time between 40 and 60 kilometres wide running from the Mediterranean, parallel to the Suez Canal and the western coastline of the Gulf of Suez, until it joined the western boundary of Zone C about 50 kilometres north of Sharm el Sheikh. In this zone the Egyptians can deploy up to one mechanized infantry division of no more than 22,000 men, field fortifications can be constructed and early warning stations established. Zone B lies between Zones A and C and here the Egyptians may deploy only four border unit battalions of no more than 4,000 men, their associated field fortifications and low-power short-range coastal warning posts. On the Israeli side of the border there is another area, Zone D, 5 kilometres wide, in which Israel may only deploy up to four infantry battalions totalling no more than 4,000 men. It can be seen that the limitations on the Egyptians are far more onerous than those on Israel – a precedent that Israel will seek to repeat in any agreement with Syria.

Egypt has always had the strongest armed forces of Israel's Arab neighbours and so posed the greatest threat to Israel, although this was much reduced when Israel captured Sinai in 1967. Today Egypt still represents a threat but in the event of another war breaking out it is likely that Israeli armoured forces, now located in the Negev, would move deep into Sinai before the two armies clashed. Nevertheless the handing back of this deep buffer zone, which ensured that any Egyptian/Israeli war was fought far from Israeli soil, was a major concession. The Israelis also gave up a valuable and extensive military training area that could be replicated to some extent for the ground forces in the Negev but not for the Air Force which lost roughly half its available air space.

The Israelis also lost a degree of early warning, particularly low-level warning, but this can be compensated for by the use of airborne sensors in either manned aircraft, remotely controlled pilotless vehicles or tethered balloons. The navy can no longer control the Straits of Tiran, some 145 km from their nearest base at Elat; however, it no longer has to patrol the extensive Sinai coastline.

On the other hand there were some advantages to be gained from the withdrawal from Sinai. Shorter lines of communication both in war and more especially in peace bring considerable financial savings. Army units located in the Negev rather than in western Sinai can be redeployed to meet threats elsewhere more swiftly. The navy can concentrate more forces to protect the heavily populated Mediterranean coastline.

Although the peace agreement has not resulted in the forging of warm relations and the opportunities for trade which the Israelis had expected and hoped for, it has endured and must show that exchanging land for peace is a successful policy.

PEACE WITH JORDAN

King Hussein of Jordan and the Israeli Prime Minister, Yitzak Rabin, in the presence of the US President, Bill Clinton, signed a Peace Treaty at the Arava Valley crossing point on 26 October 1994. Earlier a 'Common Agenda' for achieving peace had been signed in Washington in September 1993; three 'common sub-agendas' covering Water, Energy and the Environment; Security; and Borders and Territorial Matters were signed on 7 June 1994, and a Declaration which terminated the 'state of belligerency' between the two countries was signed on 25 July. Jordan and Israel would have come to an agreement some years earlier had it not been for Jordan's fears of Syria's reaction. Secret meetings between Israeli and Jordanian leaders had been taking place for over thirty years.

As with the Treaty with Egypt a number of precedents were set. Once again full Israeli withdrawal from captured territory took place but on this occasion Jordan agreed to lease back to the Israelis, initially for twenty-five years, some areas in the Arava (Tzofar) and Jordan Valley (Naharayim) which they were farming. It was agreed that the boundary line drawn by the British in 1922 would become the international border, and Israeli withdrawal from all occupied territory was completed by 9 February 1995. Water issues were addressed in the Treaty, including agreement over allocations from the Jordan and Yarmouk and the need to develop new water resources jointly. Israel agreed to allow Jordan to take an additional 40 million cubic metres annually from the River Yarmouk. A number of proposals for large-scale projects including canals linking the Mediterranean and the Dead Sea, the Red Sea and the Dead Sea, and

Main Articles of the Peace Treaty between Israel and Jordan

Establishment of Peace
International Boundary
Security
Water
Economic Relations
Refugees and Displaced Persons
Places of Historical and Religious Significance
Freedom of Navigation

The Jordan Valley south of Lake Tiberias. (Photograph: Z. Radovan, Jerusalem)

Haifa and the Jordan Rift have been proposed, as well as plans for desalination and waste water treatment projects. Israel will be keen to include water issues in any future peace treaty reached with Syria and its inclusion in the Jordan Treaty is a useful precedent.

Agreement to cooperate in a number of areas was reached; these include energy resource development, agriculture, tourism, health, and combating crime and drugs. A new border crossing site was opened between Elat and Aqaba. Access to places of religious and historical significance is to be provided and Article 9.2 states: 'Israel respects the present special role of the Hashemite Kingdom of Jordan in Muslim holy shrines in Jerusalem. When negotiations on the final status will take place, Israel will give high priority to the Jordanian historic role in these shrines.' This clause was not welcomed by the Palestinians.

Under the heading of 'Security' Israel and Jordan committed themselves to a number of measures including:

- Working for the establishment of a regional security and cooperation arrangement similar to the Conference on Security and Cooperation in Europe.
- To refrain from the use or threat of use of force against each other, to refrain from joining any alliance whose objectives include aggression against the other party, and not to allow military forces of a third party to operate through their territory. (This last is particularly important to Israel which sees Iraqi forces as a distinct future threat.)
- To work as a matter of priority, through the multilateral group on Arms Control and Regional Security to establish a Middle East free from hostile alliances and from weapons of mass destruction.

Unlike the Treaty with Egypt, it was unnecessary to set up any form of neutral observer force to monitor the Treaty, nor were any limits on the deployment of military forces necessary.

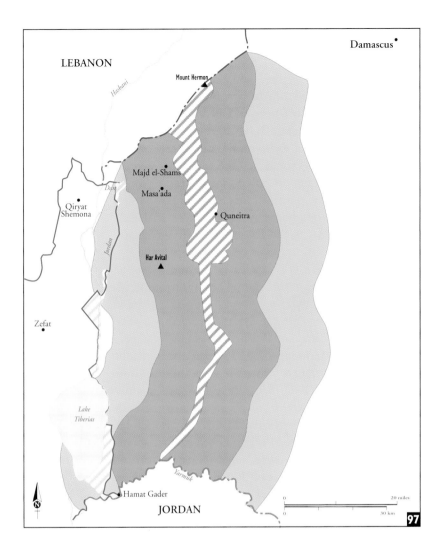

The Golan Heights

	1948 cease-fire line
	Demilitarised zone before 1967
	Separation zone (UN control)

Armament limitations	10 km	10-20 km
men	6,000	unltd.
tanks	75	450
artillery	36	160

PEACE WITH SYRIA AND LEBANON

Negotiations over a peace treaty between Israel and Syria began in 1994 with little progress apparently being made. The talks progressed to meetings between the two Chiefs of Staff in June 1995 and expectations were raised as they managed to agree on a number of general principles for the treaty but without agreeing the details. These principles were: a separation of forces agreement; the necessity for early warning provision; and withdrawal to take place in stages. Both sides are also looking for other elements: Israel will want to include an agreement over water resources in the treaty and the complete normalization of relations, while Syria will argue for complete withdrawal and look for a compensatory economic package as given to Egypt by the US.

There should be no difficulty over agreeing on the separation of forces and on zones in which force size is limited. There is already a limitation of forces agreement in place on the Golan as part of the 1973 Cease-fire Agreement. A demilitarized zone (DMZ) has been established between the

Hafiz al Assad
General of the Air Force, 1964;
Minister of Defence, 1966–70;
Prime Minister, 1970–1; President
of Syria since March 1971.

two sides. The Limitation of Forces Agreement covers weaponry deployed in two zones: that between the edge of the DMZ and 10 km from it, and the strip lying between 10 and 20 km from the DMZ; in each the numbers of tanks and artillery are limited while only 6,000 men can be deployed in the 10 km zone and no SAMs can be deployed in either zone. The agreement is monitored by a team of UN Military Observers.

The Israelis and Syrians have agreed that the DMZ should be asymmetrical, but did not agree on the ratio between the two sides. Syria proposed that the ratio should be 10:6 in Israel's favour; Israel considers this unacceptable and has proposed that the ratio should be based on the relative size of the two countries, that is 9:1 in Israel's favour. Whether the limits on weaponry should be symmetrical, as is the case on the Golan now, or asymmetrical like the Egyptian/Israeli agreement, is an issue that has not yet been addressed.

Both Israel and Syria consider early warning essential but the Syrians are totally opposed to either Israeli or internationally manned early warning stations on their territory, even though Israel has offered reciprocal arrangements for the Syrians in northern Israel. Israel has two major early warning and intelligence collecting sites on the Golan. One, situated on Mount Hermon at 2,810 metres above sea-level, can overlook both Lebanon and Syria; the other site is on the 1,200 metre high tel, Har Avital. From here, on a clear day, Damascus can be kept under observation. To some extent Israel can replace these assets by airborne sensors which could be mounted in aircraft, remotely piloted vehicles (RPV) or tethered balloons. Israel launched its first surveillance satellite in April 1995, but its replacement failed to reach orbit when launched in January 1998. Airborne surveillance cannot be guaranteed as both weather conditions and hostile activity can degrade or deny results.

The principle of a staged withdrawal has been accepted but not its parameters. The Syrians hope for the quickest possible withdrawal, and have suggested a period of eighteen months. Israel, on the other hand, is looking for at least three years in which to complete withdrawal and to establish new defences on its own territory. As in Sinai, Israel has a considerable military infra-structure deployed on the Golan. The question of where the new boundary should be has not been agreed either, although Prime Minister Rabin appears to have accepted full withdrawal: but does this mean to the pre-1948 Palestine/Syrian border that Israel wants or to the 1949 armistice line that Syria prefers. The areas which lay between these two lines in 1949 were declared DMZs and led to continual confrontation as the Syrians tried to prevent Israeli farmers living there by opening fire on them. One of these former DMZs, at Hammat Gader, is claimed by Yasser Arafat for the Palestinian entity as it was offered to the PLO by Syria at the Arab Summit in 1964. In the Treaties with Egypt and Jordan it was agreed that the British Mandatory borders should become the international border.

An agreement on water resources will be essential for Israel which relies on the waters of the Upper Jordan for some 35 per cent of its requirement. The upper Jordan is fed by the Hasbani, which rises in Lebanon; the Dan, which comes mainly from springs at the junction of Israel, Lebanon and Syria; the Banias, whose sources are in Syria; and other water which drains off the Golan Heights. In the past Syria has attempted to divert water to prevent it reaching Israel.

Withdrawal from the Golan will not have the same emotional implications for Israelis as withdrawal from the biblical areas of Judea and Samaria (the West Bank). The density of settlement is much lower: only 11,000 Israelis live on the Golan, and the Golan does not form part of *Eretz Israel* although there was Israelite settlement there during the reigns of David and Solomon.

There are conflicting opinions as to whether an international buffer force will need to be deployed between Israel and Syria after withdrawal. Some Israelis consider it unnecessary and point to the success of joint Israeli/Palestinian patrols in the West Bank and Gaza; others feel that not only is a force necessary but that its mandate should include the obstruction of any attempt to violate the Treaty and that it should include a sizeable US component.

It is widely believed that a peace treaty between Israel and Syria will lead to one between Israel and Lebanon. Israel has no border disputes with Lebanon and claims none of its land. Lebanon has never posed a threat to Israel though the presence of others' forces has. Syria may not directly control *Hizbullah* but it can ensure that it is not supplied with arms and ammunition, most of which come by air from Iran and pass through Damascus airport. The Lebanese Government will need military assistance if it is to prevent *Hizbullah* from launching attacks on Israel from Lebanese territory. The Syrians are best placed to carry out this task and the added legitimization of Syria's role in Lebanon would not be too high a price to pay for a peaceful Israeli northern border.

Failure to reach agreement with Syria could lead to another war, one in which Syria might employ its force of SSMs, known to include Russian SCUD and SS-21, and possibly Chinese CSS-15/M-9 missiles. There was an alarm in 1996 when some Syrian forces were moved closer to the Golan; however, the Israeli Defence Minister accepted the military intelligence assessment that there was no increased threat of war, rather than the *Mossad* (Israeli Secret Intelligence Service) assessment that Syria was indeed preparing for war. It now emerges that the *Mossad* report was based on information manufactured by an Israeli agent as coming from a high-level source. However, without a treaty, war is still a Syrian option. In August 1997 the Syrian Chief of Staff warned in a newspaper interview 'that his country would take back the Golan by force if it cannot do so peacefully'.

The Israeli/Syrian peace talks were halted after the Israeli election of May 1996 with the new Prime Minister insisting that any promises made by his predecessors were not binding. It has been reported in Israel that in September 1997 a secret meeting was held with the Syrians in an attempt to restart peace talks.

THE PALESTINIAN PEACE PROCESS

Although there were clauses relating to Palestinian autonomy in the 'Camp David Accords' reached by Israel and Egypt in 1979, the right-

The Exchange of Letters

9 Sept. 1993
Mr Prime Minister
The signing ... I would like to confirm the following PLO commitments. The PLO recognizes the right of the State of Israel to exist in peace and security. The PLO accepts UNSC Resolutions 242 and 338.... The PLO renounces the use of terrorism and other acts of violence....
Yasser Arafat, Chairman, PLO

9 Sept. 1993
Mr Chairman
In response to your letter of Sept 9, I wish to confirm to you that in light of the PLO commitments ..., the Government of Israel has decided to recognize the PLO as the representative of the Palestinian people and commence negotiations with the PLO within the Middle East peace process.
Yitzhak Rabin, Prime Minister of Israel

*Yitzhak Rabin
1941 Haganah; 1948 Commander
Harel Brigade; 1964 Chief of Staff;
1974 Prime Minister; 1984
Minister of Defence; 1992 Prime
Minister; 1996 Assassinated.*

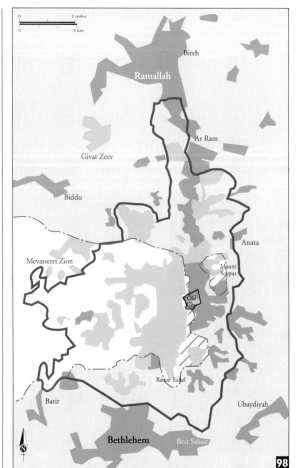

Greater Jerusalem

– – – 1949-1967 cease-fire line
The West Bank
/ / / No man's land 1949-1967
Post 1967 city limits
Arab built-up area
Israeli built-up area

98

*Yasser Arafat, Chairman of the
PLO and President of the PNA.*

wing Israeli Government had done nothing to implement them. An early indication that there could be peace between Israel and the Palestinians came in Yasser Arafat's announcements at the United Nations General Assembly – held in Geneva as the US had refused Arafat a visa – in December 1988. While he failed to make clear his intentions in his formal speech to the UNGA, at a press conference the next day he clearly recognized Israel, renounced terrorism in all its forms, and accepted UN Resolutions 242 and 338 as the basis for a settlement.

Following the Gulf War the US co-chaired with Russia a Middle East Peace Conference at Madrid in October 1991. Following this, Palestinian/Israeli talks were held in Washington throughout 1992 but little true progress was made other than Israel proposing that there should be Palestinian self-rule in the West Bank and Gaza. The biggest step forward came with the revelation at the end of August 1993 that secret talks had been held at Oslo and that Israel and the PLO had agreed to recognize each other. In September Prime Minister Rabin and Chairman Arafat exchanged letters confirming their commitments and on the 13th they met at the White House where a 'Declaration of Principles on Interim Self-Government Arrangements' (Oslo I) was signed.

The aim of the Declaration was to establish a Palestinian Interim Self-Government Authority and to hold elections for a Council to govern the

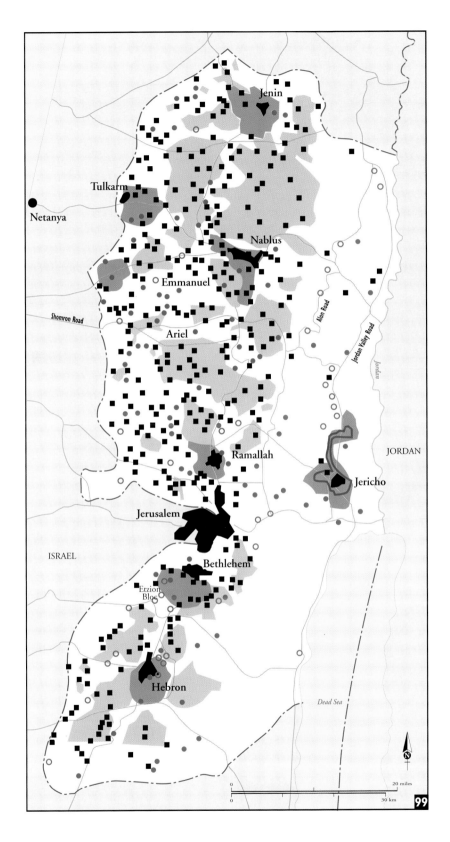

Jenin

Tulkarm

Netanya

Nablus

Emmanuel

Shomron Road

Ariel

Alon Road

Jordan Valley Road

Jordan

JORDAN

Ramallah

Jericho

Jerusalem

ISRAEL

Bethlehem

Etzion Bloc

Dead Sea

Hebron

N

0   20 miles
0   30 km

99

Settlement in the West Bank

- — · — 1949 armistice line
- ■ Palestinian villages and towns
- ○ Israeli settlements before 1977
- ● Israeli settlements since 1977
- —— Palestinian Authority territory
- ▩ Area A
- ▨ Area B
- ☐ Area C

West Bank and Gaza during the transitional period which would not exceed five years. They also included provision for permanent status negotiations; the handover of responsibility for certain civil matters (such as health and education); the redeployment of Israeli forces; the formation of a Palestine police force; and the withdrawal from Gaza and the Jericho area. It was agreed that issues covering Jerusalem, settlements, refugees, security and borders would be left to the final status talks. Following this, and despite a number of horrifying terrorist incidents, an 'Agreement on the Gaza Strip and Jericho' was signed in Cairo on 4 May 1994; Israeli withdrawal from Gaza and Jericho was completed and Jericho was handed over on 15 May 1994 and Gaza the next day. On 5 July the Palestine National Authority (PNA) was sworn in at Jericho.

The Israeli–Palestinian Interim Agreement on the West Bank and Gaza Strip' (Oslo II) was initialled in Washington on 28 September 1995. This agreement provided for the West Bank to be divided into five zones: East Jerusalem (annexed by Israel); Israeli settlements and state lands to remain under Israeli control; Area A where the PNA is responsible for security and the Israelis have withdrawn totally; Area B where Israel and the PNA share responsibility for security; and Area C where Israel retains full security control. The PNA is responsible for civil administration in all three Areas. Area A comprises the main Palestinian towns of Bethlehem, Jenin, Nablus, Qalqilya, Ramallah and Tulkarm. Once agreement was reached as to the division of Hebron, where there was Jewish settlement in the centre in an area from which Jews had been expelled in 1929, it would form part of Area A. In the initial stage Area B consisted of mainly Palestinian-inhabited areas and while Israel had overall security control its military units were redeployed from the Area.

While the Israeli Labour government was in power there were hold-ups and schedules were not met but there was some progress, with Area A, except Hebron, being handed over by the end of 1995. The future of Hebron was left to be decided after the May 1996 Israeli election which was won by Benjamin Netanyahu and the Likud coalition; immediately the atmosphere changed and progress came to a halt. Most of Hebron was handed over to the Palestinian Authority only in January 1997, nine months after the scheduled date of 28 March 1996, and after considerable local violence and the deployment of a group of international observers. Israel retained control over Abraham's Tomb and about 20 per cent of the city with 30,000 Palestinian inhabitants and 500 Israeli settlers. The handover was only approved by the Israeli Cabinet after Netanyahu went ahead with the construction of a new Jewish suburb in Jerusalem, Har Homa, which would add one more block of concrete surrounding Greater Jerusalem and which was seen by the Palestinians as highly provocative.

The agreement reached over Hebron covered other aspects, not all clearly defined: the PNA will control the entire West Bank other than Israeli settlements and as yet unspecified 'military areas'. Israeli troops will withdraw in three stages, the first in March 1997, the third no later than mid-1998. The Israelis have twice offered withdrawal packages, first in February 1997 and again in December; on both occasions the offers were rejected by the Palestinians as being on too small a scale. No plans as to Israel's final position on withdrawal from the West Bank have been published but the indications are that the Palestinians would only receive rather less than 50 per cent of the area, far less than they will accept and less than some Israelis think they should have. The main issues concern security, settlements and water. No agreement had been reached on this issue by the end of May 1998, despite the efforts of the US to broker a deal.

There are two Israeli security concerns: conventional attack through the West Bank from the east, and terrorism emanating from the Palestinian entity. The threat from the east comes from Iraq, not Jordan; Israel foresees a tank force advancing through the north Jordanian desert and across the Jordan River. The River Jordan is no tank obstacle but the Jordan Rift is and there only a few places where it can be crossed; the warning time gained by the approach march would be sufficient for the Israeli Air Force to be able to halt any force as it attempts to cross the Rift, while any elements which managed to cross could be halted on the few east–west roads by helicopter-borne anti-tank troops. Giving back the Jordan Valley and the east–west roads, which the Israeli military want to retain control of, would release a large amount of land to the Palestinians. Withdrawal from the Jordan Valley is far less of a risk than returning the Golan to Syria.

There is no guaranteed answer to the problem of terrorism, particularly to suicide bombers, and they have been active even before Israel makes its final position clear. The more territory given up the less cause Palestinian extremists will have to engage in terrorist attacks and the more willing will be the PNA to take effective measures to prevent such attacks. It is a question of relative risks, and giving up land is the lesser of these.

After Israel captured the West Bank in 1967 its policy on settlements was to build them in accordance with a strategic plan so that they would aid defence and not add to security problems. They were therefore concentrated in the Jordan Valley, on the ridge line to its west and on the east–west routes; they avoided centres of Palestinian population. After the election of Menachem Begin and the Likud in 1977 this policy was radically altered. The number of settlements has risen from 33, with a population of some 20,000, to 179, with some 140,000 settlers. A large number of the new settlements have been sited for historical/biblical reasons and are inhabited largely by hard-line 'Land of Israelites' who are unwilling to leave what they consider to be 'their' land. Yitzhak Rabin believed that separation of Jew and Muslim was the best policy but this would mean abandoning a number of settlements, a proposal to which the Netanyahu Government is opposed.

In the final status it is clear that Israel will retain some areas of the West Bank. These are likely to include settlements around Jerusalem; a finger of land from Jerusalem to Ma'ale Adummim, which has a population of 12,000; the Etzion bloc, the area where in 1948 four Jewish settlements were overrun by the Arab Legion who killed some 250 Jews; some strips of land along the 'Green Line'; and another finger of land reaching out to the large suburban settlements of Ariel and Emmanuel. A major problem will be the isolated town of Qyriat Arba, close to Hebron, which is inhabited by some of the most hard-line settlers. It is not only Hebron that has its Jewish holy place: Rachel's Tomb in Bethlehem and Joseph's Tomb

---

Major Terrorist Attacks since September 1993

Attacks by Hamas and Islamic Jihad

1994

6 April: 8 killed by car bomb in Afula

13 April: 5 killed by suicide bomb in Hadera

19 October: 22 killed by suicide bomb in Tel Aviv

11 November: 3 killed by suicide bomb in the Gaza Strip

1995

22 January: 19 killed by two bombs near Netanya

9 April: 8 killed by car bomb in the Gaza Strip

24 July: 6 killed by suicide bomb in Ramat Gan

21 August: 4 killed by suicide bomb in Jerusalem

1996

25 February: 24 killed by suicide bomb in Jerusalem

25 February: 1 killed by suicide bomb in Ashkelon

3 March: 18 killed in bus bomb in Jerusalem

4 March: 13 killed by suicide bomb in Tel Aviv

Israeli Terrorist Attacks

1994

25 February: Baruch Goldstein kills 30 praying Palestinians in the Hebron Tomb of Abraham mosque.

1995

4 November: Prime Minister Yitzhak Rabin murdered by Yigal Amir

1996

5 January: Yehiya Ayash, 'The Engineer', Palestinian bomb-maker killed by bomb installed in his mobile telephone

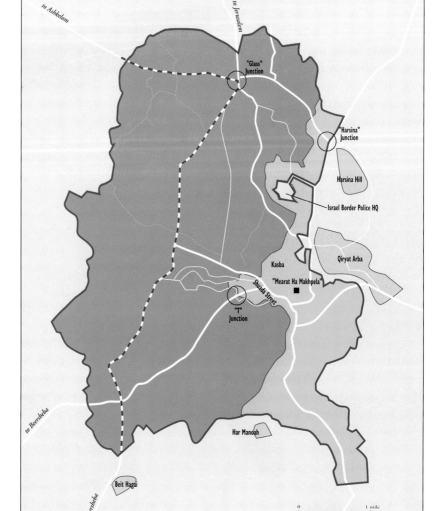

Withdrawal at Hebron

— Hebron city limits

▨ Handed over to Palestine Authority

▨ Area of Israeli control in Hebron

▨ Area C under Israeli control

▨ Israeli settlements

∎∎∎ Joint patrol road

near Nablus are still guarded by Israeli troops, and access to these may cause problems.

Some progress has been made over the question of water resources. That Israel recognizes 'Palestinian water rights in the West Bank' is contained in an agreement signed by both parties. Any additional water for Palestinians must mean less for Israelis who get some 30 per cent of their water from West Bank aquifers which are already over-used, and some other source must be found, most probably through desalination.

Two other problems to be solved are the questions of the Palestinian entity's status and the return of refugees. Already many Israelis have come to accept the inevitability of a Palestinian state and it can only be a question of time before this is achieved. There are some 2.3 million Palestinians living in neighbouring Arab countries who are registered as refugees or displaced persons. Not all of these will wish to return but the Jordanian, Lebanese and Syrian governments are likely to wish to see the departure of at least the 500,000 still living in refugee camps. Another 500,000 Palestinians living in refugee camps in the West Bank and Gaza

The Gaza Strip

Palestinian towns
Israeli controlled area
Israeli controlled roads

0   5 miles
0   5 km

Alei Sinai crossing

Erez crossing

Gaza

Nahal Oz crossing

Qarni crossing

Mediterranean Sea

ISRAEL

Kissufim crossing

Khan Yunis

Rafah

Sufa crossing

EGYPT

Kerem Shalom crossing

N

101

must be resettled. Many may claim the right to return to their former homes in Israel; this is unlikely to be allowed and will cause resentment. Whether the West Bank can absorb this extra population is doubtful but it will be less difficult if the maximum amount of land is returned.

Jerusalem remains to be discussed. In the Israeli/Palestinian negotiations it has been left as the last item on the agenda in the belief that if all the other issues have been settled neither side will wish to lose all that they have achieved by failing to reach agreement over Jerusalem. A solution is considered possible by employing euphemisms such as 'the suspension of authority' and 'functional administrative arrangements' arriving at a system of boroughs giving local autonomy without dividing the city. The future of the Holy City is a matter which unifies both Jews and Muslims in claiming what they fervently believe are their rights in the city. Whether the good will can be found to bridge the gap between their two positions must remain doubtful but without it there can be no peace in the Holy Land.

BIBLIOGRAPHY

(Works covering more than one period are shown under the earliest relevant period)

Megiddo
Cottrell, Leonard. *The Warrior Pharaohs* Evans Brothers, 1968.
Nelson, Harold H. *The Battle of Megiddo* (Doctoral dissertation) University of Chicago, 1913.

The Israelite Conquest
Aharoni, Yohanan. *The Land of the Bible: a Historical Geography* Burns and Oates, 1962.
Gale, Richard. *Great Battles of Biblical History* Hutchinson, 1968.
Healy, Mark. *Warriors of the Old Testament* Firebird Books, 1989.
Herzog & Gichon. *Battles of the Bible* Weidenfeld and Nicholson, 1978 and 1997.
Josephus: The Essential Writings, translation by Paul L. Maeir. Kregel, 1988.
Keller, Werner. *The Bible as History* Hodder and Stoughton, 1956.
Kraeling, Emil. *Bible Atlas* Rand McNally, 1956.
Oesterley and Robinson. *A History of Israel* Oxford, 1932.
Yadin, Yigal. *The Art of Warfare in Biblical Lands* Weidenfeld and Nicholson, 1963.

Pre-Roman Conquests
Barker, Phil. *Alexander the Great's Campaigns* Patrick Stephens, 1979.
Wallach, J.L. *The War of the Maccabees* Israel Society for Military History, 1979.
Warry, John. *Alexander 334–323: Conquest of the Persian Empire* Osprey, 1991.

The Romans to the Crusaders
Ali, Ameer. *A Short History of the Saracens* Darf, 1985 (first published 1899)
Gichon, M. *The Bar-Kochba War* Israel Society for Military History.
Glubb, John. *A Short History of the Arab Peoples* Hodder and Stoughton, 1969.
——. *The Empire and the Arabs* Hodder and Stoughton.
Hitti, Philip. *A History of the Arabs* MacMillan, 1961.
Josephus. *The Jewish War*, translated by G.A. Williamson, Penguin, 1959.
Norwich, John Julius. *Byzantium: The Early Centuries* Penguin, 1990.
——. *Byzantium: The Decline and Fall* Penguin, 1996.
Treadgold, Warren. *Byzantium and its Army: 284–1081* Stanford University, 1995.

The Crusaders
Holt, P.M. *The Age of the Crusades: The Near East from the Eleventh Century to 1517* Longman, 1986.
Mayer, Hans Eberhard. *The Crusades* Oxford University Press, 1972.
Runciman, Steven. *A History of the Crusades* Cambridge University Press, 1951: vol. 1 *The First Crusade*; vol. 2 *The Kingdom of Jerusalem*; vol. 3 *The Kingdom of Acre*.
Smail, R.C. *Crusading Warfare, 1097–1193* Cambridge University Press, 1995.

The Muslim Reconquest
Berthier, General. *Memoirs of the Campaigns of General Bonaparte in Egypt and Syria*, translated by Thomas White, Jordan and Maxwell, 1805.

Glubb, John. *Soldiers of Fortune: The Story of the Mamelukes* Hodder and Stoughton, 1973.
Lane-Poole, S. *Saladin and the Fall of the Kingdom of Jerusalem* Putnam's, 1898.
Rose, John Holland. *The Life of Napoleon I* George Bell, 1902.

The First World War
Babcock, G.E. *History of the Transport Services in the Egyptian Expeditionary Force.*
Gullet, H.S. *Official History of Australia in the War of 1914–1918*, vol. III: *Sinai and Palestine* Angus and Robertson.
Jones, H.A. *War in the Air*, vols V and VI. Clarendon, 1935.
Official History of the War: Military Operations: Egypt and Palestine HMSO.
Wavell, A.P. *The Palestine Campaigns* Constable, 1928.

Israeli War of Independence
Begin, Menachem. *The Revolt: Story of the Irgun* Steimatzkhy, 1952.
Carver, Michael. *War Since 1945* Ashfield Press, 1990.
Charters, David. *The British Army and Jewish Insurgency in Palestine 1945–47* Macmillan, 1989.
Lorch, Netaniel. *Edge of the Sword* Longmans, Green and Co.
Narkiss, Uzi. *The Liberation of Jerusalem* Valentine, Mitchell, 1983.

Arab-Israeli Wars
Allon, Yigal. *Shield of David* Weidenfeld and Nicolson, 1970.
Barker, A.J. *Suez: The Seven Day War* Faber and Faber, 1964.
Dupuy, T.N. *Elusive Victory: The Arab-Israeli Wars 1947–74* Macdonald and Janes, 1978.
El-Shazly, General Saad. *The Crossing of the Suez: The October War (1973)*, Third World Centre for Research and Publishing, 1980.
Eshel, David. *Chariots of the Desert* Brasseys, 1989.
Herzog, Chaim. *The War of Atonement* Weidenfeld and Nicolson, 1975.
——. *The Arab-Israeli Wars* Arms and Armour, 1982.
Jacobs, Monty. *The Birth of the Israel Air Force* Shulsinger Bros.
Lloyd, Selwyn. *Suez 1956* Jonathan Cape, 1978.
Luttwak, Edward and Horowitz, Dan. *The Israeli Army* Allen Lane, 1975.
Morris, Benny. *Israel's Border Wars 1949–56* Oxford, 1993.
Scheifer, Abdullah. *The Fall of Jerusalem* Bertrand Russell Peace Foundation, 1972.
Schiff, Ze'ev. *A History of the Israeli Army* Sidgwick and Jackson, 1987.
—— and Ehud Ya'ari. *Intifada: The Palestinian Uprising – Israel's Third Front* Simon and Schuster, 1989.
——. *Israel's Lebanon War* George Allen and Unwin, 1985.
Sharon, Ariel. *Warrior* Simon and Schuster, 1989.
Sunday Times Insight Team. *The Yom Kippur War* André Deutsch, 1975.

CARTOGRAPHIC SOURCES

Jacotin's Map. French Corps of Engineers, Carté Général de L'Égypte. Dépot Général de la Guerre, 1807.
An Atlas of Ancient Geography. Dr Charles Müller. John Murray, 1874.
Map of Roman Palestine. M. Avi-Yonah. Oxford, 1940.
Bible Atlas. Yohanan Aharoni and Michael Avi-Yonah. Macmillan, 1968.
Israel Atlas. Survey of Israel, Ministry of Labour. Elsevier, Amsterdam, 1970.
Grosser Historischer Weltatlas. Bayerischer Schulbuch-Verlag, Munchen, 1978.
Atlas of Israel (in Hebrew). Carta, Jerusalem, 1983.
Atlas of the Bible. Edited by James Pritchard. Times Books, 1987.
Histoire Universelle des Juifs. Hachette, Paris, 1992.

INDEX